√4⁵⁰

3-16-60

88.2864

MY RUSSIAN JOURNEY

BY SANTHA RAMA RAU

My Russian Journey

View to the Southeast

Remember the House

This Is India

East of Home

Home to India

My Russian Journey

BY SANTHA RAMA RAU

Harper & Brothers, Publishers, New York

TO NANDITA WAGLÉ

Much of the material in this book appeared first in articles in HOLIDAY *magazine. I would like to express my thanks to the Editors of* HOLIDAY *for permission to reprint this material and for making possible my trip to Russia.*

Contents

LENINGRAD 3

MOSCOW: PART I 75

MOSCOW: PART II 173

UZBEKISTAN 263

Leningrad

IF LENINGRAD is your first view of the Soviet Union you lead a curiously haunted life all the time you are in Russia. Always at the back of your mind, as a permanent backdrop to everything you do, all the people you meet, are the city's souvenirs of the grand, turbulent, conflicting, decisive life and events of the most dramatic two centuries of Russia's history, when Leningrad was St. Petersburg, the capital of all the Russias. It is a past that follows you even into the unaccommodating climate of modern Soviet society and lends a texture, a perspective to the most insignificant things you do or see in Russia.

From the moment that we arrived—my husband and I, with our young son, and Ruth Camm, who has taken care of him since he was a baby—for a three-month stay in Russia in late summer of 1957 we were aware of the pervasive air of dual life in Leningrad. We arrived by ship, a small Russian ship, from London, and as we approached the city we could see the domes and spires of St. Petersburg in the gray distance, and beside us along the docks and quays that we passed, in all the complex harbor of the delta of the Neva River, were great posters with the familiar Communist slogans—*Druzhba i Mir,* Friendship and Peace, *Non, a la guerre,* Youth, the Future is in Your Hands—and vast signs stamped with the hammer and sickle, all the symbols of modern Leningrad.

3

It was a truthful and a memorable introduction to the city, and even after our ship had docked and we were driving into the center of town we were aware of this ghostly mixture of the old and the new Russia. It was one of the long-drawn-out, misty evenings for which the city is famous, a pale, sentimental light that softens colors and is kind to evidences of decay. The end of summer, but too early for the sharper autumn air. Some days later a Russian acquaintance was to say to us, "There are many cities in our country where one can live, but only one to fall in love with—Leningrad." I believed him instantly only because of that first impression from the bus window, the wide streets and lovely buildings of a city that remains, in conception and design, a monument to a lavish, vanished way of life. And everywhere, at the same time, the half-obscured signs of revolution, war, and a stringent, demanding contemporary life, the flaking paint on shadowed façades, the thirteen-year-old scars of German shelling, boarded doors and windows, and the tight, shabby look of the people on the sidewalks.

Even at the quayside the atmosphere had been the same: the girls waiting on shore with traditional bunches of flashy flowers for returning friends and relatives, while on board efficient customs examiners asked us to declare only our books, manuscripts, and gramophone records. We would, it occurred to me, have been able to bring in gold, opium, firearms, liquor, but would, like a shipboard acquaintance of ours, have had to throw a copy of George Orwell's *Animal Farm* into the ocean. When we reached our hotel, there too we were greeted by the uniformed hall porter, with the age-old look of all European hall porters, tempered only by the sight of the Communist militiaman in his olive uniform trimmed with scarlet stationed in the doorway. In the lobby of the Hotel Astoria we could hear the saccharine strains of the string orchestra from the restaurant and at the same moment catch sight of the severe card informing one that "It is obligatory to remove your galoshes."

I had noticed on the ship that, almost invariably, after the usual, easy shipboard introductions the first question people asked each other was "Why are *you* going to Russia?" Had we all been going to France or Italy, I thought, we would have assumed that the other passengers were traveling for pleasure, for business, for study, to visit relatives, anyway, for some ordinary, acceptable reason. For a trip to Russia we had to explain ourselves. As it happened, we were going to Russia partly because my husband, Faubion Bowers, wanted to write about Russian theater and ballet, but mostly our motive was simple curiosity. An English friend of mine, when I had announced my plans to her, crystallized my feeling about it all in one phrase. "I can see why you might want to go," she said, "it is just about the only place that is *abroad* any more."

I think I had the feeling of being "abroad" more strongly than ever before in my life during my first evening at the Hotel Astoria in Leningrad. Standing in the suite that the Soviet tourist bureau, Intourist, had assigned to us, I looked around at the solid respectability of mahogany furniture, of plush table-cloths and curtains, of the plethora of meaningless bits of hand-made lace—antimacassars, lace covers for the pillows on the beds, lace doilies on the dressing table, under the brass lamp-stands, the marble inkpot, the mysterious marble-and-silver ornament on the desk; at all the cut glass, pin trays, pen trays, ash trays, decanters, glasses, bottles, carafes, chandeliers. It was a thoroughly Victorian atmosphere. There was only one word that captured the look and feeling of those rooms—"bourgeois"—and with the facile sense of paradox that afflicts you when you first get to Russia, I was reminded of the curious product of the first revolution to be fought against the bourgeois ideal—the bourgeois ideal.

Then I walked to the window and saw in the deepening twilight the great golden dome of St. Isaac's Cathedral and beyond it the city's even, measured skyline. A conventionally imposing view of St. Petersburg. On the street below the last of the people coming home from work, the first of the people going out for the evening, hurried or strolled along, dark, foreshortened figures cutting across the small garden in front of St. Isaac's, waiting on the corner for the traffic lights to change, queueing up for buses and streetcars, all under the curly bronze lettering in ancient Russian on the old cathedral: "O Lord, the stronger Thou art the greater the Tsar's joy."

The next morning I woke up with a sudden sense of excitement. I wandered about our suite, finding it a bit more familiar in daylight, examined the elaborate pipes, the hand shower, the long porcelain bathtub in the bathroom, the hideous marble shepherdess in our private foyer, and decided that on our first day at least we should have a proper Russian breakfast.

Faubion's knowledge of Russian is very far from perfect, but at least his spoken Russian was reasonably fluent and carried us fairly easily through most of our ordinary encounters and conversations. By the time we left the country my own Russian extended just far enough to cover some of the basic essentials of living—how to order a meal or get the laundry sent out and things like that, but that first day I was far too nervous to use even the half-dozen words I was sure of. I couldn't follow any of the complicated requests and suggestions, comments and questions that went on between Faubion and the chambermaid. However, after a considerable delay, Jai, our four-year-old son, Faubion and I sat down at the large round table in our living room to a meal of tea with lemon, mountains of sliced white and black bread, disks of cold sausage, a glass dish of caviar on ice, butter, three platters each containing three cold fried eggs, a bowl of something like cream of wheat with a dollop of jam in the middle, three apples, and a bunch of grapes.

Anyway, we felt fortified afterward.

We knew nobody in Leningrad—no friends, acquaintances, addresses. We had no idea where to go, what to do, nor, with a few exceptions, what to see.

"Well," Faubion said, when we had eaten as much as we could of breakfast, "as long as we're here as tourists we might as well behave like tourists. We'll walk about and look at the sights."

At that time we didn't realize that our Intourist coupons which we had bought in New York, in dollars, at the thoroughly unrealistic exchange rate of four rubles to the dollar, included the services of an official interpreter and guide, and the use of an Intourist car. We had assumed that they covered only our hotel accommodation and meals, and in a way this turned out to be an advantage. During our early days in Leningrad we wandered about the city as we wished, took trams and subways to explore, drifted in and out of museums, shops, churches, and walked and walked in a kind of dream through the city that Peter the Great had founded in 1703 to be the new capital of the biggest nation in the world.

I suppose we must have looked like an extraordinary group to the Russians—certainly they stared incessantly, sometimes smiled or greeted us, and constantly made a fuss over Jai, petting him, chattering delightedly—but then we would have looked pretty odd anywhere: one child of four, dressed as a cowboy, one very beautiful Negro girl, one Indian, one American. Of all of us, the only one who might have passed as a Russian was the American. However, we were all a bit too bemused that first day to take in the Russians' reaction to us.

We walked out of the hotel and on an impulse turned right. We sauntered along, constantly stopping to read the signs. I would laboriously spell them out to improve my flimsy knowledge of Russian script with its special mixture of Greek, Roman and Cyrillic letters, and Faubion would translate. We learned that it was healthy to drink tomato juice, that we should save our money, that books were our best friends. After slowly pronouncing the foreign-looking sign PECTOPAH (Russian is a phonetic language), I found that I had said the quite familiar word "restaurant." One word, painted on the pavement at all street crossings, suspended from overhead trolley and electric bus cables, read CTOII. It was a moment before I recognized one of the few English words in current Russian usage—STOP. We paused before posters announcing the week's theater programs, before cards stuck in the windows of shops or cafés advertising for assistants or waitresses or cooks. Nothing very interesting, except that because it was all Russian it was all enthralling.

We were constantly being halted by a glimpse of a monument, a palace, a church, or simply by the sight of a charming street corner; by the immense avenues and boulevards, called "prospects," softened by the pastel colors of the buildings; by the elegance that the matched façades of the houses give, combined with the almost intimidating scope of the city. Some perfectly ordinary street scene was to us entirely exotic. A Russian soldier in high, creased boots and trim uniform (there are a frightening number of uniforms on all Russian streets) holding the hand of a child; the bent, industrious figures of the ubiquitous street sweepers, old women in dingy black with scarves over their heads, working away with worn brooms and pans to keep the Leningrad streets in an almost embarrassingly hygienic condition. We were thoroughly caught in the special, evocative atmosphere of Leningrad, a city whose old days have an uncontrollable vitality—more than any other place I have known.

After a few blocks we found ourselves walking down the Nevsky Prospekt, the wide, dignified main street, named for the beloved river, the Neva, and for Prince Alexander Nevsky, cherished by Leningraders for his defense of their country centuries ago against the Germans. As we walked between the shops and the princes' town houses (now converted to office blocks), the signs and the names were reminders of the long succession of tsars who had ruled from St. Petersburg: the Alexanders, Peters, Nicholases, Pauls—some victims of assassination, some mad, some considered "good."

We came to the splendid colonnades of the semicircular plaza of the Kazan Cathedral, now part of the U.S.S.R. Academy of Sciences, a museum of the history of religion. Then, turning off the Nevsky Prospekt, we headed for the Neva itself. We crossed a couple of low bridges, followed a flowered boulevard, wandered a bit through what looked like a good residential section, peered for a second into double windows screened by thin white curtains and potted plants. From that quick, secret glimpse it was easy to furnish the room with dark, polished, comfortable family furniture, the fat ginger cat next to the ceiling-high tiled stove in the corner, the family gathered for tea, the samovar on the table, the fresh-baked pastries . . .

Later I realized that this was a picture that had remained in my mind from some Russian novel, that the room was, in fact, empty except for three white-counterpaned beds and that I had been led into fantasy by an atmosphere, by the over-all mood of Leningrad itself.

Jai announced firmly that he was dying of thirst, that his

legs were tired, that it was all very well to be in Russia, but why hadn't we brought his three-wheeler? The problem of thirst was easy to deal with. Practically every street corner in a Russian city seems to have either a soft-drink stand or an ice-cream kiosk. The Russians have a passion for ice cream. Even much later, when it was bitterly cold, we would see people eating ice cream from the street stands and were told they reasoned that at least the ice cream inside them was warmer than the air outside. That day we stopped at a booth selling mineral waters and bought our first bottle of a delicious sort of club soda called Narzan. This pleased us so much that we went into the next stall we saw and were served some sweet but otherwise tasteless red fruit syrup mixed with water. The women behind the counters, identically plump and plain and dressed in white starched uniforms like hospital attendants, were courteous and curious about us and gushingly warm to Jai. Our first Russians. It seems rather flat, in retrospect, that our conversations with them—a pattern that was to be repeated countless times in the following three months—ran something like this: *"Zdravstvuitye"* (Be healthy).

"Zdravstvuitye. You are foreigners?"

"Yes. Tourists."

"Tourists? You like our country?"

"We enjoy it very much."

"Yes. It is a good life, a good life . . ." Then a series of rapid, well-meant questions to Jai (which first bewildered him and finally bored him), ending always with some delighted comment on his black eyes. *Chorniye glaza* soon became a rather tiresome family joke—a symbol of a moment when you have to be polite in spite of your exasperation.

Eventually we found ourselves walking between big blocks of yellow-painted, beautifully proportioned buildings and ahead of us was an immense archway crowned with an angel in a chariot drawn by eight horses. We were passing the General Staff Headquarters, and when we came through the arch we were suddenly in the most dramatic place in Leningrad, the Palace Square. An unimaginably huge plaza in front of the pistachio-colored walls of the Winter Palace, now the Hermitage Museum.

It is always winter in the Palace Square. Even in early autumn, when the air is permanently on the verge of a drizzle and the expanse of clouded Leningrad sky is so grayly in your consciousness, it is like seeing a snow scene. The space is so vast, the obelisk in the center is so high, that all human figures are dwarfed by the distance and the scale of the buildings, all appear to be dressed in black, like skaters, all move soundlessly across the enormous pale stretch of stone (or ice), tiny creatures in a formal etching. Suddenly you know what January in Leningrad must feel like. Snow could only intensify the contrasts.

It was in this square in the past that the droshkies and the troikas, the sleighs and great carriages with their footmen, their bearded, fur-hatted drivers, would draw up. Here the fashionable gentlemen of old St. Petersburg with their ladies would dismount on their way to the palace dances and receptions. Here the Tsar's guard, along with the Cossacks and Dragoons, all in their fairy-tale uniforms of blue and red and gold and black, with plumed helmets and shining sabers, would parade. Here the crowds of ordinary people would gather to see the fantastic procession of the Tsar and his entourage leave for the summer palace, Peterhof, fifteen miles away on the sea.

We walked across the plaza—it took much longer than we would have guessed—and on around the palace itself, the confection of green and white and gold built in the eighteenth century and enlarged for the tiny, imperious, dissolute, scheming, indomitable figure of Catherine the Great. She didn't like the huge summer palace—it reminded her of her days of enforced seclusion there before she was able to grasp power from her simple-minded husband. She had modestly called her new residence, with its tremendous halls, vast marble stairways, its galleries filled with treasures, "The Hermitage." It was, she claimed, the refuge from unhappy past memories.

The Hermitage is now an art museum, its contents representing centuries of unparalleled good living. It was here that the shells were fired that started the Bolshevik Revolution. The city was called Petrograd then. Beyond is the wide, curving gray band of the Neva River, where the cruiser *Aurora,* manned by rebels, trained its guns to fire the first salvo on the Winter Palace. It was in the Palace Square that the rebel forces massed in 1917, only four years after the city had celebrated the three hundredth anniversary of the rule of the Romanovs. But it is necessary to remember also that besides each of those luxurious carriages I imagined there had been a knot of beggars, of ragged children, of hungry, angry men. St. Petersburg, "The Seat of the Tsars," is also Leningrad, "The Cradle of the Revolution." Both aspects of the city have an almost chilling reality at the Winter Palace.

Beyond the palace you find yourself walking along the Neva embankment, and there, suddenly, you grasp the plan of the city—the splendid sweep of the river curling around a hundred islands and headlands, crossed by the graceful arches of bridges, feeding dozens of canals and lesser streams of the delta. On each bank are the disciplined lines of the palaces and churches and ministries. In the distance are the slender spire of the Peter and Paul Fortress (the grim prison of the old days) and the distinctive rostral column on the spit of Vasilievsky Island and beside you, dominating them all, the celebrated statue of Peter the Great, his arm outstretched, poised forever on his rearing horse on top of a massive rock, the Bronze Horseman for whom Pushkin wrote, "Oh, City of Peter, be magnificent . . ."

While walking about Leningrad that first morning we noticed on many of the main streets and intersections booths that looked like cigarette stands bearing signs that read KASSA. These turned out to be theater ticket agencies although they charged no commission. One can buy tickets there for any of the shows. We decided that the best way to spend the evening would be to begin our Russian theatergoing at once, preferably with the ballet. We had seen an advertisement for a performance, that night, of *Swan Lake*.

Accordingly, after a late, slow, and rather greasy luncheon at the hotel, Faubion and I walked to one of the ticket booths. The attendant inside was again a middle-aged woman dressed in clothes that had the dingy, dark look already familiar to us. She sat on a folding chair reading a novel by Alexei Tolstoy. At Faubion's request for two tickets to *Swan Lake,* the woman looked up in surprise. "Why do you want to see THAT *Swan Lake?*" she asked.

"We just wanted to go to the ballet," Faubion said rather uncertainly.

"You are foreigners. Perhaps you do not know that the Leningrad ballet season does not open for another two weeks."

"But this was advertised—"

"Yes, yes, but it is not good," and with that special Leningrad arrogance that we were soon to recognize, she added, "It is merely some company from Novgorod."

We bought the tickets in spite of her advice and were pleasantly astonished to find that they cost only 12 rubles ($1.20) each for seats in the fourth row on the aisle.

I dressed very carefully that evening, in a sari, because I felt it was an Occasion and because I wasn't yet sure how much dressing up the Russians did for the ballet. (I needn't have bothered—most of the women in the audience were in short rayon dresses, some in blouses or sweaters and skirts, all that I saw were wearing walking shoes or low-heeled sandals.)

We took a taxi to the theater, flagging it down as it passed the hotel. It was a small, rattling car, with sagging springs in the back seat, but the driver seemed helpful and, as usual, inquisitive. Where were we from? What were we doing in Russia? When Faubion replied that we were tourists, he tilted his head with a puzzled look. "You come just to look?"

"Yes, we like to travel in foreign countries."

"I had my fill of foreign countries during the war. I was in Poland, in Hungary and Czechoslovakia. I saw enough to know we have a better life here in our country."

"But it's never the same when you travel as a soldier."

The driver shrugged and asked flatly, "How else can we travel?"

He also informed us that the ballet was at a "summer theater" in a *sad otdykha*, usually translated as "a park of culture and rest." Absurd as the phrase sounds in translation, it is, in fact, the most accurate description. You pay a ruble (10 cents) to get in, and then you take your choice of the various entertainments it offers—usually a couple of theaters (where you pay an additional sum for a ticket), an open-air concert shell (free), pavilions to play chess or checkers, an amusement park for children, a café-bar, an ice-cream parlor, a skating rink in winter, and, of course, the paths between the trees for walks. The *sad otdykha* that we went to that night was a small one, with only one theater, a big wooden barn of a place with the vague feeling of a school gymnasium. It wasn't heated and consequently was open only during the summer months to give provincial companies a chance to perform in Leningrad and provide entertainment for Leningraders during the season when their own companies take holidays.

We didn't have to pay the entrance price, were merely asked to show our theater tickets, and once we were past the turnstile we had a few minutes to stroll through the gardens, past the couples on the benches, past the groups of girls walking along arm in arm and the soldiers watching them, past the café with its striped awnings and big umbrellas over the tables, to the theater at the far end. As to the performance itself, I had been quite prepared for hard-working, rather lumpish dancing with the determined amateurism of a small provincial troupe. I had certainly not expected dancing of quite extraordinary precision and polish. The costumes were obviously cheaply made and poorly designed. The scenery was both pretentious and shoddy. But the dancers—especially Novichonok (not at all a famous name in Russian ballet), who danced Odette—were equal to any international standard.

We came out for the first intermission deeply impressed by our first view of ballet in Russia. We walked across to the café for a drink and, quite without planning it, found at least one answer to the problem of how to meet the Russians in Russia.

Watching the other people, we saw that if you sat at a table you were served by a waitress but it was quicker to wait in line at the white counter that ran along one side of the café, give your order to the attendant, and carry your own drink to a table. We took our place at the end of the queue, and immediately the man in front of us turned around, smiled at Faubion, stared at my sari, and asked what we were doing in the garden.

Faubion explained that the first act of *Swan Lake* had just ended, and before he could continue the man shouted to the barmaid, "Give this *tovarisch* his drink—he must get back to the show!" Rather timidly we ordered fifty grams of vodka each —Russians always order liquor by weight—a wineglass full, and carried it over to an empty table. Even if our appearance had not been an obvious giveaway, by that one action we would have stamped ourselves as foreigners. You never have a drink in Russia without also having something to eat. On the liquor counter was a large glass case filled with open sandwiches called *buterbrod*—slices of white or dark bread spread with butter and decorated with a scoop of red caviar, or a few grains of black caviar, or a slice of cold sturgeon, salmon, ham, sausage. Even the men who gulped down their vodka standing at the counter ordered and ate a sandwich immediately afterward.

Our ally from the queue brought his drink over to our table, sat down with us, and then gave us two chocolate candies wrapped in paper. "Please accept these from me. You must eat with your drink—it is bad for your stomach otherwise." He scarcely listened to our embarrassed thanks, but plunged at once into a series of questions about India, America (Did I know how much Russians admired Nehru? Was America really planning war?), our plans and impressions. He interspersed them with comments about Leningrad life and explanations about himself—he was a worker in a factory, was married, had two children. His wife was a worker too. They seldom went out together because they took it in turns to baby-sit, but his wife never came to this café, she preferred to visit her parents on her evenings off. . . . I think we would have been there till closing time if the warning bell for the second act hadn't rung. We sprinted back to the theater to get in before the house lights went down—no Russian theater allows you to take your seat if you are late.

In the days that followed, the *sad otdykha* became our favorite place to spend the evening. Sometimes all of us would go there after tea so that Jai and Ruth could eat ice cream and explore the park while we sat at the most conspicuous table we could find and waited for Russians to come and join us. We soon learned the advantage of being such a disparate and foreign-looking group. Almost always some utter stranger would come up to Jai and give him candies (an expensive generosity—one small chocolate wafer costs 40 to 60 cents), some bought him postcards, or a small toy. One old woman stopped near him to watch him playing, then reached into a capacious black handbag of imitation leather and pulled out a painted wooden bird on a stick. She showed Jai how to press the wooden peg that made the bird peck at its twig. Jai was enthralled, and naturally extremely reluctant to return it when we asked him to. But the old woman shook her head at us. "No, no. Let him keep it. I bought it for my grandchild who is just his age. You are strangers here and probably have not brought the child's toys. Let him keep it."

Once a Red Army officer saw him and, with the easy confidence of almost any Russian with children, picked him up and swung him high in the air. He turned to Faubion and remarked, "You are American? For the sake of this little one there must be no atom war!" and walked on down the path eying the pretty girls.

People were eternally giving Jai badges, the little gilt and enamel pins that Russians love to wear. The badges celebrated a wide variety of events and places. Many were in honor of the Youth Festival that had been held that summer, some were souvenirs of Leningrad, others were mementoes of Czech-Soviet workers' conferences, or winter sports meets, or provincial anniversaries. Soon the lapels of his jacket were encrusted with badges, and understandably the first Russian words he learned were *bolshoye spasibo,* thank you very much, or *spasibo bolshoye,* a polite Leningrad inversion—he needed to use them so often.

Sometimes Faubion and I went to the *sad otdykha* alone, or for an hour in the evening before we went on to a theater. Always we were joined by Russians, many of whom prefaced their arrival by buying us a drink. The waitress would appear, put down a glass of vodka in front of Faubion, and one of something called "portvein" (port wine) which tasted like an extremely sweet sherry, in front of me, and a plate of sweets or snacks between us. "A *droog* [friend] sends you these," she would say, and would at last be persuaded to point out which *droog* had been so kind. We would smile and invite him to our table or he would wait to catch our eye and hurry over himself. Sometimes he would simply sit down with us, omitting all formalities.

The second night we were sitting at one of the tables sheltered by a large metal umbrella. Suddenly one of the brief, light showers of rain characteristic of Leningrad began to fall. The people on the paths continued walking, partly protected by the trees, but the people at the exposed tables in the café moved to the sheltered ones until the rain was over. A middle-aged couple joined us, after asking permission, bringing their drinks with them. The man had a broad pink face and a kind of subterranean joviality. He was tightly buttoned into a dark jacket, which did not match his trousers, and he wore no tie with his dark-blue shirt. He was drinking what I took to be a tumbler of water, along with a glass of beer. His wife seemed more severe: neat, mouse-colored hair drawn back into a bun, and a prim line to her mouth. She was dressed in green-flowered rayon, absolutely without style, and drank only *limonad,* a generic name for all soft drinks. (You don't even specify the flavor of a *limonad* when you order it, and may find yourself drinking soda pop flavored with mandarin juice, apple, lemon, apricot, black currant, to mention only the ones I came across.)

We soon discovered that our companions were a minor government official (he didn't mention the department) and his wife, who was either a dietitian or worked in a food factory—we couldn't make out which. When she smiled she seemed much more friendly than I had thought, and actually she was the one to start the conversation. "You know," she said, "here we have a saying—" she waved a hand at the drizzle —"in Moscow every few minutes the weather changes, in Leningrad only the rain changes."

Faubion responded by saying, "We have a similar saying about Boston." Laboriously he translated: "You don't like the weather in Boston? Well, wait a minute . . ." We smiled politely at each other's jokes.

There was a pause before the woman asked, "Where is Boston?" This launched us on a discussion of America, and because it was the first such conversation we had in Russia it seemed to us interesting quite out of proportion to the value of what was actually said. The government official made his first remark, "The trouble is that you in America do not understand the way we live," and when we asked what he meant by that, he said, "We want only peace. We know what war is like."

Faubion, who had spent six years in the American army during and after the war, pointed out that millions of Americans had been in the war and many had been killed. But the official shook his head. "You did not suffer as we did."

Neither of us was in a mood to enter into an argument, and

in any case we were thoroughly disarmed by his next remark. "But let us not talk of sad things when we have just made new acquaintances. Allow me to buy something a little stronger than water for your wife and yourself." "Something a little stronger than water" turned out to be vodka. When he gave the order to the waitress, we discovered that what he had actually been drinking from his tumbler was vodka, with a beer chaser. His wife stuck to *limonad*.

I never did learn to gulp down my vodka in a single swallow the way the Russians always do, but before my first sip I made a toast of the only absolutely safe remark in Russian that I knew, "*Druzhba i Mir* [Friendship and Peace]," I said.

To that they replied in unison with a phrase which was new to me then but was soon to drive me into a state of bored rebellion: "*Hindi-Russki, bhai-bhai!*" This was a hangover from Nehru's visit to Russia nearly two years earlier, and evidently every Russian had been taught it. In Hindi it means "Indians and Russians are brothers." Anyway, we continued our conversation along fairly banal lines and with no further references to the war. It was only later that I learned how deeply the terrible 900-day siege of Leningrad by the Germans in 1941-1944 is burned into the consciousness of its citizens. Even now, so many years later, they remember and refer to it all the time. Once a very drunk man came reeling over to Faubion in that same park, apparently mistaking him for a German, and said in scarcely comprehensible Russian, "The war is over! We bear no resentments. I even—I *even* like the Germans."

"I am an American," Faubion announced rather crossly.

"*Druzhba i Mir!*" the man said, and tottered happily off.

At some point that evening, in our exchange of information with the official and his wife about what we should see in Leningrad and what we were interested in and why, a young man

came and sat down quietly at our table. We scarcely noticed
him at first. He whispered his order to the waitress and took
no part in our conversation, but as I watched him drinking his
beer and eating his bread and sausage I could tell that he was
listening. When it was our turn to buy a round of drinks,
Faubion included him in the order because it seemed to be the
way the Russians did it. A rather pleasant custom, I thought,
anyone joins anyone's table in any public place and, unlike, say,
the British in similar circumstances, immediately gets into conversation, orders drinks, and makes a small party out of a chance
encounter. It was certainly very convenient for us. However,
when Faubion ordered a beer for the young man, he turned
scarlet with embarrassment. "No, no," he said, blinking behind
his steel-rimmed glasses. "You are guests in our country—I
should be buying the drinks—"

"Please allow us—"

"I cannot drink more—"

"Just one more beer?"

"You are very kind. The truth is, I have not enough money on
me to pay for all."

We overruled his objections and he did, at last, accept a
beer, but remained as quiet and ill at ease as before. The
official's wife turned to us rather despairingly and said, "My
husband drinks far too much. *Even at ten o'clock in the morning*
he drinks vodka. What shall I do?"

He broke in jovially to say, "I am a good husband and I do
not disgrace myself. What more do you want?"

She looked away from him and said, "Our daughter is grown
up now. When she was small I wouldn't allow vodka in the
house. It is the curse of our country."

"But your children no longer live with you?" Faubion asked.

"They are married," she said, without enthusiasm. "My son

also begins to drink. It is easily understood. Our women are so emancipated now they no longer behave like women. Often his wife refuses to cook—*refuses to cook!* He must plead with her, indulge her, quarrel with her. Instead, he drinks. I never approved of the marriage. I was right. But he wouldn't listen—"

"Still you see them?"

She smiled. "They have a child now. I am a grandmother. It is always different with a grandchild. Is it not so in your country?"

"In my country too."

"But he shouldn't drink so much."

In spite of various protests, we all had more drinks and continued our rather slow conversation. At some point Faubion turned to the young man and said, "Tell me, what should we *do* in Leningrad?—by way of amusement, I mean."

He at once reeled off a number of plays and concerts that were on in the coming couple of weeks, but Faubion interrupted to say, "I didn't mean *culture,* I meant just, well, a good time—"

With a kind of shy eagerness he said, "For that you must go to the Astoria Hotel."

"We're staying at the Astoria—it's not very lively."

"Ah, but you can see foreigners there."

Eventually we decided it was time to leave, and when we said our good-bys the official's wife stood up. "I must thank you for the most interesting evening of my life," she said with every evidence of sincerity. Faubion and I could only stare at her, and gently she explained: "I have lived in Leningrad for twenty-eight years, and you are the first foreigners I have met."

When we got to the gate of the park we heard a voice behind us calling, *"Gospodin! Gospodin!"* Several people turned to

look, and we did too. It was the young man from our table in
his brown slacks and sweater, his light hair rumpled from
running, and his face again flushed with embarrassment. "Forgive me for delaying you—I would very much like to entertain
you and your wife—you have been most kind."

"It was our pleasure."

"Will you meet me here, tomorrow, at the same hour?"

"We would be delighted."

"Do zavtry" (Until tomorrow).

"Do zavtry."

It was naturally with great eagerness that we went to the
park at six o'clock the next evening. We half expected that
our new friend would not show up at all. We hadn't yet
learned that the Russians seem to be the most punctual people
in the world. (Much later, in Moscow, a Russian told us that
this meticulous punctuality was a habit from the Stalinist days.
"If you were not exactly on time your friend would not wait.
He would know that . . . well, that something had happened
to you." Whatever the reason, it was an odd reversal of my
preconceived idea of Russians as by nature unimpressed by
appointments, with an Asian sense that clocks are there for
the convenience of people, not for their enslavement.)

We hurried down the path to the café, and stopped with
relief when we saw the young man, dressed exactly as before,
already seated at the table we had occupied the previous night.
He stood up politely, and we greeted each other, and this time
introduced ourselves. His name was Alexandr Mikhailovich
Petrov, and as a result of firm tutoring from Faubion I knew
I should call him Alexandr Mikhailovich, *not* Mr. Petrov. Fortunately, after listening to my struggles to pronounce this
casually in conversation, he suggested that we call him Sasha,

while we became Santa (there is no "th" in Russian) and Fedya, an abbreviation of "Theodore," because Faubion was altogether too bizarre a name for him to cope with.

I had expected the usual constraints of first conversations and new acquaintances—had, in fact, thought they would be particularly sticky in Russia—but found that even with his opening remarks Sasha set the tone for ease, if not actual intimacy. "I wanted very much to talk with you yesterday," he said, "but I did not feel free in front of those others."

We wondered, of course, whether this had been because the man was a government servant, but Sasha shrugged his shoulders and said that it was only that they were *nye kulturnye* —uncultured. This was not much help because *nye kulturnye* in Soviet terminology can mean anything from a person who likes hot jazz or wears low-cut dresses to bad table manners or a genuine lack of cultivation. "He drinks too much," Sasha added thoughtfully. "I sometimes feel that Russians cannot love their wives—look at how much they drink. If they loved their wives they would give them money and say, 'Here is some extra money—buy yourself what you need.' Instead, they spend it on vodka."

"Americans drink a lot too, you know," Faubion said.

"Please do not misunderstand what I am going to say, I love my country. I could not think of living anywhere but Leningrad. But I think this is true: in America you drink out of a good life. A good life for the rich like you—"

"We aren't rich."

"You must be rich, how else could you travel so far? But in Russia we drink out of a poor life. We drink to make things better." He asked us then what our work was, and when we told him we were writers he looked triumphant. "I *knew* you were rich! All writers are rich." He quickly called the waitress and, without consulting us, ordered vodka for us and beer for himself—perhaps because that was what we had been drinking the evening before.

"But you don't seem to drink much," Faubion said.

Sasha smiled at us suddenly, a smile of great sweetness. "That is because I have other pleasures. I love the theater—classics. And I am an architect. So I am fortunate to be born in this historic city of Leningrad where it is a pleasure simply to walk down the street." It was then that we got our first indication of the rivalry between Leningrad and Moscow. Sasha, warming to his subject, said, "When you go to Moscow you will understand my meaning. A confusion of houses—skyscrapers next to fifteenth-century wooden huts—a jagged skyline, nothing like the symmetry of our city. I think it is a mistake to have moved the capital to Moscow. The history is here—even the history of the Revolution. The beauty is here, more than anywhere in Russia. Let them have their factories in Moscow. We will always keep the culture."

Sasha was the one who told us odd facts about Leningrad: how Tsar Paul I had issued the edict that no building in the city should be higher than his palace, four stories, and that by the time the edict could be flouted, in the past fifty or sixty years, there had been virtually no building erected in the city at all. And how during the building of the city the Tsar had ordered that all the bricks made in Russia should be sent to the capital to complete the royal city, while the rest of the country could build in stone or wood. And how the spire of the Peter and Paul Fortress, a thousand meters high, had been specially planned to be the highest architectural point in Russia. He also told us that the Moscow government had changed the name of Nevsky Prospekt to something commemorating the famous October 10, but that Leningraders had been so outraged at this highhanded treatment of their historic names that the main street was rechristened Nevsky Prospekt. And on and on.

He carried his loyalty to Leningrad even further. He insisted that the purest Russian was spoken in Leningrad, the best manners were to be found there—"the vulgarity of Moscow is so great—you will see—that in the busy hour when people return from work you can *even* be pushed off the sidewalk into the street. This could never happen here." He had been in Moscow once, when he was a teen-ager.

As we got to know him better he told us scattered stories about how Leningrad maintains its reputation for intellectual activity. The artists and writers it produces feel so strongly about their city that (according to Sasha) the eminent musician Shostakovich had to be forced to be flown out of Leningrad on a stretcher during the German siege because he could not bear to leave his beloved city in a time of peril. He had stuck to the official ration—three slices of bread. Shostakovich still insists that any new symphony of his be played first in Leningrad. The only exception, ironically enough, was his best known, called the Leningrad Symphony (the 8th), written to honor the heroism of the citizens during the siege, which had its premiere in Moscow.

I was captivated by Sasha's romantic love of his city—I was captivated by Leningrad too, with its slightly faded beauty, but that was partly as a reflection of Sasha. "Please, Sasha," I said, "will you show us around Leningrad—the Leningrad you are so fond of, I mean?" And while Faubion translated this, I wished I hadn't spoken. Probably one shouldn't be so direct with Russians. But luckily he smiled again, and said, "It would give me great pleasure—but it is only possible during the weekends and in the evening. I must go to my work, you know."

We thought that the best way to start our new friendship

was to invite Sasha to dinner—at the Astoria, since he seemed interested in the people one saw there—so we suggested this (also a bit timidly) and felt much more confident when he not only accepted but asked if he might bring his wife. It was the first time he had mentioned her, and his description of her, for some reason, seemed to me terribly touching. He said, "She is not like me . . ." He stared earnestly at the table under his glasses. "She is beautiful." With one of those Russian bursts of frankness he said, apropos of nothing, "She cannot have children. Perhaps that is good. Where would we put a child? She works in the telegraph office. But you will like her . . . I'm sure you will like her."

We arranged to dine the night after next.

I hadn't realized when we made the date that we had picked a Saturday. It was, therefore, something of a surprise to hear Sasha's voice on the telephone soon after noon the day of our engagement. For a moment I thought we might have invited him to luncheon, not dinner, but no. He was calling from a street phone to ask, if we were doing nothing that afternoon, whether we would like to see his favorite place in Leningrad. We accepted with alacrity and met him in the lobby ten minutes later. He shook hands with us formally, saying, "Allow me, please, I wish to take you to the apartment of Alexander Pushkin."

You can hardly help hearing a lot about Pushkin in Leningrad. You are told with monotonous regularity that he was the "Father of Russian Literature"; his work and personality seem to pursue you even into modern Soviet life. Some opera, play, or ballet based on one of his poems always seems to be playing in one of the theaters—*Eugene Onegin, Boris Godunov, Russlan and Ludmilla, The Queen of Spades*—and even in the ordinary conversation of a Leningrader you hear frequent references or quotations from him. For instance, a Russian will sometimes say of a girl in love with a man who obviously has no interest in her, "She has been dressed since morning," knowing that his hearer will know Pushkin's famous line from *Eugene Onegin* and will recall the panic of nerves with which Tatyana waited for Onegin to call and reply to her imprudent love letter.

The city itself is studded with reminders of Pushkin—statues and pictures, a school named after him and a subway station, the Pushkin Theater with, so Sasha assured us, the best dramatic company in Leningrad, "more original, also more expert than even the Moscow Art Theater." So it didn't particularly surprise me that Sasha wanted to take us to Pushkin's apartment. What I hadn't expected was that we would instantly step into the infinitely foreign, absolutely real world of early-nineteenth-century Russia. I experienced again one of those schizophrenic moments so common in Leningrad, standing in the seven elegantly formal rooms with the serious, shabby figure of Sasha beside us.

The Soviets have a pleasing custom of preserving the house or apartment of a very distinguished person as an informal sort of museum. Often, of course (as in Pushkin's case), the apartment has been taken over by other people after the owner's death, the furniture scattered. But as far as possible, in such museums, the apartment is restored to its original condition, the furniture and pictures reassembled, the décor copied from contemporary records and descriptions. To me, as I saw more of them—Tolstoy's house in Moscow, Scriabin's apartment, and so on—they formed an oddly moving aspect of Russia, the obvious contrasts with modern life, the unexpected similarities, the intimate living detail that at once attaches to famous names.

Standing in the dining room or one of the salons of the Pushkin apartment, looking out of the long windows with the looped curtains, you see one of Leningrad's many canals. "In summer," Sasha said, beside us, "sightseers and, of course, the young couples take pleasure boats along this canal." Always you would see such a boat against the background of grand buildings, still painted in the lighthearted colors of past fancies —yellow and apple green, dove-gray and rose—and almost effortlessly you are back in the flamboyant days of the tsars, when St. Petersburg was "the Paris of East Europe," the capital of all the Russias, the center of the intellectual life, a city deliberately designed for kings and their courtiers. Sasha was saying, "During the White Nights"—high summer when twilight lasts all night and the whole city changes—"lovers take such boats all the way to the Neva . . . and then on perhaps to Peterhof . . . all night. . . . It is beautiful then. You can have a picnic at midnight."

And when we turned away from the window to the cool stylishness of early eighteenth-century furniture in the room, to the satins and brocades, it was easy to fill the room with imagined gatherings of Pushkin and his friends. Clustered at the dining table, perhaps, discussing contributions to Pushkin's literary magazine, *Contemporary*. Possibly deciding to publish a story by an unknown called Gogol, or the memoirs of that amazing woman Durova, who disguised herself as a soldier and fought in the War of 1812 without being discovered. Easy to picture a group of artists and nobles seated at the round table under the huge portrait of Pushkin in the inner salon, which he saved for his special friends, talking, deciding on the spur of the moment that each would write a couplet for a song, and Glinka, Pushkin's lifelong friend, would write the music. You can see the finished product—Sasha showed it to us—propped on the music stand of the piano in the corner of the room.

The names themselves, as Sasha recited them, were an evocation of an age: Prince Volkonsky, who had the chic literary and musical salon of St. Petersburg; Prince Baryatinsky, versatile in the arts; Kiprensky, who, for lack of paints, made a portrait in butter of Pushkin when he was in exile for his part in the abortive insurrection of 1845; Krylov, who wrote the wonderful Russian fairy tales, somewhere between Aesop and Hans Andersen; Linyev the painter, Zhukovsky the famous poet . . .

"You see," Sasha said with pride, "from where comes Leningrad's tradition of culture and intellectuals?" As a sort of counterpoint to the things we inspected in the rooms—first editions of Pushkin's books, scores of holographs from musicians, writers, painters, all the memorabilia of the intellectual life of the times—Sasha told us about the high place that the university and the intellectuals of modern Leningrad hold in their country, about the Soviet writers who follow in the tradition of Pushkin, Lermontov, Gogol, Turgenev—all Leningrad writers. The only story that I remembered was one I didn't think I could repeat to Sasha. It was about Dudintsev, the author of *Not by Bread Alone* who, I had been told, had come to the Leningrad University to make one of his public apologies for the "errors" in his much-publicized novel. The apology had been accepted by one of the deans of the university, but his speech had been drowned out by yells of "No! No!" from the students who evidently didn't want to see their dean or their university fall in so spinelessly with the dictated line. In a way the story justified Sasha's conviction that Leningrad somehow maintained an inherited intellectual vigor, but at the same time it didn't seem entirely tactful to mention it to someone who so frequently insisted that Communism, the Communist way, was the only possible future for Russia and its people.

In the charming femininity of the rooms of Pushkin's wife, the other essential side of Old St. Petersburg takes on life— the social world of a major capital. There you realize that she was giddy and extravagant and beautiful, loved the palace parties (which Pushkin, as a courtier of the Tsar, was compelled to attend) and the fashionable life of the city. She could spend in a month, without a thought, 471 rubles on hats alone from the exclusive French milliner Mme. Zoë Malpart—there is still the bill addressed in French, as was proper for the nobility of the time, to "Son Excellence Mme. Pouschkine." The kind of woman who saved invitations, sentimental mementoes . . . the kind of woman who was eventually involved in a society love affair that caused her husband's death.

Pushkin's study is more casual, quite unpretentious. He must have sat at this very desk with its scuffed black-leather top, its brass candlestand, its black-stone inkpot, and wondered what to do. He must have turned for comfort to his books, massed against the wall, those famous books to which he addressed his last words. As he lay dying, mortally wounded in a duel with his wife's admirer, he said to his doctor, "I am feeling very bad."

His doctor asked, "Do you want to see your friends?"

Pushkin turned his head to look at those crowded shelves and said, "Farewell, my friends."

Sasha seemed to be almost on the point of tears when he told us this. He said, "The news of his wound had spread through the city like fire—like flood—think of it, people had stood outside all night waiting for news." Zhukovsky, Pushkin's closest friend, posted bulletins on the front door to keep them informed. Sasha pointed out the handwritten scrawls, and read: "The first half of the night he was restless. The second half he was quieter. No new complications, but no improvement and no possibility of improvement," or, "The sick one is in rather a dangerous condition." Sasha looked depressed.

From his bed Pushkin must have been able to look out his back windows to the serene correctness of the garden in the courtyard. Like most of the residential buildings in Leningrad, his is built on a design of a hollow square. Perhaps the orderliness of the trim lawns, the rose garden, the beds of scarlet salvia, the white-painted benches, offered him some relaxation from the muddle of his own life, the pressures of conflicting wishes and duties.

I understood why Sasha had brought us there. Pushkin's life, as much as his death, was contained in those rooms, the times he knew and the people, the concerns, St. Petersburg life—a whole world, really. And one was aware that it was the Soviets who had made possible this excursion into the past.

Dinner that night was quite different from our usual staid, heavy, and quite uninteresting meals. Perhaps it was simply that I was seeing the Astoria through Sasha's eyes. Before, the only remarkable thing I had noticed about the hotel restaurant was that there was permanently a sign on the door saying, "Restaurant Closed," even though you could hear the music and the chatter from inside. This, Sasha explained, was to provide an unarguable excuse to keep out undesirables, drunks, or people who obviously could not afford the prices.

In the interval between the Pushkin apartment, where Sasha had left us to go home, change and pick up his wife, and the moment we met again in the lobby of the hotel, I had wondered whether we should order dinner beforehand, but had decided that it would be interesting to see what a Russian orders of his own choice. I particularly wanted to know what the tastes of Sasha's wife, Victoria, would be.

She came wearing a blue corduroy shirtwaist dress. It wasn't quite clean, but that didn't surprise me. Faubion had sent a suit to be pressed that morning—only pressed, not cleaned— and it had cost 15 rubles, a bit more than an orchestra seat at the theater. Anywhere else she would have been described as "mousy," but my eye was becoming practiced as to Russian looks, and I could see why Sasha had described her as beautiful. She was slender, for one thing, and had good legs with trim ankles. She had a quantity of soft brown hair which flopped over her forehead almost into her eyes, and swung low at the back of her neck. She had the fine, clear skin of most Russian girls, and pleasant but quite unmemorable features. You wouldn't have looked at her twice in America. She was quite friendly, but disconcerted me from the start because she said she wanted nothing to eat or drink because she and Sasha had already had dinner. We turned to Sasha for confirmation, and he nodded and said, "Yes, yes, we have had our meal." Faubion ordered Russian cognac and fruit for all of us.

In spite of this unpromising beginning, the evening continued fairly cheerfully. Saturday night at the Astoria was much gayer than weekdays. We were used to the foreigners there— the people who had given the Astoria such an exotic appeal for Sasha. There were only two tourists besides us, but the delegations from foreign countries, invited by the Russian government, ebbed and flowed through the dining room and lobby like a shifting tide. One day there would be a Chinese military mission staying overnight as part of its tour, the next day there might be a group of French Left-Wing Socialists, of Czech trade-union leaders, of Lebanese "friendship societies," of British theater people. They always sat at the long tables at one side of the dining room, and there would be flowers and miniature flags of the appropriate nation set among the plates of hors d'oeuvres and bread. They were always accompanied by interpreters and officials, and after meals there were always speeches or songs, and many repetitions, in unison, of *"Druzhba! Druzhba! Druzhba!"* The whole elaborate series of arrangements had too organizational a flavor to suit me, but there seemed to be no doubt that the members of the various delegations were impressed—at least the few we met at the Astoria and later in other Russian hotels. Probably they were already sympathetic to the regime, possibly they were shown only the best, but there was no faking the fact that they were expertly taken care of and that there was a steady supply of interpreters for even the most out-of-the-way language.

I remember once, at the theater in Moscow, hearing what sounded like a detailed translation of the play going on in the row behind us, for the benefit of a group of Southeast Asians whose nationality Faubion and I guessed was Vietnamese. In the interval our curiosity was too much for us, and Faubion asked the interpreter what language he was speaking. "Laotian," he replied, as though it was the most natural thing in the world. And then I was really impressed. There are only about two million Laotians anywhere, and yet Russia can produce interpreters for the rare delegation that visits Moscow. I wondered whether the State Department, the British, French, Indian, Japanese Foreign Offices could do the same.

Apart from the cheerful familiarity of the waiters with the guests, the handshake at meeting, the pauses at the tables for a brief chat, the exchange of cigarettes, the use of "Comrade" (or "Dear comrade") instead of "Waiter" and "Yes, sir!" the thing that most amused me that evening was having Sasha and his wife watch the foreign delegations with a frank curiosity, while Faubion and I stared with equal eagerness at the Russians. On Saturdays, evidently, the young, smart crowd in Leningrad came to the Astoria. There were several girls in silk or taffeta dresses that *fitted* them. Some of them had short, curled hair, make-up, high heels. I could hardly believe that after only a few days in Russia they should look so unfamiliar to me. The young men with them were better dressed than Sasha (who was wearing the same brown trousers we had first seen him in, but this time with a matching jacket, a white shirt and a rayon tie) but still would have been remarkable nowhere except Russia. Actually, looking around, we soon saw that there are no dress regulations even in the best Russian restaurants. There were several men in slacks and windbreakers and many without ties.

As soon as the music started—nine o'clock—they sprang up instantly to dance, and continued all through the evening dancing with amazing diligence and energy. It was fortunate that the rests between numbers were unusually long so that they did get a chance to eat and drink a bit to sustain them. Sasha and Victoria both viewed these other young people with a certain disapproval. "Yes," Sasha admitted rather reluctantly in reply to our questions, "they *are* Russians, but we are not very proud of their sort. Their parents have worked hard and done well, so they can give their children money and advantages. But the children—they have forgotten the sacrifice of their parents for the sake of the Revolution. They live on the advantages, *even* use their parents' cars—cars that are allowed for essential work or special services. Pleasure is too important to them. I consider this immoral."

This attitude was still quite novel to me, so I watched the other young Russians with renewed interest. They didn't seem even faintly immoral to me. Perhaps they danced a bit closer than most Russians. One girl, in the corner of the dance floor, was attempting, with much laughter, to teach her partner a very simple jitterbug step. They seemed to be enjoying themselves, that was about all. But Sasha was saying, censoriously, "Some of them even have black market jazz recordings which they play at home. I find this terrible when we all have access to so much good music."

"Is *all* jazz considered bad?" Faubion asked.

"Oh, no," Sasha said eagerly, and entirely without humor. "There is *good* jazz, and *bad* jazz. We know that *good* jazz is a natural expression of the people. We encourage that. But *bad* jazz is—" he paused, wondering, I suppose, how to phrase this politely "—well, bad jazz is often a foreign influence, a bourgeois expression which is not natural to our people."

From listening to the band that evening, and on many succeeding evenings in other places, we began to get an idea of what Sasha meant by "good" jazz. The only tunes I recognized to begin with were slow, sentimental songs like *It's a Sin to Tell a Lie* and *Deep Purple*. Nothing hot and nothing fast except a few bright, bouncy numbers evolved from country dances or peasant songs. There was one song the orchestra played near the end of the evening which seemed to mean something special to both Victoria and Sasha and to the other Russians there. Sasha and his wife smiled at each other, many of the others sang the words softly as they danced or as they looked at each other across the table. It was the kind of sad, thoroughly emotional song that seemed to me exactly appropriate to the accepted picture of the Russian character and to this setting of faded luxury—the marble pillars and chandeliers, the plaster and gilt and rose-shaded table lamps.

Sasha turned to us to explain. "This song is by Peter Leshchenko, an artist in popular music, it is called *The Cranes*—this will show you how liberal is our government. Peter Leshchenko traveled abroad, and in Czechoslovakia, during the war, he sang for the Nazis. After that he was not, of course, permitted to return to Russia. But, like all Russians, he could not live happily outside his own country—naturally, he loved Russia. After the war he begged to return. Once he sang for Russian soldiers, and he sang on his knees a song he had written, *I Long for the Homeland.* It is very moving."

"And then they let him return?"

"Oh, no. But they allow his music to be played here."

We must have looked a bit blank, because Sasha elaborated carefully. "He knows his songs are played in Russia. The soldiers brought them back. Even *The Cranes* is about his wish to return—in its words, he sees the cranes flying in the sky above him, flying toward Russia. But he cannot follow them."

Luckily, at about half past ten Faubion and I were hungry enough to decide that we would have dinner even if our guests had dined before they came. Purely automatically, Faubion offered them the menu first. Sasha and Victoria ordered borsch, with shashlik after that, and something called "plombière Astoria" for dessert. It seemed to me a most satisfactorily Russian choice. We didn't finish eating until nearly midnight.

As we were saying our good nights in the lobby, Sasha suddenly became extremely formal. "My wife and I wish to thank you for your hospitality to us this evening. You have shown us that foreigners are not as we had thought. We wish to inquire whether you will come out with us tomorrow. It is Sunday, and we would like to take you to see the great palace, Peterhof. We can travel by the 'electric' at ten-thirty in the morning."

Victoria said shyly, "Please bring your little boy. I am so fond of children."

We agreed with enthusiasm and planned to meet in the lobby at ten the next morning.

It occurred to us only the next morning that, instead of making the tedious fifteen-mile trip by electric railway to the summer palace of Peterhof (the Russians always pronounce it Petergof because there is no "h" in Russian, except in the South), we might be able to hire a car at the hotel. This would allow us to arrange our time as we wanted, and if Jai got too bored or tired we could return at once. We inquired about this at the hotel desk, and were referred to the Intourist bureau. This was when Svetlana came into our lives.

I disliked Svetlana on sight for her intractable features and for the scornful chilliness of her manner. Her opening words to us in the Intourist office were "You have been in Leningrad nearly one week, and you have not applied until now to the Service Bureau."

Rather surprised by both her good English and her reproachful tone, I said, "We haven't needed anything so far."

"My name is Svetlana. That is what tourists may call me. My full name will be too difficult. I am assigned to be your interpreter and guide."

"We only wanted to know how we should set about hiring a car."

"You are entitled, on your coupons, to a Zim limousine for two hours a day for each member of the party, or to a Volga, a smaller car, for three hours a day. Since you have not used one until now, these hours have accumulated."

"Well, that's wonderful. We want a big car today at ten-thirty to go to Peterhof. I don't know how long we'll be there."

"If you wished for my services as guide, you should have let me know in advance. We are very busy."

"Fortunately we don't need you. We are going with friends."

"Other tourists?" she asked.

"No," I said nastily. "Russian friends."

Her expression didn't change. "The car will be ready at ten-thirty."

When Sasha and Victoria arrived we hustled them joyfully into the long black car, all of us commenting happily on this unexpected convenience, on the fact that the day was sunny though cool, deciding that we needn't stop for sandwiches because there was a restaurant in the grounds of the palace. We set out on the longish drive through the flat delta country, slowly leaving Leningrad proper behind and then picking up speed in the scattered suburbs. It was there that Sasha told us a sour little wartime joke—you still hear it sometimes in a conversation between Leningraders. One man asks another, "Where in Leningrad do you live?" The other replies, "At the front line."

He means that he lives in the suburbs, and everyone remembers for a moment the Leningrad siege, with a bitter relief that the days when the suburbs were quite literally the front lines of battle are over.

All the way out to Peterhof there were plenty of other reminders. Just outside the city, enshrined on the side of the road, was the first Russian tank that went out to resist the Germans. "We had only one factory," Sasha said, "producing tanks as fast as was possible. They went straight out to the front lines—to the suburbs—without even being tested."

"Were you in Leningrad during the siege?"

"Not after the beginning. I was too young. Only twelve. Like the other children, I was sent away to a camp in Siberia. There was not enough food and not enough people to take care of us. It was easier for us, the older children, but for the small ones, three or four years old, it was very hard. The long journey and the separation they could not understand. And how can one explain?" With a touch of pride he said, "But my parents stayed in Leningrad. I knew it helped them to be sure that I was safe in the interior."

Gradually we learned how important it is even to the modern Leningrader to distinguish between those citizens who "stayed" and those who left their city for safe jobs in the interior, for refugee camps, for shelter with relatives in other cities. "My mother has described it to me," Sasha was saying, "how Leningrad became a city of women and old people and babies too young to leave their mothers. The men were all at the front."

Little by little Leningrad's private war of attrition began to change the look of the city. The Germans shelled the big food reserves. People ate what they could find—even vermin. In mounting numbers the ones who had stayed began to die. The babies first; they had least resistance. Then the old and frail. Finally the young, strong women. Every morning the corpses were piled on trucks and taken away; you could hear them rattling down the street.

On another occasion a woman we met told us of the endless evenings of winter, during the blackout. There was no electricity and people had to devise ways of passing the time between spells of fire-watching duty. An artist friend who was staying with her had worn a pencil down to a stub by drawing, over and over again, the little ornaments in the room and their grotesque, flickering shadows by candlelight, enclosing the room like ghosts on every side. Our friend had the picture still, on her mantelpiece. "Things and Their Shadows" it was called. Another reminder of the slow nightmare of the siege that she had lived through.

Yet Sasha's oddly flat but proud account of those days was

somehow more arresting. A boy of twelve in a froze
organized camp in Siberia, thinking of his parents wh
"stayed" with their city. Much later, too, Faubion and I went
to see a play called *Hotel Astoria,* named for the Leningrad
hotel which had been an officers' billet during the war. There
is a scene between a mother who has just heard of her son's
death at the front and a hotel chambermaid who attempts,
rather ineptly, to comfort her. The maid reaches into the
pocket of her apron and brings out a pair of nylons. "I bought
these yesterday," she says. "They looked so thin and pretty as
I passed the shop—here, you take them. It was funny, when I
bought them the woman next to me said, 'Are you mad? These
are summer stockings and now it is winter. Too cold to wear
them now, and by next summer we shall all be dead.'" And I
found tears in my eyes thinking about Sasha and our drive out
to Peterhof, past the ruined palaces along the road, the country
houses of long-dead princes, some partly restored and made
habitable for workers' families, some still scarred and blackened
and deserted.

It seemed to me very strange, during that drive, that the
Bolshevik Revolution, which started in Leningrad (then Petrograd) and which changed so much more than just the city's
name, had not obscured forever all sense of the city's aristocracy. It was in Sasha's attitude, a modern Leningrader in a
Soviet society, in his explanation that what was once a private
palace is now a public palace—the word is still used—a palace
of work or a palace of culture. It was in his insistence that this
had never been a market town, like Moscow, or an industrial
city, like Stalingrad, Rostov, Kharkov. It had never depended
on the peasants around it. Its heart was never in trade. It still
isn't, though now you notice it only in hidden hints in the
conversation of Leningraders, in their elaborate, old-fashioned

turns of phrase, in their strict decorum and courtesy. And the holdover of the aristocratic attitude may explain why to Leningraders, as to Sasha, the favorite excursion is to take the river boat or the electric to Peterhof for the day.

There, following Sasha's lead, we stood under the golden cupola at one end of the main building and admired its ornate delicacy. With Peter the Great's palace, a smaller version of Versailles, as a background, we strolled through the meticulously planned "wilderness," through woods, along a manicured beach on the Gulf of Finland. Sharing the pleasure of Sasha and Victoria we sampled the eighteenth-century taste for careless, natural scenery, all carefully contrived, and its fine talent for the geometrically exact garden, the long straight avenues, the vistas.

We stared unbelievingly—and to Sasha's delight—at some of the most elaborate fountains in the world, cascades and sprays and jets decorated with gilded nude statues, mythological figures, dolphins, dragons. Leningraders (and Jai) are still immoderately amused by the playful whimseys of past aristocrats. There is always an enthusiastic crowd round the trick fountains, the plain-looking bench that suddenly squirts water at you when you try to sit on it, the uncannily realistic fruit tree that drenches you as soon as you try to pick an apple, the big, umbrella-shaped shelter that allows you to come in to rest, but then cascades water down all around you so that you are trapped until it stops. The whole place is conscientiously maintained, from the gilding and the lighting of the fountains to the trimming of the grass or the pruning of the trees.

It is only when you get to the palace itself that you realize what an effort this maintenance represents, and the thousands and thousands of rubles that have gone into its reconstruction since the war. The outer shell of the palace has been restored, but inside the rubble and piles of lumber and the gutted rooms that you see through the windows are as the Germans left them fourteen years ago. Showing us around the grounds, Sasha and Victoria's manner had been pleasantly relaxed and amicable, but at the palace the first trace of bitterness showed in Sasha's voice. "The Fascists used the palace to stable their horses. There are buildings intended for stables . . . but they used the palace." Following some train of thought of his own, he added, "You understand why people compare us to a bear. You can prod us with a stick once—twice—three times—but then we fight, and we are stubborn. You cannot defeat us."

But to him, as to most Leningraders we met, whatever the residue of anger at the war, there seemed no cause for resentment at the huge expenditure on public monuments and buildings, even though it vastly delayed the improvement of their own meager living conditions. The beauty of the city of Leningrad came first, certainly in Sasha's mind and also, as we were repeatedly told, in the minds of all loyal citizens.

There was something very sad about the sight of Sasha and Victoria, dressed in clothes that were just this side of shabbiness, standing in front of the shell of Peterhof. To me it was a picture—a superficial picture, admittedly—of modern Leningrad. No more princes—or paupers. The reminders of revolution and war behind each lovely building. The hard, determined, careful life that has emerged from it all.

I think it was at that moment that the idea came to me of trying to find the apartment of Dostoyevsky. Looking at those two respectable, unimpressive figures, I was reminded that there was *always* another life in St. Petersburg, even in the old days of its splendor, a life that was far removed from the palaces and parties, from the doings of grand dukes and duchesses, from the salons of the intellectuals. Its most famous chronicler was, of course, Fyodor Dostoyevsky, who inhabited quite another world from that of the almost legendary Pushkin. He wrote more than a generation later, but he never had Pushkin's view of the "Magnificent City of Peter." The titles of his books were an indication—*Poor Folk, The Housewife, The Insulted and Injured, The Idiot, Crime and Punishment* . . . This was the other life of the city.

After lunch in a pleasant open-air restaurant by the sea, we drove back to Leningrad, and at some point during the drive I asked Sasha about Dostoyevsky. Since he had taken us to the two most evocative places we had seen in Leningrad, I explained, I thought he would be the perfect person to come with us to Dostoyevsky's apartment. I wanted to see if it held, as Pushkin's had, the air and feeling of his times, of *his* life in the city. I had a vague idea that this would be the only way we might see a little of that "other life" of St. Petersburg.

But Sasha said noncommittally, "I do not know where that apartment is."

"Well, we'll try to find it, and when we do, will you come with us?"

"Please find out first. Afterwards we will perhaps arrange something."

Perhaps irrationally, I felt rather snubbed.

Leningrad is full of ghosts, full of the famous, the brilliant, the unhappy people who lived there, rich with their surroundings and the scenes that must have been familiar to them. If Pushkin still lived in his old apartment, I thought, surely Dostoyevsky, a more troublesome and assertive ghost, must haunt a room somewhere in Leningrad. Anyway, I was going to search for that room, but finding it proved to be rather less than simple. It was not listed in any of the guidebooks or

among the "places of interest to tourists." None of the biographies that I could find in Leningrad bookshops gave his
St. Petersburg address. It seemed impossible that a man of
such driving anger and despair should not have left a mark of
his presence in some house in the city that had tormented him
and held him, that had provided a setting for so much of his
writing. Not that he had been unaware of its beauties ("I love
the March sun in Petersburg, especially at sunset, in clear
frosty weather, of course. The whole street glitters, bathed in
brilliant light. All the houses seem to sparkle of a sudden . . .
it is as though everything seems brighter, as though you were
startled, or someone had nudged you with his elbow . . ."),
but he was equally conscious of its intense gloom ("Twilight
was deepening and I felt more and more melancholy . . . I
kept thinking that in the end I should die in Petersburg . . .
if only I could get out of this shell into the light of day, breathe
the freshness of the fields and woods . . .").

At last, reluctantly, I presented my problem to Svetlana at
the Intourist bureau. She asked briskly, "You are interested in
the writing of Dostoyevsky?"

"Well, yes," I said, and found myself explaining, "Possibly
it is because prose translates so much more easily than poetry."
I felt this was a pretty safe remark because Russians are constantly telling you that much of the nuance of Pushkin's poetry
is lost in English, but she replied rather coolly, "I understand
he is much admired in the West."

"Not in Russia?"

"In Russia too," she agreed with no change of tone. She
didn't add "now." After a moment she said, "Although after
his exile his mind was not balanced."

I started to protest that all his great novels were written after
his exile, but then decided against it because it is so easy to see

that Dostoyevsky presents an uncomfortable problem to the doctrinaire mind. He starts out with all the makings of a revolutionary hero of literature—bitter indictments of the conditions of the poor, of the grasping degeneracy of the aristocracy— and he himself was poor and sick and battened on. Then there was his arrest for revolutionary activities and his death sentence. His own description is the grimmest account of it: "Today, December 22, we were led out to the Semyonovsky Platz. There the death sentence was read out to us, we were given the Cross to kiss, swords were broken above our heads and our last change of costume was made (white shirts). After that, three of the accused were placed by the post for execution of the sentence. We were called out in threes. I was in the second three and so not more than a minute remained for me to live." In that last minute it was announced that "His Majesty the Emperor has decided that their lives be spared" and the sentence commuted to four years' hard labor in Siberia and lifetime service in the army as a private. I read that translation of Dostoyevsky's letter to his brother in a Soviet publication, *Soviet Literature.*

So far Svetlana would, I'm sure, have approved thoroughly, and if, during those four years of hard labor, which Dostoyevsky remembered with the sensations of "a man buried alive, nailed down in his coffin," he had in fact died, he need never have been the subject of controversy. But after an experience like that he returned believing in sin and atonement, in individualism and compassion, in Christian love—what was a Svetlana to do with a creature like that?

I asked her, with some malice, whether she had ever read a book by Dostoyevsky called *The Possessed* (a scathing attack on revolutionaries—the Russian title is more accurately translated as *The Demons*—which I had been told was banned in the Soviet Union).

"I have read it," she said without much interest.

"Is it available here?"

"It is available. Do you wish to buy a copy?"

"Well, no . . . no," I said, disconcerted. "I just wondered."

Actually I didn't believe her, but later I was glad that I hadn't made an issue of the point. Nowadays all Dostoyevsky's books *are* in print in Russia (including *The Possessed*).

"Is there," I continued to Svetlana, "any memorial to Dostoyevsky in Leningrad?"

"He was born in Moscow."

"But he lived and worked here."

"There is no memorial. Maybe in Moscow . . ."

"Well, can you find out where he lived in Leningrad?"

"I will try."

Again I didn't think that Svetlana was going to do anything about it—she had seemed unenthusiastic to the point of disapproval. But the next day she announced in her efficient way, "I have discovered the address of the apartment of Fyodor Mikhailovich Dostoyevsky."

"Wonderful! However did you manage it? I couldn't find it in any of the—"

"I asked."

"Oh." Then, matching her tone, I said, "If you would be kind enough to write it down for me?"

"You wish to go there?"

"Yes."

"I think it will be of no interest to you."

"I think it will be of great interest to me."

"It is not a museum," she insisted.

"I dare say," I replied equally stubbornly.

"You will not be able to go inside."

"Then I shall have to be satisfied with looking at the *outside*."

Svetlana got up from her desk. "In that case I will come with you."

"Please don't bother."

She said, with a kind of resigned formality, "It is my job."

"If you'd just write down the address—"

"You may have difficulty in finding it."

I gave up. I decided, too, that this was not the kind of expedition on which I wanted to invite Sasha—one is full of worries like that in Russia. Would it harm Sasha in any way to be seen with us, foreigners, by someone as strict as Svetlana? Would he no longer trust us—if he trusted us? Anyway, there was the practical problem of how to get in touch with him. He could always reach us at the Astoria by telephoning or leaving a message, but we never learned either where he worked or where he lived—or even if he had a telephone at either place. At best we could hang about the *sad otdykha* and hope that he might turn up.

With a thinly disguised hostility between us, Svetlana, Faubion and I climbed into one of the Intourist Zims that afternoon and set off. In silence we swept around the plaza in front of the Astoria, past St. Isaac's, past the small park, past the pillared façades of government buildings. We drove along the Leningrad streets, stringent in their atmosphere, gracious in their design, all of us assiduously concentrating on the passing city. It was not, as it happened, a long drive, but it took us to a part of town that I suppose tourists seldom visit. Clearly it was a poor section of Leningrad, run-down and neglected. The car stopped at a nondescript corner. Svetlana made no attempt to get out, but pointing through the window, said, "There is the house, I think."

Faubion and I climbed over Svetlana's ankles to open the car door. We stood on the windy sidewalk staring blankly up at the apartment house. It was a corner building, with an arch-way leading into the courtyard from a cobbled alley on one side, and on the other, where the car had halted, a wider street with another entrance—double doors with cracked glass panes. The building was on what the Russians call "a side street," meaning a short, narrow alley of a more important street.

The walls of the house, like all of Leningrad, were painted plaster over brick, but here the yellowish-tan paint was chipped and peeling badly. Large patches of plaster had been blasted off by shells, presumably during the siege. The faded, pitted red brick showed through in irregular, fantastic maps. A big pile of lumber had been stacked in the alley. Presumably some kind of reconstruction was about to begin, or had begun, on some of the buildings. On the corner there was a red-and-white striped cigarette booth and across the road a green-painted soft-drink stand, but at this dead hour of early afternoon there were no customers and no traffic on the road. We could catch a glimpse of a canal a block away—not one of the charming ones, simply a stretch of grimy, utilitarian water.

Four small children crouched in the gutter, playing some game with a handful of pebbles and a stick. They stopped to gaze at us with the canny, self-assured look of street urchins. We in turn gazed at them, at the torn canvas shoes and woolen stockings on their thin legs, the boys in dirty sweaters and hand-me-down shorts, with shaved blond heads. One girl in a short black apron had wide organdy bows on her pigtails. Then we turned back to the drab, uncommunicative façade of the building.

I don't know just what I had expected to see, but standing there in the pale, misty light so typical of Leningrad, a light that carries its own special sense of desolation, I had to keep reminding myself, This is what Dostoyevsky looked out on when he was writing, this quiet, dull scene. I suppose I had been prepared for shabbiness, but not for inactivity. It could have been even poorer and more depressing—but full of life and people.

I didn't notice when Svetlana joined us. I heard her say "There is nothing to see" in an I-told-you-so voice. There isn't even a plaque saying, "Fyodor Mikhailovich Dostoyevsky lived here."

"Which do you suppose his apartment was?" I asked, looking up at the windows. Almost all with thin white curtains behind the glass, two with narrow iron balconies holding a straggle of pink and red flowers.

Svetlana said, "I do not know."

"Could we ask somebody?"

Svetlana called out something to the children, but they only stared at her in that particular cautious silence of slum children. A man came hurrying out of the alley and we stopped him. Svetlana repeated her question. The man glanced at the long black Zim parked at the curb, then back at us. He shook his head and walked on. We waited for a few moments, but there were no other passers-by. Eventually we climbed into the car again, but this time on the return drive to the hotel I watched carefully for landmarks and turnings.

We did a number of other things in our few remaining days in Leningrad—went to the theater several times, but most of the plays that Svetlana recommended to us as the best or the most popular turned out to be translations of foreign plays. A rather strange fantasy-drama from Spain called *Trees Die Standing Up* or a French comedy called *Sixth Floor*. The one that interested me most—not because it was a particularly good play but because it was the first Soviet play that we saw—was

a story about teen-agers at school, *I'll Find You,* and its theme
and content came to me as something of a surprise.

We had invited Sasha and Victoria to the theater with us
that night and, at their insistence, had met at the box office five
minutes before curtain time. Victoria looked quite festive in a
short dress of dark-blue rayon taffeta, spoiled only by a long
uncovered zipper which swept up her back in a shiny silver
streak. Sasha was still in his brown suit. During the play he
kept adding to Faubion's whispered translation comments and
explanatory remarks of his own. Certainly the story and the
attitudes in the play appeared to be quite familiar and acceptable to him.

The play opens with a teen-age boy and girl who have suddenly fallen in love with each other during the rehearsal of a
Shakespeare play that their class is performing. The dialogue
is openly sentimental—for instance, the girl says, "But you've
known me for nine years. I've always been the same Katya—"

He replies with intense feeling, "No. . . . Since the rehearsal
I've discovered you—a new Katya, a girl I never knew before."

In a series of short, changing scenes, interspersed with long
soliloquies, one learns some of the boy's background, that his
father is a respected doctor who was deserted by his wife, that
the boy is filled with bitterness about this betrayal, that Katya's
family consider him unstable and disapprove of the romance.
The action itself concerns a new schoolteacher, a woman, who
shares that disapproval and reprimands the two young people
for their behavior. They are, of course, indignant, and so are
all their friends. By now it is clear that the teacher is the
villain of the piece. She makes this even clearer by refusing to
allow the class to publish its magazine because it contains some
passionate love poetry written for Katya by her young admirer.
Then, as a final act of meanness, she gives the boy disgracefully

low marks on an assignment, an essay on Gorki, while a plodding, conventionally conscientious student is given the top marks.

At this point the students protest and take the papers to the director of the school to ask if he thinks the marking was fair. He calls the teacher into his study and gives her a long lecture on the principles of teaching. He tells her, among other things, "You have given the paper with the orthodox interpretation of Gorki full marks. But can't you see that this other paper shows that the student has *thought,* has found something new in Gorki? You must appreciate that." Her punishment is pretty drastic. The director, who had been planning to marry her, announces that he has "woken up at last" and no longer wishes to marry her and, besides, she is dismissed from the school.

Sasha's whispered comment on this was "You see how we encourage the creative—the inquiring mind." But during the intervals, when we sat in the theater café and ordered cognac and candy, he elaborated a bit on this remark. "Things have changed a great deal in the last two or three years. When Victoria and I were at school this situation could not have been. Then the teacher would have been considered correct."

Victoria spoke up with sudden vehemence. "It is good that this is changed. Part of your life must be for yourself alone— the teacher has a right in your schoolwork but not in your life inside yourself!"

Sasha said, "But if the schoolwork suffers because you are in love—?"

"*Still* she has no right—"

"But if she is trying to help—"

"Help?" Victoria turned on Sasha. "I know that help! In such a time only a friend can help—not a comrade—a *friend.*"

I was to hear that distinction made many times during our

months in Russia—a *tovarisch,* who could be anybody, even an enemy in a veiled way, and a *droog,* a tested, reliable, loyal intimate—but Victoria's words were the first indication of aspects of Soviet life that I had only read about before: the changing official attitudes, a cautious liberalization, the difficulties of establishing trust, the quiet, nervous interior world of "comrades." I began to see why this diffuse, insignificant play should have been a success—the sympathies of the audience were engaged by the situation and they were delighted to see the brisk resolution, everything coming right at the end, young love triumphing, the rigid mind being defeated.

We had a drink after the theater, but then, as usual, they insisted on going home by subway. Ever since we had acquired our Intourist car we had offered to take them wherever they were going, but they never allowed us to see them home.

In the daytimes we continued with our sightseeing, sometimes just wandering about the city and sometimes going to a museum with Svetlana. As we expected, the Hermitage was the most impressive of the museums we saw, and even Svetlana's dutiful presence couldn't spoil the magnificence of the rooms and rooms full of gold and silver plate, of ancestral portraits, of furniture, of coats of arms, the galleries and galleries filled with royal collections of painting, jewelry, weapons, miniatures, sculpture, china and on and on. . . . From the echoing marble corridors, from the countless halls and wide stairways, you look through tall windows to the river, to the Palace Square, to all of modern Leningrad.

At the Hermitage I had particularly wanted to see the Rembrandts and the moderns—Picasso and Matisse especially—and had explained this to Svetlana on the way there. When we arrived, she bustled up to the inquiry desk and immediately I was involved in one of my maddening exchanges with her. The

Rembrandts were easy to find. We were given directions for the correct room at once. But for the moderns we were told that we must have come to the wrong place.

"Please ask her where the Picassos are," I said to Svetlana.

"There are no Picassos here."

"But I *know* there are. Possibly she knows where the Matisses are."

Svetlana repeated my question in Russian, and then both of them turned back to me shaking their heads.

Svetlana asked me, "What nationality is this painter? The rooms are arranged according to nations."

"Well, Matisse is—was—French and Picasso is Spanish, though he may be a French citizen by now."

More conversation in Russian, and then Svetlana said, "We will go to the French gallery, perhaps these painters are represented there."

The Rembrandts did turn out to be, in my untutored opinion, some of the finest anywhere. But in the French gallery, although there was a charming Watteau and a Fragonard, there were also a number of very dull pictures and, of course, no moderns. Here Faubion asked the gallery attendant for further instructions and everything was suddenly extremely simple. She told us exactly how to find the right rooms—at the top of the palace, and an interminable walk from the entrance—and we hurried up the stairs (Svetlana silently keeping pace with us) and looked up on the last flight to see the huge panel of Matisse's dancing figures on the wall above us.

We caught our breath, and then walked slowly through the almost clinically clean, freshly painted rooms all looking out to the Palace Square. They were empty except for the pictures and the half dozen or so visitors. A roomful of Matisses. Another of Picassos—lovely ones. Several rooms of Impressionists and other French painters, of which I liked the Cézannes and the Gauguins best. Altogether an astonishing collection.

Svetlana said nothing, and at last I asked her what she thought of this kind of painting. She replied, "I prefer our own artists. They are more real."

As we left, we stopped at the postcard counter to buy some prints of the moderns we had seen to send to friends. There were none.

Other days either Ruth or I or sometimes both of us would take Jai to one of the Leningrad parks, and between us we had a number of minor experiences that added up to a growing picture of park life and the world of mothers and children in Russia. The parks themselves are scrupulously neat. There is always a small group of industrious old women, wearing red armbands, eternally sweeping, cleaning, tidying up the gardens and the paths. The children arrive in the mornings with their mothers or, more often, their grandmothers and on weekends with their fathers. They play in sandboxes and with a few toys —a little rocking chair shaped like a swan, a miniature see-saw—which are permanently maintained in the park for any-body's use. Often there is a group of high school children who have been brought to the park for an exercise period, the girls in baggy trousers caught in at the ankle and blouses or sweaters, the boys in shorts and sweaters, all supervised by a gymnastics instructor who leads the drill. Sometimes there are children from the state nurseries or kindergartens with the appropriate teachers or nurses directing their play.

Whenever Ruth or I sat on one of the park benches, often near an imposing bust of Stalin that still decorated the gardens, watching Jai tearing about under the trees or digging in the sand, one of the women near us would start a conversation, and with a few words of ill-pronounced Russian and much sign language we would try to respond and learn a little about them. They were invariably fascinated with Ruth, wanting to know where she came from and what life was like for her in America, and always commenting with amazement on how well she dressed. One woman told us that she knew life in Russia was better than in America because she had a sister who had gone to America and now lived in a one-room apartment. "Here it is better. Here we have two rooms for my husband, myself and our daughter."

Often utter strangers would come up to us to tell us that Jai was too lightly dressed and that this was bad for his health. Naturally both Ruth and I had looked around when we first went to the parks to see how Jai differed from the other children there. The first thing that had impressed us was how bundled up the Russian children seemed to be. Even in mild weather they wore layer upon layer of woollies until they looked like little toy animals, unable to put their arms down to their sides, and what we could see of the pink cheeks and wide blue eyes of the babies was always framed in an uncomfortable-looking mass of wool.

The Russians have, we learned, an inordinate dread of something they call "angina," which, according to the many descriptions we were given, we assumed to be a bad cold with a sore throat—after all, they couldn't *all* have had real angina. To guard against angina, the children wear scarves and knitted caps under another wool or fur cap, several sweaters and a couple of layers of long underwear (always brightly colored), a heavy coat over the whole lot, socks over wool stockings and boots. In contrast, even on cold days, Jai was dressed in snow boots, windproofed, lined pants, a fleece-lined jacket over a sweater, and a leather cap with earflaps. After having been told repeatedly that this was dangerously little clothing for him, I used to ask him at regular intervals whether he was cold. However, he never seemed to need more clothes—and he never got angina. I decided that the explanation might simply be that the newer fabrics like windproofed or rainproofed cotton, nylon, and nylon fleece that enable a child to dress warmly but lightly are virtually unknown in Russia.

Sometimes, when it was a bit too chilly to sit on park benches, we would walk through the gardens to the river for tea or a *limonad* on one of the boats turned into floating restaurants that are moored at the bank. We noticed that at specified times these boats ran excursions down the river as far as Peterhof (one and a half hours each way for 2 rubles and 50 kopeks) and there are shorter trips among the islands too.

Once on a rather threatening morning we took a tram from the park, across the river and to the place where the battle cruiser *Aurora* is permanently anchored. Luckily we didn't have to state our destination—we didn't know the name of the locality—but found when we boarded the tram that all adults paid 30 kopeks for any journey within the city limits, and that small children traveled free. Copying the other passengers, we sat rigidly still, not talking to each other and shushing Jai whenever he made loud, foreign-sounding comments on the passing sights.

We inspected the *Aurora,* meticulously maintained, painted and polished and trim, and the sailors waved to Jai running about in the children's playground on the riverbank. Afterward we walked across the street to look at the shell of a Greek Orthodox church. It was an *Arabian Nights* confection of onion domes and painted pillars twisted like sticks of barley sugar, similar to the "Temple on the Blood" built on the spot where Alexander II was assassinated by an irate mob. There seemed to be a good deal of construction going on, and from one of the workmen we learned that this ex-church was being converted into workers' flats. We had already been told that there are eighteen or twenty functioning churches and synagogues in Leningrad. Most of the churches are Greek Orthodox, but there are some Catholic, some Protestant, and even one Southern Baptist. Still it struck me as funny that in the conversation of the workmen engaged in transforming the church we heard constantly the expressions *"Bozhe moi!"* (My God), *"Spasibo"* (Thank you, but literally God save you), and once *"Blagadaryu"* (Blessing on you) to Jai as we were leaving.

One day for a change from the park we went window shopping along Nevsky Prospekt. It was a weekday, so the shops were relatively uncrowded. (On Mondays stores are closed, and Sunday is the busiest shopping day.) But still there were queues outside certain shops, mostly shoe shops, bakeries, and dairies. Ruth and I diligently compared prices and found that a pair of decent men's shoes cost 400 to 450 rubles ($40-45), but cheaper and much shoddier ones were displayed too. Women's shoes cost less and we saw some very flimsy plastic summer sandals for as little as 30 to 100 rubles. Rayon stockings were 28 to 35 rubles, rayon nightdresses and lingerie 200 rubles and up. TV sets were 1,200 to 2,000 rubles for rather clumsy old-fashioned models with small screens. Cameras were 700 to 2,000 rubles. We saw one rather sleazy nylon blouse, proudly labeled and given a full window to itself, but evidently it was so expensive that there was no price tag on it. Food seemed fairly cheap on the whole although there was little variety, few vegetables except cabbage, and no frozen food. Ruth and I were interested to note that the price of eggs was given as 2 rubles each, and we watched fascinated while some of the women did, in fact, buy just one egg.

The women shoppers all seemed to be well over middle age, and we assumed that this must be because the younger women were at work leaving the *babushkas*—the grandmothers —and the women who had passed the age of retirement from jobs to take care of the marketing and the daily household chores. They were all dressed on so closely the same pattern that they almost seemed to be wearing a uniform, a familiar enough uniform among the poorer classes of Europe, certainly —the dark, ill-fitting dress, the heavy, homemade sweater, the wool stockings, the run-down walking shoes, the scarf over the head, the scuffed shopping basket. But it seemed more striking partly because of the contrast the slow, seedy figures presented to the famous façades of the Nevsky Prospekt and partly because they were not counterbalanced, as they might have been in other European cities on an average weekday, by the young, the smart, the people out simply for pleasure or for a hairdresser's appointment or for an early lunch date. The contrast is, of course, most apparent to Americans and to Western Europeans. To Asians the Russians don't seem so badly off.

We were mildly puzzled by trucks that we saw from time to time, labeled KVAS. One of them would cruise slowly down the street or park at a corner. Soon people would come up, would be given a drink of something from a tank on the back of the truck, would pay, and would then go on about their business. Later *kvas* was explained to us as "bread juice"—I still don't know what that means, but it is supposed to be "strengthening."

At some point we went into a big bookstore to look around, and found it decorated with slogans from famous Russian writers urging people to study their classics or assuring them, in the words of Turgenev, that "so great a language could not have been given to any but a great people." We bought a book for Jai, in English, because we were told that it was the favorite Russian children's story. It was called *The Little Humpbacked Horse* and, rather to my surprise, turned out to be about a young prince. We also learned from a student standing next to us at the counter of a rather useful system that all Russian bookshops maintain. If there are certain books that you want— new, out of print, secondhand, anything—that are not in stock at the time, you fill out a card with your name, address, the names of the books (or the authors or the subjects), and leave it with the attendant. Within a few days, or longer, you receive a notification telling you which of the books have been found. If you don't reply within a week, it is assumed that you are no longer interested, and the books go to the next person who asks for them.

Coming home that day we traveled by subway, or métro. It was the only time we did. The subways are, as promised, the deepest in the world, with vertiginous stretches of escalators far down into the marshy land of the Neva Delta. The stations are exactly the monstrous marble palaces decorated with statues of eminent Russians that I had imagined. The trains are quick and quiet. And I couldn't see any reason for depriving myself of the beauty of Leningrad streets for the sake of all that efficient ugliness.

However, through all our various activities in Leningrad—the parks, the sightseeing, the theaters, the evenings with Sasha—I never quite forgot the look and the air of the seedy side street where Dostoyevsky had lived. We had seen many beautiful and impressive things in Leningrad, but somehow that cold, undistinguished street corner was more memorable—or rather memorable in a different way—than all the palaces, museums, gardens. It had the solid feeling of real life. Faubion and I decided that we would go back there—without Svetlana this time—and see if we could learn a little more about the place. We didn't realize that we had launched ourselves on an unintentional excursion into modern Leningrad life.

The day we left Leningrad was moist and cold. Leningraders said that the summer was really over now. No more long mild evenings. Now autumn would spread, like the penetrating chill from the Neva, through the city. All afternoon I had been reading *The Insulted and Injured,* that early, inept, and curiously moving mixture of autobiography and fiction that Dostoyevsky had written nearly a century ago in St. Petersburg. When I came to passages like "he pointed to the foggy vista of the street, lighted by street-lamps dimly twinkling in the damp mist, to the dirty houses, to the wet and shining flagstones, to the cross, sullen, drenched figures that passed by, to all this picture hemmed in by the dome of the Petersburg sky," I had only to look out my hotel window to find an almost theatrical re-enactment of the scene. Although it wasn't actually raining, the Leningrad sky was soft with clouds and St. Isaac's golden dome was transformed by reflection to a somber metallic gray.

After tea Faubion and I walked to Dostoyevsky's apartment. It was already deep twilight, the premature evening of misty weather. When we again stood outside the building we could feel the damp seeping up from the canal at the end of the next block. The first trickle of people coming back from work had begun and there were customers at both the cigarette stall and, surprisingly, at the cold-drink stand. Three women in dark winter-looking clothes with woolen scarves over their heads and holding shopping baskets stood talking on the corner. They looked at us with curiosity, two foreigners idling about indeterminately on the sidewalk, and then went back to their gossip and news.

Imitating Svetlana, we stopped the first person who passed us on the pavement, a middle-aged woman with an occupied air. Faubion asked her whether she knew which was the apartment of Dostoyevsky.

She looked at us unbelievingly. "*Which* apartment?"

"Of Dostoyevsky. The writer."

"You are a foreigner?"

"Yes. American."

"I too am a foreigner. Czech. I know nothing of this." She smiled and added "Good evening" politely.

The entrance to the building was on the alleyway half blocked by the pile of lumber and building materials. "There is an alley, dark and narrow, shut in by huge houses. . . . The second house from the corner was under construction and was surrounded by scaffolding. The fence around the house came almost to the middles of the alley, and a footway had been laid round the fence." The place must have looked very much like this when Dostoyevsky wrote that passage, I thought.

We walked through the archway to a dank and messy courtyard. Firewood was stacked all across one side, partly covered with a length of tarpaulin. Next to it was a small shed or outhouse with a rotted door hanging unevenly from its hinges. Moisture had collected in shallow puddles between the flagstones. The children we had seen on our first visit were playing there, taking turns in climbing to the outhouse roof, jumping to the firewood, and then to the ground across a wide sheen of water. They stopped their game to stare at us, until we turned away uncertainly to examine the wooden board hung on a nail just inside the archway. It gave, in white painted letters, the names of the tenants and their apartment numbers, but that, of course, was no help to us.

We were trying to collect the courage to knock on the door

of one of the apartments—any apartment—when the biggest of the children, the shaved-headed blond boy, came over to us.

"Foreigners?" he asked without smiling.

"Yes."

"Poles?"

"No," Faubion said, "I'm—"

"Hungarian?"

"No, American."

"Chewing gum?" the boy said hopefully.

"No chewing gum," Faubion said, sorry to disappoint the child.

But the boy was already busy unbuttoning his coat and fishing in the pocket of his shorts with a chapped and dirty hand. He produced a small rather tarnished gilt and enamel badge, made like a lapel pin, and held it out to us on the palm of his hand. On the badge, in Russian characters, was inscribed "1957 Youth Festival U.S.S.R.," obviously a souvenir of the previous summer. "Foreign money?" he asked.

"I'm sorry. But we will buy it for rubles if you want."

"Rubles?" He turned down the corners of his mouth and put the badge away in his pocket. He looked resigned more than disappointed. While he was busy with the badge he said suddenly and casually, with his eyes averted, "You are searching still for the same apartment?"

"Yes."

"Second entrance, third floor, on your left." He raced away to join his companions, leaving us wondering. Had he expected a tip? If so, he hadn't allowed us time to give him one. Had he had been unwilling to talk the first time we saw him because of the intimidating presence of Svetlana and the official-looking car? Had it just been the general caution of people who live in a cautious world? Shyness? And then, this time, was he just being kind? Had he been pleased that we had offered to buy his badge, even in rubles? But why had he approached us anyway? We never came to a satisfactory explanation of his behavior. It occurred to me much later that it is only in Russia that one searches so diligently for motives.

Inside the doorway marked "2" we found ourselves in a stone-floored hallway, colder than the evening outside. The stairs were uncarpeted stone too, with iron railings and a small fogged window with iron bars on each landing. On one landing a metal bathtub was propped against the wall with its four little claw feet sticking out toward the stairs. On the third floor two doors faced each other across the small hallway. Both were heavily padded and had strips of felt hammered along the edges to cover the cracks. We rang the bell of the door on our left.

All the way up Faubion had been composing sentences in his politest Russian. "Please forgive us for disturbing you, but is this the apartment that was at one time occupied by Fyodor Mikhailovich Dostoyevsky, the writer?" But when the door was opened to us by a gray-haired woman in a dark dress with a sweater over it, he could only blurt out, "Good evening—did Dostoyevsky live here?"

Understandably, she looked astonished. "*What* did you say?" she asked, and added as an afterthought, "Good evening."

The second time it came out sounding better, and she smiled. "Ah, Dostoyevsky. You are foreigners?"

"Yes. Tourists. And we are so sorry to trouble you."

"Ah, *tourists*. It is no trouble. Please come in. You are interested in Dostoyevsky?"

"We think him a great writer."

"Come in, please come in. Yes, this used to be his apartment." She beckoned us through the outer and the inner door, equally padded, an arrangement like the light baffles of public buildings during wartime blackouts. I was suddenly aware of how drafty and freezing the Leningrad winter must be. She locked both doors behind us, and remarked pleasantly, "You would like to see this apartment where he lived? It is nothing very special."

A woman's voice from behind a closed door called out something to which our hostess replied, "Come here, come here," and, smiling at us, explained, "My sister—my younger sister."

The door on our left opened and a small round woman, dressed in black, emerged. She had a face like a bun, with bright, inquisitive raisin-colored eyes, and dark hair drawn into a knot on the back of her neck. "Foreigners," her sister said, as though only that one word would explain our presence. The four of us stood uncomfortably close together, packed between the padded black bench on one side of the foyer and a tall white-painted cupboard on the other. There was an old-fashioned wooden coatrack in one corner, and simply no room for any other furniture.

The older woman said, "I have often thought what kind of furniture Dostoyevsky had. This hall must have been empty— you can see that would be better. Really, there is only space for the waiting bench and the coatrack. Probably he had not much furniture to put here—he always had to sell things to pay doctors' bills, debts." She smiled at us rather apologetically. "I know all this because I have lived here so long—thirty years, even before I was married. When we first moved here there were still old people in the building who remembered Dostoyevsky. They are dead now, of course. But they used to tell us. Movers would come up the stairs. Another piece of furniture taken away. Another bill paid. He was very sick, you know. I was young when I heard these things, and it all seemed to me sad." She shrugged her shoulders. "Now . . ."

Now worse things have happened to all of us? I wondered. Or, now I have other things to think about?

But Faubion said politely, "Now he would have had free medical care?"

She laughed as though we all shared a secret together. "Yes. That is true."

With a rush of housewifely indignation she said, "You should have seen the place when we moved in! Dirt? Incredible! The people who had taken this apartment before us had done nothing to it. Of course, practically none of Dostoyevsky's things were here even when *they* came—even the books had been sold. Only this cupboard remained." She pointed to the tall, cheap cupboard in the hall. "It used to be in his bedroom. He kept his books in it. We had it painted white and moved here. There is so little space."

The younger sister opened the door behind her. "This was his room," she said in a soft, deprecating voice. "The coldest and darkest room in the building. This is where he lived." *The Insulted and Injured* had opened with the hero looking for a place to live: "All that day I had been walking about the town trying to find a lodging. My old one was very damp and I was beginning to cough rather ominously." We followed the sisters into his room. Smallish, with two narrow windows set close together in the wall opposite the door, it too looked crowded although there was actually not much furniture. Two iron beds, one under each window, a cupboard, a round table covered with a plush tablecloth, a couple of straight chairs. I walked over to the windows, squeezing past the table, and stared out at Dostoyevsky's view. The dingy courtyard, the dark thin little figures of the children playing, the Leningrad evening closing in.

Behind me one of the sisters switched on the light and said, "He worked here too, so I was told. He was in bed much of the time and had to do his writing here."

I turned away from the window to face the Victorian look of the room in the lamplight, the pink-flowered wallpaper, the tablecloth edged with little round bobbles. "Dostoyevsky's wallpaper was still here when we came to this apartment. It was a dark green, about this color." She indicated with her fingernail a fragment of leaf in the design of the present paper, a rather murky sage green. "But it was so badly stained and torn that we had to change it."

I could think of no questions to ask, could not even imagine the sick, tormented figure lying under that tidy white counterpane, writing away in the coldest, dampest room.

We crossed the tiny foyer to the door immediately opposite. This room was a bit bigger, with French windows opening on a narrow iron balcony that we had seen from the street. Here, too, there was a bed, but apparently the room was also used as a parlor—that is what it had been in Dostoyevsky's day—and there were three armchairs covered in white cotton and another round table. The wallpaper too was rather more formal, a plain, milky green the color of celadon, with a decorative border of rather fanciful urns. "The sun comes in here in the afternoons," the gentle voice of the younger sister said, "when we have some sun." We all smiled with her. Leningrad weather, like London weather, is always good for a mild crack.

While we were in this room the doorbell rang. The older sister hurried out to answer it, and we could hear fragments of a muttered conversation in the hall. Almost immediately our hostess returned with another woman of stocky build and slightly severe expression. She was still in her outdoor coat and scarf and was carrying a string bag filled with a bunch of onions, a large cabbage, a loaf of black bread and some packages wrapped in newspaper. She was introduced as "my older sister. This is her room."

In the awkward silence that followed I said, "How nice that the family is all together." When Faubion translated this, our hostess replied, without much interest, "Yes. We all lived here together once, when we were young. Now we all live here together again. Three old women."

"And in between?" my husband asked.

"In between, we married. And the war. All three husbands killed. Again we live together—like girls." She laughed to emphasize the absurdity of her description.

Back to the foyer and then into a thin sliver of a pantry next to the bedroom-parlor. Obviously part of the passageway had been partitioned off to make this pantry. The older sister was there unpacking her purchases. Eggs in a plastic bowl on the table, cookies on a blue china plate. There was a small electric hot plate on the table too, which transformed the narrow pantry into a makeshift kitchen. There was no proper kitchen and no bathroom. I supposed they must share those with other families somewhere in the building.

With a touch of eagerness the youngest sister led us through the pantry to curtained glass doors which opened into yet another bedroom. "My daughter's room," she said, almost whispering, and motioned us to follow her. She went directly to a baby's crib in the center of the room, and when we all stood round it, staring at the small pink child asleep in his closely wrapped shawls, she said, after an admiring moment, "My grandson."

I looked around at the rest of the room. Two large wardrobes were placed side by side, jutting into the room to form a kind of screen for the double bed in the corner. A desk and a bookcase. Two or three chairs. And the baby in his crib. "My daughter is a schoolteacher. Her husband too. They are not yet back from work." Rather timidly she asked, "Perhaps you will stay and meet them?"

"Oh, no," Faubion and I said together, suddenly aware of how long we had been there. He added, "We have already disturbed you far too much."

"But at least you will stay and have some tea with us?"

"No, really. We must go." We stepped back into the pantry.

"But *some*thing," the middle sister said, looking worried. She picked up the plate of cookies and handed them to us. We each took one and, since there wasn't room for more than one of us to sit at the pantry table, we all stood up nibbling cookies and smiling at each other with some constraint.

"Have we shown you what you came to see?" she asked.

"Yes, exactly," I answered firmly, lying shamelessly, for nothing could have held less of Dostoyevsky's atmosphere than this neat, cramped life, the quiet, the three old widows, and the sleeping infant.

"I have been wanting to ask you something." The first touch of diffidence came into her voice. "What is it that you find in Dostoyevsky's writing?"

Before I could answer she went on hastily, "I do not ask out of ignorance. I used to be a doctor, I am retired now. I get a pension of a thousand rubles a month." (I assumed that this was intended as an indication of her accomplishment during her career.) "My husband, before he was killed, was an engineer. So you understand that we are not uncultured. I have read Dostoyevsky—with particular care, since we live in his apartment—but still I must ask, what do you see in him? Why is he great?"

I couldn't think what to say, how to describe Dostoyevsky's

calamitous power with words, his overwhelming sense of guilt and tragedy, the dark, dark world he lived in. At last I said, rather feebly, "He wrote of such extraordinary things—such strange, unhappy people—"

She listened to Faubion's translation with growing bewilderment. "Extraordinary?" she said. "Strange? But Dostoyevsky wrote of everyday, *ordinary* things and people. When I finish a Dostoyevsky novel I forget it before I put the book down. What is there to remember? Now *Tolstoy*—a truly great writer. Who can ever forget Anna Karenina?" Anna Karenina, the rich, the aristocratic, the eternally romantic woman.

"To *us*," Faubion explained, "Dostoyevsky's world is extraordinary. And powerful. And remembered forever."

For the first time the oldest sister joined in the conversation. "You are foreigners," she said.

Faubion and I were silenced for a moment, hearing this familiar remark in an entirely new way.

At last the oldest sister continued. "Is it permitted to ask what country you come from?"

Faubion said, "I am American. My wife is Indian."

"America and India," she repeated wonderingly. "And you have come such a long way just to see *this* apartment?"

After dinner that evening, under Svetlana's chivvying, we were at the station an hour before the train was supposed to leave. We arranged our luggage in a four-berth compartment. Svetlana called the attendant to have the beds made up. Even under her strict gaze we tipped the porters—a matter they accepted without surprise. (We had been told before we came to Russia that if you tipped a Russian he would certainly return the money to you with indignation, saying, "I am not your servant. I am doing my job." In all our stay in Russia we never found this to be true. Anybody we tipped either accepted the money with eagerness or as a matter of course.)

Then we sat down to face the dreary prospect of talking to Svetlana for the rest of the hour, since she was committed to staying with us until the train left. But when we looked out the window, to our great pleasure we saw Sasha and Victoria waiting on the platform. Evidently they had come to see us off and I was disproportionately moved by this courtesy. We waved to them through the glass that we couldn't open and made excited gestures indicating that we would join them in a minute. Svetlana was clearly rather torn in her sense of duty—whether to stay with Jai and Ruth to be sure there was no trouble about our reservations or to come with us and be sure we didn't miss the train.

Faubion and I rushed out to the platform and found that Sasha and Victoria had brought a bunch of flowers for us and a picture book for Jai, the story of a cat who teases the goldfish, stares longingly at the canary in its cage, preens herself in front of the mirror, steals a herring from the dinner table, but eventually settles down when she has a kitten of her own and has to teach him manners.

We went to the station buffet for a farewell drink and there, inevitably, the usual constraint between departing travelers and seers-off fell over us. To fill in the silences Faubion and I gave them an account of our small adventure that afternoon. They listened with an almost identical expression of polite attention on their faces. When we had finished, Sasha said, "You have seen a little of how we live."

There was such a long pause that I thought he had made his only comment on our visit to Dostoyevsky's flat. With a change of tone he said, "Victoria and I have wanted to do something for you—"

"But you did—Peterhof, and so many drinks in the *sad otdykha*—"

"Hospitality is a great tradition in Russia—anywhere you go in our country, any village, any house—people will say, 'Please eat. Please drink.' Even if there is not enough for the family, they will put everything on the table and say, 'Eat, eat.' But perhaps now you will understand why Victoria and I could not invite you to our house—to our room."

In the confusion of paying the bill and running for the train we were all in a cheerful flurry. Svetlana beckoned us into the compartment with undisguised relief. We waved and blew kisses to Sasha and Victoria, said a more sedate good-by to Svetlana. Within a couple of minutes the night train to Moscow was pulling out of the station.

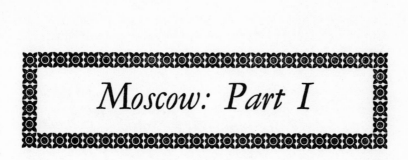

Moscow: Part I

YOUR FIRST sight of the Kremlin after you arrive in Moscow cannot fail to be impressive. However often you have seen photographs of it, however often you have heard descriptions of its massive red walls, its towers and crenellations, its golden domes and turrets, still that first view, across the slow Moscow River, holds wonder and fantasy and excitement. On the outside it symbolizes everything that is fascinating about the old Russia and on the inside everything that is terrifying in the new Soviet Union. Certainly the Kremlin dominates Moscow, architecturally and emotionally, and you understand at once why the *Kremlyevskiye kuranty* (clock chimes) are as evocative and moving to a Russian as Big Ben is to the English, why people stop in the street in the evening to watch the big red stars light up on top of the five main Kremlin towers, why patriots call the Kremlin "the heart of our people."

Since daybreak that first morning I had sat staring out the train window watching the countryside near Moscow slowly take shape. It seemed pleasant enough but not dramatic, rather flat with stands of pine and birch woods, everything a misty green. An occasional sparse village of one-storied wooden houses, the windows outlined with tiny patterns of wooden fretwork and capped with ornate gables. Many of the houses seemed to have warped and stood at crazy angles with sagging

porches and piecemeal patches of repair work. In that comfort-
less early light the paper cutouts of flowers which I saw pasted
on windows, a grim attempt at charm, only accented the dreari-
ness of the little farms and village houses. Gradually we entered the suburbs, the factories, industries, railway yards. We
passed sections that were a mad mixture of skyscrapers next to
fifteenth-century wooden huts, and at last came by taxi into
the heart of the city, and had our first view of the Kremlin
towers. Only then did I feel the real exhilaration of being in
Moscow.

The rest of Moscow, in that first short look, was the predictable hodgepodge of a big city, department stores and office
buildings, apartments and theaters, a tangle of small streets
cut here and there by wide tree-lined avenues opening into
neat plazas or ending in parks. All of it was given a slightly
seedy air by the fading remnants of signs and decorations that
had been put up the summer before for the great Youth Festival.
By early autumn the posters of welcome were looking rather
worn, the stages on the street corners where there had been
music and dancing by various national groups from morning
to midnight were deserted. The huge models of open books
in one of the parks that had represented Russian classics now
seemed a bit forlorn among the falling leaves. There were
peeling pictures of doves everywhere. Leningrad had been
shabby too, but it was an elegant shabbiness. Moscow, harder
in atmosphere, brisker in pace, with more traffic on the streets
and sidewalks crowded with pedestrians, seemed altogether
a more forbidding city.

I had read somewhere, in a Soviet magazine, that during the
Youth Festival the main road from the Exhibition Grounds to
the Central Stadium had been renamed "Happiness Road."
"Happiness," the article had continued, "is of course com-

pounded of peaceful Labour, Friendship and Love. Hence Pervaya Meshchanskaya will be called 'Labour Street.' There will also be a 'Friendship Street' and 'Love Square.'" Nothing, I thought on my first day in Moscow, could have been more inappropriate to the city than so much cheeriness. From the determined expressions on the faces of the people in the streets, from their air of bustle, from the harsh intonation of Moscow Russian, I thought we should never get to know anyone there. They would be too busy to spend time on foreigners. If we met any of them it would be a coldly formal occasion, and no laughter. Certainly we would never make a friend.

As it happened, I proved to be entirely wrong.

We knew only one Russian in Moscow, Edward Ivanian of the Ministry of Culture, whom we had met in London and had liked at once. We decided to wait until we had found our feet a bit in Moscow before we called on him. Our only other contacts were Ambassador and Mrs. K. P. S. Menon, friends of ours for years, and Mr. and Mrs. Ratnam, also of the Indian Embassy, whom we had known in Tokyo.

Sitting rather drearily in our very plushy suite at the Metropole Hotel, in that sharp depression that comes after the muddle and activity of arrival and settling in is over, before you have managed to put the ash trays in places where they can actually be reached from a comfortable chair, before a certain litter of letters and newspapers makes the desk look a bit friendlier, we decided that we should go at once to the Indian Embassy. There, as we might have predicted, we were instantly surrounded by the ease, informality, intelligence, and information that seem to be a special formula of the Menons. We drank quantities of coffee, caught up on old news, were invited to dinner that night with Mrs. Roosevelt, who was touring

Russia at the time, and to the preview of a Russian film before. We returned to the Metropole filled with an urge to go out and see more of the city, to walk about and watch the people on the streets, to get both a sense of direction and a sense of character in Moscow.

That afternoon, following our Leningrad formula, we went to the Gorki Park of Culture and Rest, took a table in the open-air café, and sat back to enjoy the mild afternoon. It was there, that first day, that we met Boris Alexandrovich Shorin, who seemed to us even then one of the most appealing people that we had met in Russia and eventually came to be our best friend there.

Boris had deliberately chosen to join our table because, as he told us at once, he could tell by our clothes that we were foreigners. He described himself to us as a "philologist"; by this, we discovered, he meant that he was a foreign language student—specializing in English and French—in his last year at the University of Moscow. "The greatest university in the world," he added, as though it were a most commonplace remark. He was longing to practice his English and French, and Faubion's Russian certainly needed all the practice it could get. So we embarked on the first of our many trilingual conversations, forgiving each other our verbal clumsiness, and gradually, over the weeks, reaching the affection of *droog* rather than *tovarisch*.

The first formalities passed without embarrassment with Boris. He ordered vodka and sandwiches and port wine for me (I was too shy at the time to tell him I hated the nasty sweet sticky stuff) and then plunged straight into a series of questions about America. What was life like there? Did we enjoy it?—Ah, but that must be because we were rich.

"We're *not* rich," Faubion protested.

"You must be. How else could you travel?" The echo of Sasha's words in Leningrad made me insist that we had come to Russia because we were interested in it and wanted to write about it. "Ah, *writers*," he said. "I knew you were rich!" And the questions went on. What did we pay for rent? For clothes? For food? Is there free education in America? Free medical care? Is there a writers' union? And more and more and more.

It was time for us to go back to the Metropole to change before we had time to ask any of our own questions. Rather uncertainly we asked Boris whether we might meet him again.

"You wish that we make an appointment?" he asked, sounding surprised, and I wondered whether, just as we had been told that Russians were hard to meet, even harder to get to know, the Russians in turn found foreigners equally elusive. He looked around the park, the calm, and the trees in the late afternoon. September is a pleasing time of year in Moscow. The brief, intense heat is over, the fogs and chill rain of early winter haven't yet begun, the days are cool and filled with a misty, fitful sunshine.

"I like very much these days," Boris said. He added with restraint, "I like to come out by myself—things are somewhat crowded in my flat. Soon college will begin, and then—work, work, work!"

"Then shall we meet here again tomorrow?"

"Thank you," he said. "I shall wait for you."

The movie that evening was shown in a small projection room in one of the movie studios on the outskirts of town. We drove past the huge skyscraper that houses Moscow University —there is little diversity in the Moscow skyscrapers, they all look rather like the Chrysler Building—into a quiet exclusive section of town called the Lenin Hills. This is where most of the chief politicians and the top party officials live, though the people we asked, including taxi drivers, never seemed to be certain who lived in which house. It was a wide road with a narrow pavement down the middle and space for three-lane traffic on each side, but you never knew how long it would take to cover the Lenin Hills road, so we were told, because it was often cordoned off or studded with police road blocks to allow the easy and discreet coming and going of Russian VIPs.

The studio itself was an ordinary grouping of utilitarian-looking buildings inside a large, dark compound with guards stationed at the outside gate under the big sign saying MOS-FILM and at the entrance to each of the buildings inside. The movie was called *The Cranes Are Flying,* and sitting with us in the audience, along with the Menons, Mrs. Roosevelt, and a couple of members of the Indian Embassy, were the director of the film, Kalatozov, and the star, Samoilova, a girl in her late teens or early twenties with the wistful, haunted beauty of a young Luise Rainer.

The opening sequences of the film were among the most lovely I have seen, a lyrical stream of photography, almost without words, of a day in the life of a young girl and boy in love. It is the day, however, that the radios all over Russia are announcing war, and after the joyful and springlike opening the movie progresses from pathos to courage, to tragedy and despair, and finally to a kind of stern stoicism. The boy, a factory worker, enlists in the army without telling his girl—they even miss their chance to say good-by because in the confusion at the embarkation point they cannot find each other in the crowds.

She lives on in the city, working at her job, visiting his parents, confident that she will hear from him. Then the air raids begin and the long nights of sleeping in subway stations, never knowing the shape of the city that would be revealed in the morning light. Her home is bombed and her family killed. She goes to stay with her fiancé's family, lives in his room, and in a state of shock and numb incredulity is seduced by his cousin.

Here the movie shifted its pace to the bitter grind of endurance during the war years. The evacuation from the cities, the cold, endless work in base hospitals in Siberia. She has married the cousin, but is still convinced that one day her long-awaited letter from the front will arrive. She was never informed that her young man had died early in the war. Slowly her disillusion with her husband grows. She learns how he evaded active duty and got himself placed on the "defense list" by a combination of bribery and string-pulling. Still she waits for the letter.

After the war she joins those tragic queues waiting for the troop trains to come into the stations, searches among the wounded, the crippled, the tired men on the platforms for a familiar face, a friend, a member of the same unit. At last, from a fellow soldier, she hears the story of her young man's death and walks away from the station in tears, giving the flowers she had brought for him to anyone she passes on the way. A strange, inconclusive ending, but much better, I thought, than the kind where everything is neatly sorted out. I was eager to tell Boris about it the next day, but when I actually did, he said, without much interest, "We have had many films on that theme," and seeing my look of surprise, he quickly added, "I think it is *good* that we have many such films. We must be reminded of the war. I am too young to remember much of the last war, but I, too, must be reminded so that I will work for peace as our leaders wish."

Dinner after the movies, even though it was at the Indian Embassy, set a pattern in my mind for the correct conduct of a

formal meal in Russia, which I was to see repeated on a number of subsequent occasions. There was always quantities of
food, far more than anyone could eat, and all of it excellent.
Vodka, as well as wines, is served throughout the meal and
toward the end conversation is punctuated with a series of
toasts—to the friendship between nations, to world peace, to
welcome Mrs. Roosevelt, to applaud the acting talent of
Samoilova, the directing skill of Kalatozov, and so on until
everyone at the table has been mentioned. Often the toasts are
accompanied by brief or lengthy speeches, but this is not essential—Samoilova, for instance, sitting across the table from
me, very still, entirely remote behind that beautiful, sad face, was
too shy even to look up from her plate when the toast was
addressed to her. She wore a short, black street dress, no make-
up at all, her dark hair pinned up loosely on the back of her
head. She spoke only when she was asked a direct question and
the rest of the time sat quiet, scarcely touching her food. It
seemed to me quite unusual behavior for a film star, but, it was
explained to me, she couldn't really count herself as an established star yet although she had had considerable success. This
modesty was correct in someone so young.

Among the other members of the film company there was
increasing joviality and cordiality and when they learned that
Faubion was in Russia to write about the theater and ballet
they focused their full attention on him. For the second time
that day he sat answering questions about America: Who were
considered the great directors there? What had become of
Garbo? Of Charlie Chaplin? Were Russian movies shown in
New York? There was no doubt about it, the interest in
America was enormous—on any level that we had so far met
in Russia; there were suspicions, of course, guarded or openly
expressed, but no disguise of the genuine wish to know. I

wondered whether Americans are equally curious about Russia, of all spheres of Russian life, or whether there is, perhaps, too concentrated an attention on Russian politics.

Like most such evenings, the party ended early. The lesser members of the film unit had to be sure of catching the last métro home. The ones who had access to a car all left together with their colleagues.

Gradually a certain order and routine evolved itself in our days in Moscow. Jai went to school every morning. We had wanted to send him to a Russian school, but discovered that a child has to be able to speak Russian before he can be admitted to a Russian kindergarten. Although he was picking up a certain amount of basic Russian quite quickly, he was nowhere near fluent enough to qualify. He went, instead, to the Anglo-American school along with children of assorted ages from the various foreign embassies.

Often Ruth and I would go window shopping or museum visiting or would manage to accomplish one of those minor errands that you think will take only a few minutes, but in Russia almost invariably lead you into elaborate complications. Once I received a post-office notification that a package had arrived for me and that I must appear in person to collect it. The Intourist people told me that the only post office where foreign packages may be accepted is in the Ostankino section of Moscow, clear across the city, easily half an hour's drive each way. At the post office I had to show both the notification and identification. Fortunately I had my passport with me; otherwise I suppose I would have had to return to the hotel for it. Then I was given a form to fill out with my name, the details of my passport, my nationality, my profession, my address in India and in Moscow (including the room number in the hotel), whether I had any diplomatic status, and the number of my customs book. The fact that I had no customs book seemed to worry the man at the desk, but when he checked my Russian visa and saw that I was a tourist he looked a bit happier. He picked up my package and calmly opened it although it was stamped "BOOK" in large letters all over and he did speak a little English.

I was, by now, quite absorbed in the procedure and watched with interest to see what would come out of the package. It turned out to be an advance copy of a book I had written called *View to the Southeast.* I was longing to see what it looked like in print, but the man hadn't nearly finished with it yet. First he laboriously spelled out the title and the name. Then he began to flip through the book, pausing here and there to spell out a chapter heading or a random sentence. At last he came to the back cover of the book and saw a photograph of me on it. He stared at it with a look of almost comical alarm and incredulity and called out something in Russian. Other officials hurried over. In a confusion of chatter, none of which I understood, the book was handed around, the photograph examined, and always followed by a searching look at me as though I were a ghost. Some of the girls shook my hand, one spoke to me in German. Someone said, *"Hindi-Russki bhai-bhai!"* At last the book was returned to me along with a torn piece of paper saying that the charge was 5 rubles and 60 kopeks.

Rather foolishly I explained that I had no Russian money with me and pulled out some American traveler's checks instead. The post office couldn't change those, and I thought I would have to go back to the hotel after all. In a flash of inspiration I decided to borrow the money from the Intourist driver of the car and pay him back at the Metropole. After all, it was only a matter of 56 cents. I led the driver to the desk, and

in a weird mixture of elementary English interspersed with
Russian words, continually interrupted by the postal official,
tried to get the situation across to him.

"Ponimayu, ponimayu" (I understand, I understand), he said
after a while. He dug out a worn zipper purse from his
pocket, opened it, and emptied the contents on the desk.
We added up the single dirty note and the pile of small coins.
It all came to 3 rubles and 20 kopeks. There followed a heated
discussion in Russian of which I only caught the word "tourist"
from time to time. At last I was allowed to leave *with* the
book. At the hotel the driver asked an interpreter to explain to
me that he had given his word to the postal official that he
would return at once with the money. It was only on that
condition that I had been permitted to take my package.

After a number of comparable encounters we began to settle
into the pace of Moscow, never attempting to do more than
one or, at the most, two things in the course of any morning.
The first time Ruth and I went shopping, for example, was
to buy a bottle of vodka to keep in the room (room service in
Russian hotels is unbelievably slow) and some fruit for Jai.
We went to a sort of combination grocery and liquor store
across from the hotel to accomplish this errand, which we were
certain could not possibly take more than ten minutes. We saw
there was a queue at the liquor counter and we joined the end
of it, not realizing—then—that we were learning the complex
mechanics of shopping in Moscow.

When, after a longish wait, we got to the head of the liquor
line we were asked by the girl at the counter what we wanted.
We pointed to a bottle of vodka. She scribbled a price on a
piece of paper, and sent us to join the end of the line in front
of the cashier's desk. Eventually we got to the head of *that*
line, paid for the vodka, and returned to the end of the line

in front of the liquor counter. Then we waited to get to the head of *that* line, presented our receipt from the cashier to the girl there, received our bottle of vodka. Then we started all over again at the end of the line for the apple counter.

I never understood the purpose of this cumbersome system of grocery shopping—it doesn't operate in department stores or bookshops—and I wondered how a woman with a job, who would certainly have to do some of her shopping on her way home from work, ever managed to get supper ready at a reasonable hour. You can't shop by telephone in Russia. Few people have servants to help them. Russian women must spend hours every week in queues. I thought it might be a circuitous way of making people buy the absolute minimum that they would need to prevent food shortages, but judging from the displays in the shops and markets there seemed to be plenty of food.

Our museum visiting took us, naturally, first of all to the Kremlin, where once again we were surrounded by the splendor of Old Russia and had to discipline ourselves for a moment to remember that it was all part of the same city as the crowded grocery stores and the hurrying pedestrians in the Square of the Revolution. Inside the yellow-painted palace were the fantastic collections and trappings of centuries of tsars and tsarinas. A huge hall full of state coaches alone, gilded and painted and upholstered in rare fabrics, some given by other European monarchs to their Russian counterparts—one from Queen Elizabeth I of England, a curious affair that is so constructed that it cannot turn a corner. Another from Marie Antoinette, a lovely and delicate confection, painted on the outside with pink and blue pictures by Boucher. A room full of jewel-studded thrones, Persian and Byzantine, extraordinary designs in precious metals. Cases of crowns banded with sable and glittering with gems.

Coronation robes and royal regalia. Catherine the Great's wedding dress, fitted to a child of fifteen, impossibly slender of waist, and then her later dresses, the clothes of a woman who was old and fat and powerful. Gold and silver, belts and boxes, clocks and trinkets, ivory and rare woods, incredible saddles and trappings for horses, swords and shields, and yet more jewelry. We came reeling out of the museum scarcely able to take in the simple whitewashed lines of the royal churches across from the palace. But we also understood a lot about the Revolution.

Faubion, who is allergic to both shops and museums, used to spend his mornings seeing the various people connected with the theater and the ballet whose information and views he would need for his book. Early in our stay in Moscow we had called on Edward Ivanian. He received us in a downstairs reception room at the Ministry of Culture, a brown, rather cheerless room with a tape recorder in one corner (which was not switched on). Edward himself is a good-looking young man from the south of Russia, the Armenian Republic. He speaks perfect English and greeted us with the same blend of courtesy and concern that we met everywhere from the Russian officials we encountered. His first question, after the inevitable tea and cookies had been served, was "Now tell me, how can I help you? Who do you want to see?"

It struck me at the time, as Faubion was reeling off a list of directors, actors, dancers, musicians, that the great, the famous, the more distinguished are far more accessible to the foreigner, even the casual tourist, in Russia than anywhere else in the world. I dare say this is partly because they are "requested" by the appropriate official and do not feel that they can refuse, but I think it is also partly because of a difference in attitude among Russians. They do not, on the whole, feel that they have a right to privacy. Some Americans we met in Moscow told us that when they were visiting the music conservatory, on the spur of the moment they asked if they could see David Oistrakh. They were shown straight into his room, without an appointment, talked to him for an hour, and were treated throughout with an absolutely unruffled graciousness.

The only name on Faubion's list that made Edward look at all doubtful was Galina Ulanova, the great star of the Bolshoi Ballet. However, he said he would do his best, and we left after making an appointment for lunch. ("Good, good!" Edward said. "I will take you to an Armenian restaurant. In Moscow often I long for our own food. This northern food has little flavor for us.")

Sometimes in the afternoon we took Jai to the park or for a walk, occasionally stopping for a drink or a snack at the Automat. There one could buy cold drinks, tea or coffee, or wine by the glass. The banks of glass-fronted boxes along one side of the room contained many varieties of *buterbrod*, expensive things like sturgeon and caviar, as well as cheaper ones like herring and salami. There were complete meals too, hot as well as cold. Each customer carried his choice to one of the high, marble-topped tables where he stood to eat and drink—there were no chairs. Smoking was forbidden in the Automat, and so was the consumption of hard liquor, though we did see groups of workmen taking surreptitious swigs from a bottle which they passed to each other under the table and then hid in somebody's pocket. The harsh glare of neon lighting on the scrubbed marble counters, the virtual silence of the customers, and the lack of ease and comfort all gave the Automat a cold, unfriendly air, and we did not go back very often.

While it was still warm enough to sit outdoors, Faubion and

I frequently returned to Gorki Park and often met Boris there, sometimes by appointment and sometimes by accident, seeing his untidy blond head and purposeful walk between the trees and waving to him to come over. There we would sit sipping our drinks, nibbling on fruit or sandwiches or candy, and we would talk. Bit by bit we learned a good deal about Boris, that he was considered a very good student and received a relatively large government stipend because of his high grades, that he was a serious worker in his Young Communist League group, that he was ambitious, that, unlike Sasha, he was not particularly interested in sights and monuments and visual art, but preferred reading and had devoured any novel in English that he could find. But he was reticent about his home life, and it was only after a rather unexpected conversation one day in the park that we began to know more of how he lived, the moment, really, that we began to be friends.

It was a pleasantly mild, sunny afternoon at the moment just before evening when the sun is slanting low between the trees. We were all sitting at our usual place and looking around at the other people making the most of the short season. Autumn is, in any case, a sentimental time of year, and as we watched the couples strolling along the paths or sitting on the park benches under the yellowing leaves of the trees, eating ice cream, smiling, talking to each other in low voices, I asked Boris, "Tell me, have you equivalents in Russian for a saying like 'All the world loves a lover,' or 'All's fair in love and war,' or 'It's love that makes the world go round'?"

Boris thought for a moment. "Sometimes we say, 'Love is not a potato, do not throw it out the window.' Ah, yes, and— this is very difficult of translation—'Love is so—so,'" he thumped his head with his fist in exasperation, "'so cruel-and-stubborn, you can even fall in love with a mountain goat.'"

"Those don't sound very romantic," I said.

Boris looked astonished. With a characteristic gesture he pushed his blond hair back from his forehead, which only made it messier, and said very seriously, "But we are the most romantic people in the world! We—especially students—think of it all the time. Often it interferes with our study—"

"Are there many college romances?"

"Of course, many."

"With girls that you meet in class?"

"In class, or at a *vecherinka*" (any evening party, sometimes given by schools or clubs or the Young Communist League), "or, if he has a job in the vacation, then in the office can also be. But really, it is time for the boy to fall in love—he is in love even before he speaks to the girl."

"And then he makes a date with her?"

"So quick? No. He sees her at an evening party, in school, in the office. He is too shy to dance with her. His friend urges him, but he says, 'No, no! Never with no one!'" (Boris never grasped the principle of the double negative—in Russian it is a perfectly reasonable construction.) "He will perhaps be braver on the phone, but still so shy that he is rude—abrupt?— and she is very annoyed. 'Who is this boy? He is very uncultured.'" Boris made a face of extreme scorn. "At last he has the courage to ask her to the cinema. He is certain she will not come. He waits in front of the cinema watching every person getting off at the bus stop. Perhaps she has decided to come by métro? He runs to the corner to watch the métro entrance. He runs back to find her waiting in the lobby. Will she forgive him for not reaching there first? He is so proud to buy her ticket, he thinks that even the woman in the *kassa*—what is *kassa*?"

"Box office."

"So. Box office. Even the box-office woman notices him with

his girl." Boris sat back in his chair looking vaguely at the golden leaves above us. "After this he *knows* he is in love. He cannot concentrate. He walks about the streets in a dream. He sees the flower seller on the corner. He stops to stare at the flowers—the raindrops are still on them—they look so fresh, they remind him of his girl, and he buys some for her."

Boris' words immediately brought to mind the scene I had often noticed on Moscow streets, of an elderly Russian woman in her knitted shawl and shabby jacket from a man's suit worn over a black dress, sitting on a folding stool, hip-deep in flowers. Stiff bunches of chrysanthemums and snapdragons stuck into tall tin cans all around her on the sidewalk. She always caused a small eddy in the stream of pedestrians hurrying back from work in the early evening—she used to make me stop too whenever I passed her. I liked the sudden sight of the massed reds and yellows and purples against the sober coloring of Moscow's streets and, besides, she seemed to me such an odd reminder of pre-Revolutionary life in Russia—the bright flowers and the dingy clothes—in my mind I had peopled the street corners of old Russian novels with women like her.

"At last the day comes," Boris was saying, "when the girl invites him to meet her parents. Terrible! He has too many feet. He falls over the furniture. He does not dare to pick up his tea glass for fear it spills. When he has gone, her parents say, 'How can you go out with such a clumsy boy, an educated girl like you? Whatever else, we have always had good manners in this house.' Then she goes to meet his parents and is so shy that she cannot talk. Afterwards they say, 'She may be a sweet girl, but evidently she is too dull even to speak.' The young people decide that their parents do not understand them. They are old-fashioned and have forgotten what it is to be in love. From then on they meet in public places."

As you live in Moscow you learn that there are a number of popular rendezvous places—the steps of the Bolshoi or the porch of the Lenin Museum right next to Red Square—but the favorite one, the equivalent of under-the-clock-at-the-Biltmore, is the statue of Pushkin. There are always flowers on its pedestal or its steps, and always a few impatient young men pacing about nearby, glancing up occasionally at the sad, dark face with its curly hair and long sideburns, then looking quickly back at each girl that crosses the square. If a young man has brought flowers for his girl, she will certainly pull one out of the bunch and throw it to join the others on the steps before she turns away and takes her escort's arm.

"And then what do they do?" I asked Boris. "Since they can't go home, I mean."

"In any case they cannot go home," he said casually. And I realized a bit guiltily that I should have known that privacy must be one of the biggest problems that young couples have to cope with. Conditions at home are almost always, in Boris' phrase, "somewhat crowded." On the whole, you are lucky if your family has an apartment to itself and does not share at least the kitchen or the bath with other families. Even then it is very unlikely that such an apartment would have a separate living room. If a married couple has a grown son they are usually entitled to an extra room for him; often there is only a flimsy partition between the two rooms, or simply a curtained glass door. If they have two sons, of course the boys share the second room. And then (again if they are fortunate and the kitchen is large enough) the kitchen becomes the dining room as well, and one of the bedrooms doubles as a living room. In these circumstances it is quite understandable that romantic exchanges are impossible at home. Besides, private automobiles are extremely rare, so access to the family car is no solution.

"So they just walk about the streets together?" I asked Boris.
"Or the parks," he said. "Everything else costs money."

Apparently, if they can't afford the theater or a movie, they
wander about the city. Often they can be seen standing close
together against the first chill of the late evening, in plazas and
some of the wide sidewalks, listening to the recorded music
pouring from outdoor loud-speakers, perhaps the clear brilliance
of Oistrakh's violin mixing strangely with the sound of traffic.
Russians seem to enjoy listening to music in the open air—even
in cold weather—and for the young people street concerts have
the added advantage of costing nothing.

Somewhere in this conversation I began to realize that Boris
was telling us about himself, and I listened carefully, picturing
him in the middle of a romance, while he told us how young
Russians love to take long walks along the Moscow River,
under the walls of the Kremlin, sometimes crossing one of the
big bridges to the island in the middle of the river, pausing on
the bridge to watch the water and the boats go by. Often they
sit by the river and read poetry aloud to each other. "To a girl
at one time I read *Eugene Onegin* by Pushkin. She was very
moved. She determined to learn it all by heart."

"But it's immensely long."

"Of course. Nearly as a novel. The boys and girls are always
very serious," Boris assured us. It was easy to believe, for
frivolity is, in any case, strikingly absent in Russian life.

"Also," Boris continued, "they have long conversations. They
criticize each other. He says, 'You should study harder. It is
as important for a girl to be intellectual as a man.' She says,
'You have no sense of money. You spend too much on me—on
everything—you must save.'"

In extreme cases, if being in love is clearly interfering with
a student's work, if he is spending too much time on romance

and his grades are getting low, then a friend—or sometimes even his girl—can report him to the local head of the Young Communist League, who will reprimand him, and this can well mean a black mark on his record.

"That doesn't sound very nice," I said carefully. "What business is it of his?"

"It is a good thing," Boris said with emphasis. "A Komsomol leader must know that the members of his group are reliable and serious."

"I see. Well, how do they prove that? By getting married?"

"Perhaps. If they are really in love. They decide to get married." This time when they meet each other's parents things are very different. "They show their maturity. Now they have confidence." Now the young man will not only pick up his girl from her apartment whenever they have a date, and drop her home every evening (instead of leaving her at the street corner), he will also be expected to spend a short while with her parents before they go out and will often come to meals at her home. He will, in fact, behave like a fiancé rather than a beau, even though he will not give her an engagement ring or make any formal declaration of their intention to marry.

Their wedding is a simple, unromantic signing of forms at the marriage registration office. Usually there is no fuss beforehand and possibly only a celebration party for a few friends that evening. The parents, even if they disapprove of the match, have to take an accepting attitude. They can express their displeasure, of course, but can do very little about enforcing their wishes. A father cannot, for instance, cut his daughter off without a penny. If she is a student she is, in any case, receiving a government stipend to cover both her tuition and her living expenses. If she is a very good student she may receive as much as 800 rubles ($80) a month, though the stipend varies according to her grades and capabilities. This amount, combined with her husband's allowance, will give them enough to live on.

"But sometimes," Boris said consideringly, "they are not really in love. They do not get married." During the time of their courtship perhaps another man has come along, and "the girl realizes that the other was only a friend, or because he was the first she had no judgment," and mistook a passing fancy for love. They break each other's hearts, they are miserable. They talk together for hours about how they can't bear to hurt each other. "Then the girl marries the second man. At least," Boris finished abruptly, "that is how it was with me."

"Cheer up, Boris," I said. "There are other girls, and one day you'll be glad you didn't marry the first."

"But I *am* married," Boris replied.

"Oh." I paused to work out the situation. "So you were the second man?"

He smiled. "To *her* I was the second man."

He appeared to feel that this rather cryptic remark needed no explanation, so rather timidly I asked, "But to some other girl you were the first?"

"Ah," he said, "that is the difficulty."

Certainly, I thought, he had been describing his own romance, but had it been with a girl who had jilted him and caused him to marry his wife on the rebound? Or had he met someone since his marriage who made him wish he *hadn't* been the second man to his wife? It was some time before we learned the answers.

Most of our evenings in Moscow were spent at the theater or ballet. I soon came to divide the Russian theater, in my mind, into the Good Old Stand-bys and the Problems of the Soviet Society. There was another category that could have been called Sheer Entertainment, but we discovered that only much later, through a friend of Boris, and even then there was not a great deal of it. For the most part Russian theater seemed to me heavily cultural, long drawn out, with no expense spared on settings and costumes, and an atmosphere of dedication rather than enjoyment. Above all it was Serious.

All Russian theater works on the repertory system, and every week the programs are posted on street corners and billboards, in offices and hotel lobbies, listing just what each of the couple of dozen companies will be playing on each of the coming six nights. Monday is a holiday for theaters. Any week there are plays, by some assortment of the Good Old Stand-bys—Pushkin, Chekhov, Tolstoy, Gorki, Turgenev, Gogol, Ostrovsky, Goncharov, and so on. Russians—Russians of any level of society and in the widest geographical distribution—love their classics, and even though there is a good case for the people who say that this is inevitable because there is nothing in Soviet literature to equal the giants of the nineteenth century, still the feeling of the Russians for their great literature is both impressive and worthy of respect. Any foreigner in Russia has had the experience of asking a receptionist in a hotel lobby or a cashier in a restaurant what is that book she keeps on the side of her desk to read during lulls in her duties and has been shown in reply a book by one of the great names in Russian literature. Once I asked a taxi driver to show me the book that was beside him on the front seat. To my considerable astonishment it was a library copy of the collected poems of Ribindranath Tagore. "Have you heard of him?" he asked me.

In a way the Good Old Stand-bys were among my most memorable moments in Russia. In that literal form, on stage, they gave an almost tangible reality to a world that I had only imagined before. Much of it, in my opinion, was not good theater. All of it was an enthralling kind of re-enactment of history. And I found it fascinating (perhaps naïvely) that in a "classless society" there should still be, on stage, such a solid comprehension of class and aristocracy.

Inevitably the first play we went to in Moscow was *Anna Karenina* at the Moscow Art Theater—MHAT, as it is known for short. Even after more than a generation of fairly steady performances (the play is part of the basic repertoire of MHAT), the theater that evening was so crowded for *Anna Karenina* that extra folding seats were set up at the sides of the aisles. As in all Russian theaters, the names of the actors who will be playing on any given evening are not announced. After you buy your program you see that opposite the name of each character two or three actors are listed. A pencil check against one of the names will tell you who will be playing the part that night. The idea, of course, is that you are supposed to be interested in seeing the play and a *team* of actors performing it, not an individual star. That evening, however, apparently word had got around that Anna was to be acted by a relatively new actress, Andreyeva, who had only recently started doing the part. Faubion asked the girl sitting next to us whether this was the first time she was seeing *Anna Karenina*. She looked astonished. "Oh no, I have seen it many times. I have come back tonight to see the new Anna."

Andreyeva, herself, was too untried an actress to have received any of the awards with which the Soviet Union decorates its artists—a "worker" in the arts is the lowest of the awards, then comes a "merited artist" of a particular province, then a "People's artist" of a particular province, and finally the top honor, a "People's artist of the (whole) U.S.S.R.," which signifies both long experience and high achievement. Beyond the awards come the prizes—the Stalin prize, the Lenin

prize, and the Laureate of the Lenin Premium which goes only
to two or three supremely distinguished artists, like Ulanova.
On the MHAT program I noticed that only two of their large
company of actors were People's artists of the U.S.S.R., though
a number had lesser honors and would probably receive yet
more in coming years.

The performance itself was magnificent to look at, the meticulous precision, detail, and fidelity to period of the scenery, the
gorgeous gowns and jewelry of the women, the uniforms and
well-cut suits of the men, the velvets and satins and laces. I
couldn't resist turning away from the stage from time to time
to watch the girl next to us in her dark sweater and skirt. The
light from the stage emphasized her expression of almost dream-
like absorption. When Vronsky came on stage she smiled and,
catching my glance at her, leaned across to whisper, "He is the
best-looking actor in Moscow—although he's old."

The woman in front immediately turned round to say,
"*Tishe!*" (Quiet!) in an angry tone.

I looked more carefully at Vronsky. By Western standards
he was rather fat, but he had a fine profile in the Barrymore
tradition.

As the play continued in its long rambling adaptation—more
than a dozen scenes, each with a different, though equally elaborate set—I began to wonder why it all seemed vaguely un-
satisfactory to me. Our neighbor was clearly loving every
minute. At last I decided that it was because the whole play
was in one unrelieved mood—poor Anna cries almost all the
way through, and by the end of the evening even the back rows
must have been able to see how bloodshot her eyes were. And
then I was sorry that Kitty and Levin were entirely omitted
from the play, as were the gaieties, the joys, and the excite-
ments of the early days of Anna and Vronsky's love. The whole

play concentrated on the long, tragic struggle and disillusion-ment that leads Anna in the last scene to fling herself, most realistically, in front of a train that rushes full-tilt from the back of the stage toward the audience. This brought a roar of applause, and when the curtain rose again for the bows, the people from the back of the theater scrambled down the aisles to the orchestra rail where they stood clapping and clapping. The girl next to us was clapping too, with tears streaming down her face. "Beautiful, beautiful!" she repeated.

The Soviet plays that we saw—at least to begin with—were both less well attended and less enthusiastically applauded. The first one we went to was called *The Golden Carriage* and was set in the troubled, disorganized days immediately after the war. The hero is a geologist. I was to discover later that geology is a very enviable profession in the Soviet Union. As a geologist, you are a Scientist, and therefore privileged, and one of your chief advantages is that you have the freedom to travel within the country on practical work or on research be-cause the testing of rocks or the analyzing of soils for the improvement of Russian agriculture or the development of its natural resources is considered of great importance to the nation.

The play opens with the return of the hero and his grown son to his native village the day after the war is over. In the years since he left he has become famous as a scientist, re-spected as a person, and rich. Gradually one learns that he had left his village because he was poor and had no obvious ad-vantages to offer his sweetheart. She had promised to wait for him but the years and the war have separated them. Both have married. Both have been unhappy. When they meet again they wish it were possible to go back, to do it all again differently. "I used to dream," she says, "that you would return in a golden carriage to fetch me away." But they realize that they must accept their lives as they, and circumstances, have formed them.

Meanwhile, predictably enough, his son falls in love with her daughter. Here, however, the pattern changes. The daughter rejects the attractions of the comfortable life, position, travel, and money that the young geologist offers her and decides instead to stick by the village boy whom she loved before, who fought in the war as an ordinary soldier, who returned home blinded, who is trying to rehabilitate himself on a collective farm.

The play did not seem to me inspired, but it interested me. I was, for instance, enthralled to find that wealth and position did, after all, count in a Soviet society; that parents could impose their will, even in romantic matters, on their children; that there was a sharp differentiation in manners, dress, language, and behavior between the workers on a collective farm and the more sophisticated or "cultured" urban types. The farm workers wore aprons, overalls, handkerchiefs on their heads, they got drunk, flirted, made mildly dirty jokes, and spoke in broad dialect. The geologist and his lost love and their children dressed and behaved in a neatly bourgeois manner. They drank tea or a moderate glass of wine. Their manner toward the workers was implacably patronizing—even to the understanding and regretful smile with which the heroine sits down to a meal of boiled potatoes with an impoverished couple in the village and her gracious acceptance of their flustered pleasure at having her stay to dinner.

However, when I recounted all this to Boris a couple of days later, he had the same noncommittal expression that he had shown when I told him about *The Cranes Are Flying*.

I asked, "Is this another theme that you have seen too often?"

"Never too often," he replied quickly. "It is good that we

are reminded. There were girls that deserted their men during
the war. That is bad. Also there are women who are influenced
by money and position. Also, that is bad. We must be reminded."

"Well, what would you recommend for us to see?" I asked.

"I do not very often go to the theater," he answered, as
though that ended the matter.

As the weeks went by and we saw many more Soviet plays,
I began to grasp Boris' unexpressed point. So much insistence
on the war and the problems during and after it does get tiresome. What is worse, the message loses its impact. To the young
people in Russia who scarcely remember the war it must be both
irritating and boring.

After a minute Boris said, "You must meet my friend Shura.
He goes to the theater sometimes. To one kind of theater that
he likes."

I didn't think anything was going to come of this suggestion.
I had the feeling that, although we liked and enjoyed Boris
very much indeed, he, perhaps, was not quite so much at ease
with us, that he was, perhaps, afraid of being indiscreet, that
foreigners were all right as chance acquaintances but not such
a wise choice for friends. After all, we had never met except
in public places, and often very casually.

Shura, when at last we met him, turned out to be a very
different sort of person from Boris. One afternoon Boris remarked in an offhand way, "Today perhaps Shura will come.
I have asked him." With a touch of constraint he added, "He
is my friend—not simply my comrade, one has many comrades
—my *friend*."

Faubion felt that this was a good opportunity to ask, "What
is the difference? When does a comrade become a friend?"

Boris said thoughtfully, "A comrade can be—*can* be—

another member of the Komsomol who knows something about you that he can report. You know something about him also. Neither of you reports. You are comrades."

"And a friend?"

"A friend would not report. Even you know nothing bad about him, he will not report."

"How do you decide when someone becomes a friend?"

"Ah, for that you must test him."

"*Test* him," Faubion repeated incredulously.

"First you tell him something small—even can be a lie. Then you wait. If he has repeated to others, you will hear. Then you try with something not so small . . ."

"And at last you have confidence in each other?"

Boris nodded. "But sometimes can also be betrayal."

"How long did it take you to be sure of Shura?"

"Seven years," Boris said promptly. "We were at school together."

"Well, anyway, if he is your friend, we will like him too."

"Thank you," Boris said with great sincerity. "But do not judge Russians by Shura. He is only interested in pleasure."

It is difficult to come across a truly pleasure-loving person in Russia. Not that Russia is without pleasures of many different kinds, but mostly, to the foreigner, they seem to be over-shadowed by some rather worthy aim. Good health, or a desire to excel internationally (as in Russian sports), or the acquisition of "culture" (as in much of the theater), or a wish to familiarize oneself with Russian history and attainment (as in much of the sightseeing). It was the quality of lightheartedness, of uncalculated enjoyment, that I missed most in Russia. So that day Faubion and I waited with particular interest for Shura.

Shura turned out to be a charming, volatile young man. He

liked to describe his appearance as "very dark," though in reality his hair was light brown and his eyes a curious brownish-yellow. He was a fellow student of Boris' at the university, though he was studying to be an engineer. We had also learned from Boris that Shura was poor at his studies and would have neglected them altogether if he hadn't been bullied and tutored by his friends into a passing grade. After we met Shura we learned that we needn't have discussed him behind his back at all. His own remarkable frankness would probably have told us all that and more. He breezed into the park, slapped Boris on the shoulder, bowed to me in a very courtly way, gripped Faubion's hand and said, in Russian, "American? Ever since Boris told me he had met you, I have been asking, 'Where are your American friends? Why do you hide them?' To me Americans are very good. You will be surprised—I *like* Americans."

He sat down with us, beckoned to the waitress, smiled and said, "Not bad," in an undertone, ordered vodka for us all, and continued his chatter in Russian, which had to be translated for me by Boris and Faubion between them. It didn't seem to inhibit him a bit. What he liked best about America, he announced at once, was American jazz. He liked American clothes too. He even admired American girls—at a distance. "I danced with an American girl during the Youth Festival," he told us. "I wanted to see what it was like. But I could not tell what kind of girl she was. She looked so nice, but she danced so close."

We quickly fell into a pattern of half-joking intimacy with Shura even though we never learned his last name.

The first indication we had of Shura's attitude toward life in Russia came on a later occasion, one evening when we were having a drink together in one of the parks. Usually, until the weather makes it impossible, there are open-air concerts in those parks—a military band, a classical orchestra or "light music,"

Viennese waltzes and the like. That evening a recorded concert was played over the loudspeaker that reached even the remoter areas of the park. It opened, I remember, with a Tchaikovsky symphony, and immediately Shura broke off in the middle of some inconsequential remark, clapped his hands over his ears and said, "Oh, no, no, no . . ."

"What's the matter?" Faubion asked, rather startled.

"This government! They are always forcing *culture* on us. Can't they ever play something that isn't *good?*"

Faubion had to translate this particularly slowly for me, not only because my Russian wasn't equal to it but because I didn't quite believe it. Russians speak to foreigners much more freely than I had been led to think, but even so it is relatively seldom that you hear criticism of the government flung out in such a casual way. With considerable interest I asked, "What kind of music would you *like* to hear?"

Shura smiled broadly and said, in English and with an obvious air of daring, "Rock-roll. You know?"

We admitted that we knew rock and roll but wondered where Shura could have heard it, since it is forbidden in Russia. "A friend of mine has a tape recorder," he said, as if no further explanation were necessary. Eventually we learned that with a borrowed short-wave radio a tape recorder is a valuable asset. You can tape the music from foreign radio stations to play for your friends. "Of course he could make a lot of money selling his recordings." Shura opened his cat-eyes wide and added, "You know—black market," to be sure we understood. "But he would never do that." We all nodded virtuously. "But even other music," Shura went on, "Louis Armstrong . . . Woody Herman. . . . Do you know *Lullaby of Birdland?*" He whistled the first few bars. "That's what I'd like to hear. I would enjoy that."

"You don't like serious music at all?"

"Once I went to the Bolshoi. Some kind of opera. I was so bored I walked out after the first act."

"What is your idea of a good time?" I asked Shura, charmed by his openness and the heady air of insouciance. "If money were no object, I mean, what would you do to enjoy yourself?"

"A really good time," Shura said from some remote day-dreaming corner of his mind. "And with plenty of money. Well, I would eat every night in expensive restaurants. Yes, yes, yes, yes," he said in that rapid, emphatic way the Russians have as they get interested in something. "And I would order black caviar . . . sturgeon . . . ."

"And lots of wine?"

"Of course. A fish needs to swim. If you order sturgeon you must drink with it. But I would order vodka *stolichnaya*—the best. Once I tasted whisky. A friend got a bottle from a foreigner and gave me a drink. He told me I had to *mix it with mineral water!* No, no, no, there is no substitute for vodka."

"And what else would you do?"

"And what else? I would dance between the eating. With a very beautiful girl, very beautifully dressed—in really high heels. I too would have many good clothes, foreign clothes. Italian style is best, do you agree?" Coming suddenly down to earth, he added prosaically, "But to do all that one would have to be a government minister's son, or at least be connected with a high party official." Even without the advantages of useful family connections, money and more particularly foreign exchange, Shura dressed quite distinctively, quite unlike Boris. He was what we soon learned in Moscow is called a *styliagi*—"a stylish one"—meaning that he dressed in the closest approximation of foreign clothes that he could manage. No processed cardboard shirts for him, and usually he wore tapered slacks (a sharp contrast to the baggy, almost bell-bottomed look of most Russian trousers), a turtle-necked sweater of heavy navy-blue wool which, together with his short cropped hair, gave him a vaguely college-boy look. He affected a consciously foreign, springy walk made even more pronounced by the thick crepe soles on his brown suède shoes. The one time we saw him in a suit he quickly pointed out that the suit itself was nothing much, but with it he was wearing a white shirt with a button-down collar and a bow tie. He pulled off the tie to show us how neatly it was fastened to his shirt with two little metal clips. "American style," he said.

"Of course," Shura was saying, back in his dream, "to live really well I would have a car. I mean, my own car." And I was reminded of *The Cranes Are Flying,* of one of the scenes in the movie at a hospital base deep in the interior of the country during the war. In the middle of a rather hectic wartime party one of the girls comes out on the porch for a moment's respite from the feverish atmosphere inside. She turns to the man with her and says, with all the nostalgia in the world, "In Leningrad after parties like this—before the war—we used to drive and drive late at night. . . . Can't you get a car? . . . Please get a car . . ."

I suppose the way Faubion and I lived in Moscow must have seemed pretty enviable to Shura, even though it was the cheapest visit to Russia that Intourist could arrange for us without putting us on the kind of guided tour where you are required to spend two days in Rostov, a day and a half in Stalingrad, where you visit collective farms and factories, and so on. Naturally we lived in the usual tourist accommodation that Intourist had arranged for us at the Metropole, a drawing room, a bedroom, a dressing room, a bathroom, a hall, and a long iron balcony reached by French doors—considerably more than the ordinary Moscow family can expect of its own apartment. Ruth and Jai had exactly the same space and comfort. Inevitably we ate most of our meals in restaurants. As tourists we had cars at our disposal. Our American clothes, which have never excited a moment's comment anywhere else, came in for a good deal of interest in Moscow—by Russian standards the material was surprisingly good and the price ridiculously cheap.

Shura apparently liked to visit us at the Metropole. He had no hesitation about coming to our rooms—again, contrary to my expectations—but he clearly preferred the hotel restaurant, a vast hall full of Victorian echoes. It had a fountain in the middle, a stained-glass dome, curly marble balconies, evergreens in pots, massive lampstands of intricately worked brass with tasseled shades. Shura would walk alertly through the swinging glass doors, hands in the pockets of his slacks, restless eyes picking out the pretty girls and the strategically placed tables. He would sit down on a plush banquette with his back to one of the huge mirrored wall panels, order 300 grams of vodka and some fruit, light a Prima cigarette (a cheap brand but, like American cigarettes, filled to the top with tobacco—unlike the Russian *papirossi,* which are half tobacco and the rest a hollow paper cylinder), and then he would lean back and watch the world go by.

Once he said to us, "*This* is why it would be terrible to have to leave Moscow. No life like this in the provinces. It is worth working a little hard to stay in college here." (Actually, it is more than just the pleasures of restaurant life that make it worth while for a Russian student to work to stay in college. The longer you can stay in the university the smaller your chances of being sent off to work in some factory, or being posted in some obscure town for a lifetime of provincial school-teaching. There seems to be no allowance for the person who develops late, who finds his academic, technical or artistic feet only in his late teens or twenties.) Shura's attitude, however, was relatively simple. He did the minimum work necessary to stay in college because he wanted a good time, and if some of the things he had heard about America attracted him on this score, he still remained profoundly Russian. I don't think he would have wanted to live anywhere but Moscow. Moscow meant, to him, a good time. And when he was enjoying himself his delight was immediate and infectious. We decided that he was the perfect person to show us the night life of the city.

He looked rather surprised when we suggested this to him. "You mean go to many places in one evening?" he asked. But I suppose he put it all down to foreign eccentricity. "I see—an American evening!" He agreed with endearing enthusiasm, and said, "There is a girl I want to impress. Not bad. Shall I bring her?" He turned down the corners of his mouth with a look of slightly comic despair. "Perhaps this will persuade her to kiss me."

We took this with relative calm because we were fairly used to Shura by then. There had been an occasion, once before, when he had turned up for a drink with us carrying a parcel wrapped in brown paper. He slapped it down on the table and said, with a touching air of triumph, "I got a present for my *devushka*. Something she wanted. A little nylon blouse."

"For your little girl?" Faubion asked in astonishment, accepting the literal meaning of *devushka*. "I didn't know you were married."

"Married? Never! No, it is for my—" he searched helplessly for a synonym—"for my—you understand—my *devushka*."

"Oh, I see," Faubion said. "Is she meeting you here?"

"No, outside. This evening," Shura continued vaguely, "is

just walking around, walking around." He brightened up a bit. "But next weekend will be better."

"What are you doing then?"

"Taking her out of town," he said promptly. It was then we learned that, as a Russian, you can't get a hotel room in your own town. To get a hotel room at all you have to show your identity card, and if you have, say, a Moscow address, then you can't stay at a Moscow hotel without all kinds of special official permissions. Even spending the weekend out of town presents its difficulties, not only of cash but also of coping with travel restrictions. "But with a little trouble things can be arranged," Shura assured us. And you can usually manage a few days in youth hostels or rest camps in the country.

"Will you marry this—er—your *devushka?*" Faubion asked.

"Oh, no. She isn't the first and she won't be the last." Shura smiled winningly. "I'm not a steady type like Boris."

An evening of night-clubbing, even if there were night clubs in Moscow, doesn't seem to be a Russian idea of a pleasant or amusing way of spending time. Even an English pub crawl would provide an uncomfortably rapid change of scene and atmosphere. Russians, when they go out of an evening, evidently like to go to *one* place, settle down at leisure, and stay until the place closes. If you merely want a drink you can go to a *pivnaya,* the simplest kind of bar, in which there is usually not even a place to sit. You walk in, order your drink, knock it straight back the way the Russians always do, eat the inevitable snack, and walk out again, all within the space of a few minutes. Usually there are no women in a *pivnaya* and the surroundings are unpretentious to the point of dinginess. If your tastes run to something a bit classier (and more expensive) you go to a *stolovoye*—literally, an "assembly of tables"—where you order only "refined" liquor, cognac or wine, that is. No vodka, except for *pertzovka* vodka, which is made with pepper and is, for some reason, considered "medicinal." *Buffets* and cafés, which again vary slightly in grade and chic, are often attached to theaters, railway stations, or parks and can give you only snacks or ready-cooked food with your drink. So if you really want to enjoy an evening on the town you go to a restaurant. This is considered pretty *luxe*—a restaurant stays open until midnight, there is always music and dancing, even in the small places catering to regional tastes. You can get any kind of Russian wine or liquor, and all food is ordered à la carte. There is no cover charge or minimum, but everything costs a bit more. Altogether it provides the most expensive way of spending an evening in Moscow.

Like many foreigners, when I first got to Russia I thought the service in the hotels and restaurants incredibly slow and inefficient. Only later did I realize that this is, quite simply, the pace the Russians enjoy. You may order vodka and *zakuska* (hors d'oeuvres) when you are first settled at your table; after an hour or so perhaps you choose the main dish of your meal (which, in turn, may take another hour to arrive). At midnight you are very possibly still nibbling fruit with your wine or cognac. It has, in short, been An Evening Out.

We chose a Saturday night for our date with Shura. Sunday is a holiday in Russia too, for everything except shops and places of entertainment, and like all big cities, Moscow develops a kind of electricity in its atmosphere on Fridays and Saturdays as the focus of the week changes. Shura met us in the Metropole restaurant at exactly eight o'clock. Like all the Russians we met, he was either extremely punctual or, as we had by then learned, never showed up at all. He was wearing his navy-blue suit, still with the crepe-soled shoes, but even the neat sobriety of the suit didn't diminish his cheerfully raffish look. He introduced the small pretty blonde with him as Irina Ilienishna. She smiled and greeted us with that self-contained, uncommunicative air that so many Russian girls seem to have. She wore a maroon sweater and skirt and walking shoes, no make-up, and her light fluffy hair fell to her shoulders in rather untidy waves. She didn't seem at all the vivid, laughing type I would have thought Shura would prefer. She was silent and uninterested while we discussed where to go—in fact, she said practically nothing at all while we were together. I was very surprised when, a couple of days later, Shura told us, with that charming, mildly wicked smile of his, that the evening had been a great success.

"The best thing," Shura said at last, with the air of making a joke, "is to stroll down Broadway and see what is happening." As he pronounced it, it came out "Brodvei." Broadway, or "Brod" for short, is Gorki Street, a wide tree-lined street of good shops, restaurants, and a few theaters. It is locally known as Broadway because, as Shura explained it, "the lights are so bright that when it rains they even reflect brightly from the wet pavement." By real Broadway standards, however, the lighting is dishearteningly subdued. "It is a wonderful thing to do," Shura continued in his mood of exhilaration, "to 'stroll down Broadway.' That is a line out of a song, you know. But I cannot repeat to you the rest because the words are too vulgar."

It took some persuasion to get him to tell us the rest of the words: Faubion's rather free translation ran:

> How rakish it is to stroll along Broadway,
> To stare at the smart ladies and the virgins!
> You can be successful there—
> If you are wearing stylish pants.
> All this is degenerate, no doubt.

> You need plenty of cash for the dives,
> And if you have none—
> Then you're sunk.

This seemed to me puzzling rather than vulgar—compared with *some* songs, after all, it had quite a high moral tone. Possibly this was because a lot of the hidden meanings are lost in English.

Shura laughed and chattered as we walked around Sverdlov Square, in front of the Metropole. He made a rude noise in the direction of the lighted portico of the Bolshoi Theater as we got a glimpse of it over the trees. He caught Irina's arm and muttered something fast and funny which made her laugh, and led us all on into Revolution Square.

There, at the place where it opens on to Red Square, he halted us and made an expansive gesture toward the city around us. "This is a place and a moment of a Moscow evening that always gives me pleasure," he said. One couldn't help catching a fragment of his delight, understanding why Muscovites are sentimental about their city and stirred by its moods. Red Square looked magnificent, flanked on one side by the brick-red crenellations of the high Kremlin wall broken by narrow irregular towers, and the night sky studded with the Kremlin's glowing red stars. In front of us, beyond the slight rise of Red Square, we could see the inspired fantasy of St. Basil's Cathedral, the gold-topped central spire and massed asymmetrically around it the giddily painted, twisted domes of the lesser towers, like a bunch of crazy onions. "Beautiful!" Shura said, and added solemnly, "I disapprove of religion, you know, but those people had joy in their buildings." The late evening and the distance softened the colors of St. Basil's and hid the uglier details of the GUM department store on the other side of the square. And all the time there was music pouring out from a street loudspeaker somewhere behind us.

The evening was not unpleasantly raw, but it was too cool to loiter about for long. The first snow of the season had fallen a few nights before, and had melted immediately, but had left the distinct presence of approaching winter in the air. We soon turned away from Red Square and walked to the corner of Gorki Street.

Strolling down Broadway turned out to be at least informative, if not precisely the distillation of high life and gaiety that I had half expected. For instance, when we asked Shura who were the young men who stood in close groups on the street corners or talked earnestly together in doorways, and what they were doing, he said casually, "Beezness, beezness. They could be anyone who wants a little extra something—money, clothes —anything. Gorki Street is the best place for beezness." Business, the word said in English, seemed to mean any slightly shady deal, buying spare clothes off tourists, or exchanging foreign currency, or any small black-market operation. We looked with interest at the businessmen, and at the more respectable strollers out for an evening's pleasure. We stopped in front of a number of lighted shop windows, shoe shops and food shops and some antique shops with rather lovely silver and china.

"All Russian," Shura said. "The old families sell piece by piece every year." One handles this transaction through a "commission"—an approved dealer, that is, who sells the antiques (or simply secondhand goods) and keeps 8 per cent—flat—of whatever he gets from the customer.

There were several dressmaking establishments, of the rather somber variety, displaying a couple of models in the window with several opened bolts of materials behind them. Here Irina did show some animation, and I thought that perhaps window shopping or buying things might provide her (as it does many women) with a major pleasure. I asked her, on an impulse, whether she and I might go shopping together sometime. She seemed interested, even amused at the idea, and said she would be glad to show me the fine Moscow shops as long as we made it on a Sunday. It still struck me as odd that everything should be open on Sundays, but when I said something of the sort to Irina, she replied seriously, "But that is the only day we have leisure to shop—for enjoyment. What do American workers do? It must be very difficult for them."

After a couple of long blocks, Shura turned us off Gorki Street into a small plaza where a lighted entrance and sign marked the Aragvi Restaurant. "You will like this place," he said. "It is very distinguished, and at the same time intimate. Many people say that the Prague is the best restaurant in Moscow. Only because it is very expensive. To me, I would as soon eat in a factory." I rather agreed with him. The Praga (or Prague) occupies several floors of a big building and seemed to me showy without being particularly good.

There was a long line of people waiting for tables at the Aragvi, but Shura elbowed ahead to talk to the headwaiter. He explained in a loud voice (as much for the benefit of the people waiting as for the maître d'hôtel) that he was with foreigners, that visitors to the country must be shown every consideration, and added with a flourish, "And, dear comrade, let us show them how good is the best!"

We were immediately led under low archways, through a series of what appeared to be interconnected cellars, each filled with tables of diners. In the end room we were placed at a table right under the orchestra that played in a small balcony halfway up the wall. The headwaiter took our order himself. Shura asked for black caviar, a couple of things I didn't recognize, and of course vodka.

"This place is famous for Georgian dishes," he explained to us; "you must taste the great variety in our country." (In con-

versations with Russians I was often impressed by the kind of
deep-seated patriotism that makes them so frequently speak
of "our country" rather than the Soviet Union, say, or Russia,
or even their particular province.) He pointed to the members
of the orchestra, who were just taking their places, to the wooden
ceiling of the restaurant, painted with the kind of peasanty-
looking designs that I had until then connected with Bavaria
or Swiss chalets. "All Georgian," he announced with satisfac-
tion. Suddenly he smiled widely and leaned forward, his yellow
eyes very bright. "I will tell you a joke about Georgians. You
know that both Stalin and Beria were Georgians? Good." His
voice sank to a whisper. "One Georgian and what do you get?—
A Cult of Personality. Two Georgians?—An Enemy of the
People. Three Georgians?—Thank God we have never had
three Georgians!" He thumped his fist on the table and leaned
back laughing. Even Irina smiled.

In Russia, caviar is an experience all its own. Very delicate in
flavor, far less fishy tasting than the varieties that are exported,
it has to be eaten in the Russian way with plain white bread
and butter. When we told Shura of the barbaric foreign tricks of
adding lemon or onion or egg white, he looked properly horrified and said, "How can you ruin these black jewels?" The
Georgian delicacies turned out to be a dish of cold, chopped
eggplant in a thin peppery sauce and one of lumps of cold
turkey with a thick, slightly grainy cream sauce that tasted of
peanut butter.

When the orchestra began to play, Shura relaxed in his chair
and told us to listen to the music and absorb its mood. Georgian
music is apparently famous for its sentimentality. "An excellent
way to start the evening. Later on it is easy to be sentimental.
In the beginning you need to be persuaded."

We didn't dance, although other people sprang up as soon

as the music started and Irina looked wistfully at the dancing couples. But Shura insisted, laughing, that this was "an American evening" in which we were not permitted to enjoy ourselves, only hurry, hurry.

Actually we had to move pretty fast because Shura, in spite of his casual attitude, had clearly planned an itinerary for us, and Moscow hours gave us all what Faubion called "a Cinderella complex"—an abnormal dread of midnight. From the Aragvi we moved farther up Gorki Street, to the Kiev, where the waitresses were in Ukrainian dress and served us chicken à la Kiev and more vodka. There some Red Army officers from the next table formally asked Shura's permission to dance with Irina. She looked absolutely uninterested, and Shura, even though he was patently irritated, said yes.

While Irina was dancing, Faubion asked Shura, "Is it serious between you two?"

Shura shrugged. "Impossible to tell. I must see her more. Perhaps I can persuade her. I must see her alone."

"But isn't that almost impossible?" I asked, remembering our talk with Boris.

Shura started to laugh. From him we learned that the principle, if not the phrasing, of "love will find a way" exists in Russia too. "There is always a friend," he explained. *Someone* you know will probably have an apartment to himself because his parents are away on holiday or visiting relatives in another city. It does work out a bit expensive to arrange. First you have to phone around to see which of your friends can help you. Then, the decent thing is to buy him a couple of tickets to the movies so that he, too, can enjoy himself while you entertain your girl, play his gramophone records (very cheap in Russia—about 70 cents for an LP) or watch his TV (about the same as a medium-priced TV in America). And as a last resort there is always the immense tract of Sokolniki Park in northern Moscow which always offers a measure of seclusion—but the summer is a short season. Still, if you are young and determined you can extract the maximum of romantic adventure there, confident in the knowledge that the subways start running again at six o'clock in the morning to get you to work comfortably on time. "Do you know," Shura said, "before the war there used to be nightingales in the Moscow parks?"

From the Kiev we walked across Gorki Street and across another plaza to the Peking Hotel, just "to see the décor" Shura insisted. "It is very new and many delegations from foreign countries—especially Asia—are accommodated there. It is very respectable." I gathered that by this he meant "dull." The décor was certainly striking. Huge red-painted pillars, a dazzling green-and-gold ceiling, designs of dragons and good-luck signs. Behind a fretwork moon-gate a Western orchestra in scruffy dark business suits played slightly faded, slightly soupy tunes. I wondered what the Chinese delegations must have thought. The Russians were obviously delighted and the small dance floor was packed with people.

The menu was in Chinese, but Shura waved it aside and asked for vodka and ice cream with jam. When it arrived, Faubion mentioned casually that this sort of ice cream would be known in America as a sundae. Shura was immediately fascinated, and asked for a detailed description. Chocolate sauce? he repeated. Nuts? Whipped cream? At last he burst out laughing. "Then *this* we must call a Monday!" he said.

Irina looked a bit nervous, though her only comment was that Shura drank too much. He replied, "As long as it makes the world good and you don't fall down, it is all right to drink."

"Doesn't the world normally look good to you?" I asked. (One finds oneself asking far too many of this sort of questions of Russians.)

"Yes, yes, yes, yes. I'm an optimist." He leaned forward, smiling in anticipation. "Shall I tell you the difference between a pessimist and an optimist in Russia? A pessimist says, 'Things were bad in the past; things are still bad; things will always be bad.' An optimist says, 'Things used to be bad, and things are bad now. But nothing can be worse than this!' " He shouted with laughter, and Irina looked still more uncomfortable. I think she was relieved when we left the Peking for the Astoria restaurant.

The Astoria, Shura had told us, was "the best place in Moscow"—the climax of the evening. Certainly, it was crowded; so crowded that the doors had to be locked against the people waiting on the street for tables. Shura's magic formula, however, got us in, and I looked around trying to discover why the Astoria was so popular. Not for the food, which was supposed to be only mediocre. And surely not for the decorations, which seemed to me quite startlingly ugly—seminude marble women with their backs to the pillars, holding up the ceiling, thick lace curtains at the arched windows. The only distinctive feature was a row of partitioned booths along one side of the room, each containing one table. Shura drew our attention to these with a sly movement of his head, and I noticed that one could shut a booth off completely by drawing the plush curtains across the entrance and in that way get some cherished privacy.

The music was quite ordinary—the orchestra at the Metropole was much better—but the tiny strip of dance floor in front of the band at the Astoria was so crowded that many of the couples were dancing between the tables and on the carpeted aisle.

We asked Shura what sort of people came to the Astoria, and he said in a vaguely inclusive manner that Russians often use, "Just workers," as one might say, "Nobody special, just anyone." Apparently they were relatively rich workers, for the girls seemed better dressed than most, though many of them still wore heavy, serviceable shoes, and they all looked rather younger, on an average, than the customers in other restaurants. I decided that the Astoria must be "the best place" for one of those elusive reasons, like a particular ease in atmosphere or the right people going there, that are responsible for the special popularity of certain places of entertainment all over the world.

In the Astoria we all danced. I had expected Shura to be a very good dancer because Irina had said, quite unemotionally, that it was his only talent. As it turned out, he held me a good distance from him in the usual Russian way and jogged about between the tables in a rather uninspired sort of foxtrot. And he talked the whole time even though I couldn't understand more than a word or two, sang snatches of the tune the orchestra was playing, raised his eyebrows appreciatively at a couple performing something that looked like a tango.

During the first pause Shura asked for vodka and fruit. By now his expansive mood was thoroughly established, and he insisted with emphatic gestures that the waiter bring us a full bottle, not the usual cut-glass decanter of vodka, to be sure that it really was *stolichnaya*. "At this time in the evening," he told us cannily, "they think you won't notice." Vodka is always described, and priced, by its alcoholic content, but *stolichnaya* is considered the best because, although its alcoholic content is relatively low (about 30 per cent), it is much smoother to drink. The usual size bottle, somewhere between a pint and a fifth, costs 33 rubles ($3.30) in a restaurant and 29 rubles in a shop. Our bottle was brought to the table and Shura opened it himself with the magnificent flourish that Russians like to use for this fairly prosaic job. He scraped off the sealing wax at the top, and then slammed the bottom of the bottle on the palm of his hand with a colossal thump. The cork flew out, the vodka spurted onto the tablecloth, and Shura filled the tiny glasses. "Here is the milk of the crazy cow—vodka!" he said as he lifted his glass. He gave one to the waiter, who shrugged his shoulders, drank the vodka in one gulp, said, "Good health," and went about his work.

"This is the stuff the government stands on," Shura was saying excitedly. He leaned forward. "Just think. It costs them two or three rubles a bottle to make. They sell it for thirty-three. What happens to the other thirty rubles? I tell you, the government stands on vodka!"

The informality of the Astoria was all around us like a fog. People from other tables came over to join us, sometimes out of curiosity to talk to the foreigners (evidently foreigners didn't very often get to the Astoria), sometimes to offer us a drink, sometimes because they were rather drunk and just felt confusedly friendly. Whenever we decided to sit out one of the tunes, someone would come up to either Irina or me and ask us to dance. At first I accepted, but when the combination of the language barrier and the uniformly bad dancing got too much for me I declined. The refusals did not disconcert them in the slightest. They would give something between a bow and a nod, walk away, and often come back for the next free dance. There were a number of men there, unaccompanied by women. I guessed that this was most likely because of baby-sitting problems at home. One man, who I thought was about thirty years old, joined our table fairly early and simply stayed there. He didn't dance, and apparently didn't drink much either, although he bought the polite round of drinks for the rest of us. I couldn't think why he had come to the Astoria at all, and when Faubion asked him, he only said, "One must go *somewhere* in the evening sometimes."

His name was Nikolai Nikolayevich Svobodin, and he told us that he worked for a firm of building contractors. He was a quiet, rather humorless man, and his chief interest seemed to be in looking at paintings. When he heard that we had not yet been to the famous Tretyakov Museum he was shocked. "The best of Russian art is there! It contains the whole history of Russian painting! Please permit me to accompany you when you go." We made a date for a few days later, and even though it was by then late for a Moscow evening and even though the atmosphere of the Astoria was conducive to easy, meaningless promises, I felt certain enough of Russian ways to know that he would keep the date.

For the hours before midnight we stayed on at the Astoria, dancing and drinking, talking and drinking. Shura sat with his arm around Irina during the rests between the dances, and she didn't seem to mind, although she retained her remote air. At midnight the orchestra played *Dosvidaniya Moscvichi,* (Good-by, Muscovites), their invariable closing number, and everyone got up to dance it with a certain solemnity, like a ritual. Actually the restaurant didn't really close until about one o'clock. After the band left, people stayed on to finish drinks, to eat a couple of open sandwiches quickly in an attempt to sober up slightly.

The Russians do two things as a cure for drunkenness that still seem to me entirely mystifying. If you feel yourself getting drunk you should hold a piece of black bread to your nose, then take a deep sniff and this, the Russians swear, helps to keep you sober. If you are drunk to the point of insensibility—and it is amazing how many people one sees in that condition in public places—then the waiter, policeman, or whoever is responsible for getting you on your feet will twist your ears, certain that this will sober you up at least temporarily. At the

Astoria the men who had reached the stage of drunkenness where they just wanted to rest their arms on the table and sleep were forcibly ejected. A couple of waiters would come up to a drunk, shake him, twist his ears, hustle him to the street door, and push him out with that offhand violence which the Russians use on drunks. I never saw a Russian woman require this treatment, though I did see a few, from time to time, who had reached the bleary, staggering stage.

Before we left, Shura carefully counted out the tips for the waiters. Then we stood on the sidewalk outside the Astoria. Shura had his hands in his pockets and rocked back and forth on his heels thoughtfully. "There is one place in Moscow that is still open," he said. "I don't know what it is like. I have never been there. Shall we go? Let's go! This is an American evening, after all."

We took a taxi across town to the Ukraina Hotel. The Ukraina is a very new, very expensive, modified skyscraper of a hotel which was finished just in time for the Youth Festival. In Moscow it is considered "modern," which means only that it is a little less old-fashioned than the other hotels. It has banks of elevators on each side of the large lobby instead of the two metal cages, with all their cables and pulleys showing, of the Metropole. But it still has a profusion of red plush, lace curtains, cut glass, and chandeliers.

The Ukraina café, for no reason that I could determine, is open all night. It hasn't music or dancing, but you can drink and eat there. When we walked in, Shura looked around the neat, hygienic-looking room, less than a quarter filled with quiet people, and reflected my thoughts exactly when he said, "This is no good. It has not had time to find its place yet." We stayed for only one drink and then took a taxi home.

In the taxi Shura, sitting next to the driver, turned to face us over the back of the seat. "Have you enjoyed yourselves?" he asked over and over again. "Has it been a good evening?"

"A splendid evening," we kept repeating.

"As good as an American evening?"

"Well, different. But just as good."

"Really?"

"Really."

"You see, with money one *can* live in Moscow."

I was about to say that the best things in Moscow—the Muscovites—were accessible without money, but it sounded sentimental, so I didn't. Shura was saying with a kind of wistful seriousness, "It *could* be a good life . . ."

During these days we were meeting another kind of Russian too, a kind that would probably have been shocked or disapproving about Shura or would at least have felt him unrepresentative of Russian youth. Edward Ivanian had taken considerable trouble to arrange a number of formal interviews for Faubion with people in the theater and ballet worlds, and I went along to the ones that sounded the most interesting. Although Russians seldom bring their wives to any occasion unless they are specifically and pressingly invited (this includes diplomatic parties), they are not at all surprised to see a foreigner's wife appear at a business interview. Another thing that interested me about the people we met "respectably" (as opposed to the chance park or restaurant pickup) was that, with one exception, we never saw or heard from any of them again. Certainly no friendship, scarcely even an acquaintanceship, developed from those meetings, although the meetings themselves were as cordial, helpful, and interesting as one could have hoped.

Among the most informative of the people we met in this way was Alexander Solodovnikov, the director of the Moscow

Art Theater. He was a charming, gray-haired man who received us one afternoon in his office in the MHAT theater, a simple, severely furnished room, decorated with portraits of Lenin, Stanislavsky, and Nemirovich-Danchenko and lined with crowded bookcases. Much of the interview was uncompromisingly technical, but every now and again evidences of Solodovnikov's humor, experience, and problems would come through, and those were the moments that interested me.

By then we had seen a number of MHAT productions besides *Anna Karenina* and *The Golden Carriage.* Lillian Hellman's *Autumn Garden,* which was written in three acts with one set, was, with the Russian passion for elaboration, converted to a four-act play with four different sets. This was not the only foreign play that MHAT performed. There was Shaw (*The Devil's Disciple*), Shakespeare (*The Winter's Tale*), A. J. Cronin (*Jupiter Laughs*), to mention only the most popular. My favorite had been Turgenev's *A Nest of Gentlefolk,* possibly for the wrong reasons, but it had seemed to me a most moving reconstruction of the slow, sad pace of life in the great country houses of another century. The restrictions, the emotional upsets, the grip of a certain society and its decay, all so tellingly presented. It was, therefore, quite extraordinary to hear Solodovnikov explaining how hard MHAT has to work to produce this effortless-seeming result. "Remember," he said, "that any of our actors under forty—they never knew an aristocrat. They cannot be expected to know how an aristocrat behaves." Andreyeva, he pointed out, who played Anna Karenina, had seemed a good choice for the part because she had genuine feeling and sincerity and was easily moved. The trouble was that she came from a simple family and had been brought up in the provinces. She had, in fact, started her acting career in Kharkov before MHAT spotted her. She had no idea of aristocratic manners and deportment. This is true of many of the actors in MHAT productions of, say, *The Three Sisters*, in which all three women are the daughters of a general, or in *Mary Stuart*, where the characters are almost exclusively of the royal circle. Now, MHAT hires "ex-princes," in Solodovnikov's phrase, to teach these manners and habits to the actors, to give them additional training in drawing-room technique, and to re-evoke the atmosphere of the past. "It is difficult," he said, "because an aristocrat does not like to show his feelings openly. But our actors must be expressive and still appear aristocrats."

The system on which Russian theaters and theatrical companies are run interested me too, partly because it seemed to be the exact reverse of the American and partly because it had a great deal in common with Asian theater. A would-be actor, for instance, enters the MHAT training school at sixteen or seventeen, after he has passed the competitive examinations. After four years' training in the Stanislavsky methods and techniques, he faces the final examinations. The pressure is enormous. In 1957, an average year, eight hundred youngsters applied for the training school, twenty were accepted, and of these only four or five were chosen for the company itself—the others could, of course, try their luck with other theaters. But once they are in the company, their future is assured. They need never worry about jobs or parts or being "type-cast." They need never concern themselves about whether or not money can be raised for a production—all theaters in Russia are either subsidized or "collectives," running on the same principle as a collective farm. Each company has its own theater, so there is no fuss about finding a place to put on a show. They can, in short, settle back to the steady, predictable routine of an American man in a safe business job.

This system does, however, carry its own penalties, though

more for the directors than the actors. Solodovnikov outlined the most persistent trouble. "There is a contradiction in our art, in my point of view. We are told that by December so many plays *must* be ready, but we cannot foresee that a given play *will* be ready. Art cannot be standardized in this way. We want to have a clear perspective to know how many plays we will do, how busy the actors will be. In the United States you play every day the same play until it is finished, but we are preparing eight plays at this moment."

Just which plays MHAT decides to do is decided by the literary board in consultation with various directors. The modern plays come pouring in at the rate of forty or fifty a month, of which one or two may be chosen for the whole season. Most recently, Solodovnikov explained, there had been a play which MHAT had finally decided to accept largely because the younger actors were so keen to do it. (There is some friction between the younger and the older actors because a number of the veterans are suspicious of the new generation, who did not work with Stanislavsky personally even though they were all taught according to The Method. "We call this skepticism," Solodovnikov said severely.)

The play that the young ones wanted is the story of the son of a railway worker who has traveled about with his father on his various jobs. When the father is honored for his long stretch of good work by being given a *dacha,* or country house, of his own to live in, the romantic life of wandering from place to place is finished for his son. The boy decides to come to Moscow for higher education, but fails his exams. He sits in Sokolniki Park trying to decide whether he should go back to the country and a life of boredom or stay for a chancy future in Moscow. Here he meets an actress, an older woman, and when she hears his problem she says, "We haven't enough servants in our house—come and work for us. You need a job, we'll give you an apron, and you will have a place to stay."

He takes the job as cook, dishwasher, and server, but he also falls in love with the actress. This, combined with the fact that he is young and handsome, deeply shocks her family. They don't want to keep him as a servant, but at the same time they know that his alternative is sleeping in the park.

The actress, after all, marries the man she was engaged to before, but soon they realize that they are unhappy and separate. The husband goes to work on a government project in Siberia. In the end, after a few more complications, the boy decides that adventure is still possible for him, but in a different way. He joins the husband in Siberia to start a new life and to serve his country. "I think this will be an interesting comedy," Solodovnikov said, while I was wondering what Shura would have thought of the denouement. A new life in Siberia? When there was a possibility of staying in Moscow? At least everyone seemed to agree on the boredom of life in the provinces.

Jai had his fifth birthday while we were in Moscow. It was rather an odd birthday for him, partly because we knew virtually no children his age—or rather no children who spoke English—whom we could invite to a party (even at school, most of the children his age spoke some other language) and partly because it marked his first grown-up dinner in a restaurant. It had to be dinner because our only guest was a boy of fourteen called Valery. He was Boris' younger brother. We had met him only once when we had asked Boris to bring his wife to have a drink with us because I was longing to meet her. Boris had accepted politely, but had appeared with Valery instead, without comment or explanation. He had taught Valery some English, and although that first time the boy had been almost totally

silent, he had occasionally produced a careful, stilted phrase
for us.

The day before the birthday I had walked the couple of blocks
from the Metropole to the huge department store called Children's World which caters exclusively to the needs and pleasures
of children. Walking through the confusing maze of depart-
ments and separate little shops within the big store I noticed
that you could buy a snow suit for a child for the equivalent of
$8—and remembered that an ordinary suit for an adult would
cost at least $100 or $150. (Often on the Moscow streets in
winter you will notice a curious reversal of, say, the American
procedure. You will frequently see small children in fur-
trimmed cloth coats or in fur coats. I never saw a grownup in
a full-length fur coat.)

However, that day I was looking for toys, and eventually
found the right section. After a good deal of thoughtful pricing,
calculation, and comparison, I settled for a small, rather flimsy
truck, the kind you wind up with a key. This cost $3.50 and
seemed to me pretty expensive. Then I bought a box of painted
blocks which you could set up to make a Russian village. That
was $1.55, which seemed average. A pencil with a rather tricky
plastic case enclosing a tiny model of one of the Kremlin towers
cost $1.40. Two colored picture books were extremely cheap—
70 cents each. Then, because a birthday doesn't seem to me complete without them, I looked around for a package of balloons.
In Russia, however, you buy them singly, and the reason is immediately clear. They cost 10 cents each for the kind of balloon
that normally comes in a package of twenty for 15 cents. I
prudently bought only four. Two each for the children, one to
burst and one to play with.

Then came the problem of the birthday cake. I went to several bakeries in the neighborhood, but could find only small

pastries, no big cakes of the sort that one decorates with candles. At last I returned to the hotel defeated. Faubion suggested that we telephone the restaurant where we were to dine the next night and ask *them* to arrange for a cake. They would certainly know where to get one and if we gave them a day's notice the whole thing should be perfectly simple. Accordingly he telephoned, first of all to make a reservation.

The restaurant we had chosen specialized in Azerbaijan food and was called the Baku, after the capital city. It was decorated with Caucasian tiles, mosaics and motifs to give the atmosphere of that particular part of Russia, an Azerbaijan orchestra of flutes and drums and strange, beautiful stringed instruments played the music of the province, but most important to us was the fact that they cooked delicious pilaff and shashlik, both typical of the area and both Jai's favorite Russian dishes. We knew from experience that one had to make a reservation there because people from the outlying republics of Russia who find themselves in Moscow seem to get very homesick for their own food and atmosphere, and the small restaurants with provincial specialties are always crowded. The man who answered the phone promised us a reservation and seemed to understand perfectly about the cake. Yes, we could certainly have a cake. No notice was necessary. There were always cakes. He would on no account forget about it.

It remained for us only to buy the candles, but this proved unexpectedly complicated. The first department store we went to had no candles, and the puzzled salesgirl whom we asked where we might find them said, "But why do you need candles? All of Moscow has electricity now." We asked in another department store, in a grocery shop, in the kind of shop that sells magazines, postcards, souvenirs, cigarettes, and in a hardware store. No candles. Someone suggested that we go to a church or to a shop carrying religious supplies, but by then we had decided to do without candles.

The next evening at 6:30 Valery appeared in our hotel room. He was wearing his suit. (In Russia you hardly ever need to specify "his *good* suit." Most people have a suit, and then they have their work clothes, and sweaters and slacks.) He looked painfully neat, pink and clean, damp brown hair slicked back. When I commented on his fine appearance he explained that he had just come from the public baths across the street, which were better than the ones his family usually patronized. The pinkness was the result of having splurged on a session in the steam room.

One of the minor mysteries of life in Russia is what exactly are Russian mealtimes. I don't think I ever met a Russian who did not say, "Thank you, I have had my meal," when he was offered something to eat. This seemed to be true even when they were invited specifically to lunch or dinner. Mrs. Menon, the wife of the Indian ambassador, told me an amusing story. A friend of hers had grown so desperate after hearing this refrain from Russian guests—especially when she had gone to a lot of trouble to prepare a really excellent meal for them—that she waited impatiently for her first invitation to a Russian party. When at last it came she went to the house of her Russian friends, and as her hostess announced dinner, she said, "Thank you, I have already eaten," feeling that she was getting her own back.

The Russians, however, had the last word. Her hostess smiled and said, "You have eaten? We too have already eaten."

After we had exchanged formalities with Valery I asked him if he was hungry and would like to go straight to the restaurant or whether he would prefer to have something to drink at the hotel first. It was with no surprise that I heard him say, "Which

you prefer. I have already eaten." Jai settled the matter by demanding *limonad,* and Valery decided on beer. He took his
duties as a guest very seriously. The two boys played football
with the balloons for half an hour, and between goals Valery
would sip his beer and make conventional inquiries about our
health, whether we were enjoying Moscow, what we had seen
of the city, and so on.

Dinner at the Baku was excellent (Valery appeared to have a
good appetite in spite of the beer and his previous meal) and,
what with the music and the crowded southern atmosphere, it
began to feel like a real party. Russians are, in any case, extraordinarily accommodating about children. Children seem to be
allowed anywhere, except at evening performances at the theater. Waiters in restaurants seem delighted to serve them and take
special pains to see that they are properly taken care of. There
appears to be no age limit for alcoholic drinks, though when we
once remarked on this to a waiter at the hotel, he said, "Well, I
disapprove of serving drinks to young people. But what are we
to do?—it might be a government minister's son."

"And he could get you into trouble?" Faubion asked.

"We have two kinds of ministers. One would thank you for
not giving his son a drink. The other would have you fired."

That evening at the Baku the waiter appeared in the middle
of dinner with a bottle of sweet muscat wine, which he poured
for us, announcing, "This is a present to your little boy from
the *tovarisch* at the corner table." We swiveled round in our
chairs and smiled and beckoned to the comrade across the room
to join us.

He came up with a bunch of grapes and two apples which he
placed between the boys. A short, dark man with a jolly manner.
"It is the black eyes of your son," he explained when we
thanked him for the wine. "Very unusual in Moscow. I come

from the Caucasus, and they reminded me of my own boy."

We clinked glasses. Faubion, entering into the spirit of the occasion, said, "May they be friends when they grow up."

The comrade from the Caucasus shrugged. "May they grow up," he said, and drained his glass.

At last the moment came for the birthday cake. We signaled to the waiter. He nodded reassuringly and hurried off in the direction of the kitchen. A few minutes later he returned carrying a plate which he set down in the middle of the table. On it were four chocolate eclairs.

By then we were in too good a mood to fuss any further about the cake. Instead, we improvised a birthday cake from Azerbaijan bread. It is baked in thick spongy disks about the size of a dessert plate and you tear off pieces to soak in your soup, or to mop up sauces, or to eat with the meat instead of rice. We used one complete disk into which we stuck five matches. With proper ceremony we lit the matches. Jai blew them out with one puff and made his wish. We cut the bread in slices and added a Russian touch to the whole performance by eating it with salt. Bread and salt are the two traditional gifts for all auspicious occasions.

Valery chose this moment to produce a narrow package from his pocket. "My present for the birthday," he said. It was wrapped in white writing paper and tied with the kind of string that is really made of paper. (I never saw any gift-wrapping paper in Russia, and colored ribbon that will be thrown away immediately is, of course, a senseless extravagance.) Inside was a bone-handled penknife in a scuffed leather case. "It is not new," Valery said gravely. "It was given to me when I was young. But for eight years it has been my friend, and I have nothing else to give."

For a moment none of us could comment on the magnificence

of this gesture, but at last I found myself repeating stupidly, "Valery, you shouldn't have done it. Really you shouldn't have done it."

Valery's voice was quite matter-of-fact. "But for a child, everything must be done."

I suppose Jai's response to the present was the only satisfactory one. The penknife instantly became his most cherished possession—far surpassing the blocks, the books, the truck. He wouldn't let it out of his hand all evening.

I often had occasion to think of Valery's remark in the months that we stayed in Russia. Certainly it did seem that everything is done for children—not only in the sense of nurseries, schools, hospitals, but also in a wealth of children's entertainment that I have seen nowhere else, and most of all in the spontaneous warmth of the people toward any child. Yet I found it an odd contradiction that most of the young Russians we met did not seem to want children of their own, or, if they already had a child, did not want a second, and in spite of state encouragement were determined not to have a large family. Possibly attitudes were different in the villages, where the congestion of living is less oppressive.

Another thing I found hard to explain was that, although Russian children appear to be surrounded with every possible indulgence, they are still extraordinarily disciplined. I never saw a child misbehave in public, be wild or noisy or unmanageable. Like almost any foreigner, I was struck by another fact: in the parks, on the streets—anywhere—we scarcely ever heard a child crying.

I never did come to any convincing conclusions about these aspects of Russian life, but now and again I happened on partial explanations and hints that seemed to me significant. Once, for instance, when Jai was getting out of a taxi, he tripped, stumbled through the door and fell on the sidewalk. He began to cry. Before I could get to him, the taxi driver, a woman, whisked out of her seat, picked him up and said sternly, *"U nas nie plachet"* (Among us, we don't cry). My instinct was quite different; I wanted to comfort him, but not to keep him from crying. Possibly out of surprise at the severity of her tone, he did, in fact, stop crying at once.

Later I had many opportunities to see examples of a kind of public discipline, a group rule that governs the life of a child in Moscow. Anyone seems to feel quite within his rights in telling a child—any child—not to litter the streets. By the time a child is three years old he has learned that all city parks and streets in Russia are well provided with metal urns for rubbish, and small children can often be seen toddling dutifully off to such an urn to get rid of a candy paper or a used bus ticket. I never saw a Russian mother strike a child, but I often heard from mothers and strangers that tone of uncompromising admonishment that seems to be equally effective. A child soon seems to learn that, for instance, "among us, we do not litter the streets."

Once in a park Jai was playing in the sand pile. He was looking rather enviously at a little girl who was digging with a shovel. The child's mother saw the situation, noticed that we were foreigners, and made her daughter give the shovel to Jai. The little girl started to protest—so did I—but we both stopped when we heard the familiar severity of the voice, "Among us, we share our tools." The mother turned to me and smiled. "She must learn," she said with finality. The child returned to her digging . . . with her fingers this time. Eventually, I suppose, this concerted barrage of strictures has its own effect on a child, an effect that is given solid weight by the example of the parents, their discipline, their diligence, their respect for (or fear of) authority, and of course the constant molding action of their society itself.

On one occasion it was suggested to me that the docile calm that lies over Moscow parks, children's playgrounds and nurseries can be explained by the fact that the Russians swaddle their babies. As soon as a child is born he is washed, and then his arms are either crossed over his chest or held straight to his sides and he is snugly bandaged in strips of cloth from his neck to his toes until he looks like a miniature mummy.

In other countries where I have lived the general feeling seems to be that a newborn child should have as little restraint as possible, wear the minimum covering consistent with the climate, so that he can kick about, exercise his muscles and grow up strong and healthy. There is, in contrast, something rather creepy about seeing a nurse in a Russian maternity ward carrying two or three swaddled babies at a time, and handling each rigid little form as casually as if it were a log of wood.

The most cursory glance at the Russian population shows that the practice doesn't appear to do any obvious physical damage but, I was told, the imprint on the personality of the child is apparent both to a psychologist and to the mother. I asked a number of Russians what the purpose of swaddling was—and got a number of different answers. Predictably, they all agreed that if you swaddle a child you ensure that he grows up strong and healthy. One young woman I met in a Moscow park, where we both used to take our children every sunny weekend, said, "Is it not done in every country?" And when I told her that in my country mothers wanted their children to be free to move about as much as they could, she asked (making a more general observation than she realized), "But doesn't that make them very hard to handle?"

Other people told me that a child is swaddled so that his

limbs will grow straight. Or to keep an infant from scratching himself in his early, uncontrolled movements. Or to be sure that he doesn't kick his covers off and catch a chill. Or to keep his neck from flopping back when he is lifted. Or to give his spine support.

A foreign woman I knew, whose husband was stationed in Moscow, had her baby at one of the Russian Polykliniks. She told me that a mother is invariably kept in hospital for ten days after her baby is born. In that time she has no say in the treatment of her child, and any protests she may make about swaddling are politely but firmly overruled. What's more, she has no allies because even her husband is not permitted to visit her or her baby until he comes to take them home. (A minor by-product of this I learned when I saw a Russian movie called *A Man Is Born*, with a long sequence in a maternity ward, is that the wildly desired bed is next to a window in a ground-floor ward —no private rooms for maternity cases—because there the more intrepid relatives can dodge the guards and visit through the window.)

The effects of swaddling become really clear only when you take your baby home and remove the bandages to give him his first taste of freedom. The child, I was assured, invariably starts yelling and keeps right on yelling until he is tightly wrapped up again and feels secure and cozy, if immobile, once more. You have to unswaddle your child in very gradual stages—a few minutes a day—and even then you will find that for months afterward if you want him to go to sleep quickly and quietly the simplest method is to swaddle him again.

Most women in Russia work—I mean work in offices, factories or farms, not simply in their own homes—so any private objections or convictions they may have about the early care of a baby can be followed only if they happen to have a mother, grandmother, or aunt who is past working age and is free to look after the children. Otherwise, when the mother's four-month maternity leave is over and she resumes her job, the baby is placed in a state day nursery, and immediately the pressures of "group discipline" begin and the child has started on his long career of public care and education.

The day after Jai's birthday Boris telephoned us on Valery's behalf to thank us for the dinner. "He came to my flat afterwards to tell me how good was the food."

"We were delighted to have him—and he gave Jai such a wonderful present."

"A present? He did not tell."

"A penknife. Jai likes it better than anything else."

A pause. "Ah, yes. His penknife."

"Boris, he shouldn't have done it—"

"No, no. It is right. He should give. He gave his penknife?"

"Yes, he said it was his friend—"

"It was. I remember his face when it was given him. Now it will be Jai's friend."

"Boris, we do want to see you."

"At your convenience."

"Shall we go to the theater? We've been wanting to see *Hotel Astoria*—we stayed there in Leningrad."

"Again it is from the war."

"Would you rather see something else? We don't mind—"

He said slowly, "Let it be *Hotel Astoria*. It will be interesting for you. For me also."

In fact, *Hotel Astoria* turned out to be more interesting than I had expected. For one thing, it was the only Russian play we saw that had only one set and used suggestion and lighting to shift the action from the private salon of the Astoria to other places—the bank of the Neva or the hotel corridor. There were no curtains to the stage, and the beginnings and ends of acts were marked by the playing of a full orchestra. Much of the action was punctuated and heightened by mood music too. But it was the story itself that interested me most of all.

It takes place during the war at a time when the Germans had practically encircled Leningrad and the Astoria was an officers' billet. All through the play you hear spasmodic bursts of shelling and occasionally see the red glow of fires in the city. And you get the mood of the city at that time through brief exchanges between the characters, embedded in more important dialogues. A professor, a deserter from the army, says to the hero, an air force major, "Do you think the Germans will win?"

A pause. "Do *you?*"

No answer.

Or a journalist, seeing the hotel maid standing at the window, "What is burning up now?"

"Food. Our food stocks. They could have been distributed to the people two days ago, but the authorities decided to wait. And now, it burns—our sugar, our bread . . ."

Or the hero, walking through the city during the shelling, quoting Pushkin, "O City of Peter, stand fast. Be magnificent, as all of Russia . . ."

The hero, rather to my surprise, was a controversial character, a man who had been unjustly accused of treason during the terrible purges of 1937-1938 and imprisoned for four years. While he was in jail his wife deserted him, then divorced him and married his friend, an important factory manager, so that she could assure a safe future for their son. Now the son is grown up, and when the major, whose only wish during the war is to fight for his country, returns to Leningrad, he sends a message to the young man asking him to come to the Astoria.

Instead, the boy's mother, the major's ex-wife, appears to beg for his forgiveness. It was for the sake of their son that she was unfaithful, she explains. No one knew what had happened to the prisoners. She had to think of the boy. The major replies bitterly, "Because you loved him you had no faith in me?" and he rejects her apology, "I asked to see my son—not you."

Her present husband, his old friend, comes in, and he too tries to justify the frightened atmosphere of the time. "Women never looked at me as they did at you. I knew she still loved you—the only way I could show my love for her was by helping her at that time." But the major remains inflexible.

What fascinated me about all these characters was that, for once, none of them was presented as entirely good or entirely bad. The major, torn between a continuing, helpless love for his wife and disgust at the events of the past, determined to fight for his country but, remembering most painfully its injustices, seemed to me to crystallize so much of what so many Russians must feel—the love, the hope, the sorrow, the fear, the bitterness toward their country. The wife too—you could understand her predicament and her despairing effort to salvage what she could. And the man she married, his kindness and his weakness, above all his courage to act in the only way he could to save the woman and her child, and later to relinquish them with grace.

Even the professor who deserted from the front lines produces his moment of sympathy. He tells his story to the major, begging help to escape from Leningrad—he has seen enough of the war. He and his unit were cut off by the Germans. Eight of them escaped. Of those, seven died. "I ran. I hid. I drank swamp water. Eat?" He laughs. "Nothing to eat. I decided I would die. I dug my grave. But instead I buried my party card and my documents. Then I was no one. A man without identity. I deserted, yes, but can you blame me? What, in the end, did the party do for me?"

The major replies, "You say that to *me*? What could be worse for a sincere Communist than to be imprisoned as a Fascist? But I did not lose faith in this country or in Communism. Yet you *buried* your party card?"

In spite of the major's indignation, I could see the professor's point. Evidently the author could too, because there were a number of cracks about the party in the play. The one I liked best was delivered by the only entirely unsympathetic character —a party bureaucrat. At one point he announced with rigid conviction that anything the party says must be right. The major asks, "No one may ask questions?"

"Oh, yes. Certain questions."

"Which ones?"

"Those printed in the newspaper as suitable."

In the end, however, the play works out reasonably happily. The major, who because of his jail sentence, is still not trusted by his superior officers with a flying command, does manage to persuade them of his worthiness. His son is killed in the defense of Leningrad, but he sees the boy's young bride bravely prepared to work for the better future of Russia. He never takes his wife back, but he is ready to forgive her and accept her reasoning. Even the journalist, who acts as a kind of informal chorus, relating outside events and the progress of the siege, decides to give up the cynicism that he had acquired after the civil war in Spain, when the Russians who had fought there had gone as heroes and returned, too often, to face charges of treason. He decides to "stand" with Leningrad and Leningraders in defense of the city, in defense of Russia.

Boris and Faubion and I all left the theater in a rather thoughtful mood. We went back to the Metropole for supper, and there, in a conventional way, I said to Boris, "How did you like the play?"

"It had much meaning," he said slowly. "Especially for me."

"Why especially for you?"

"We have suffered in this same way."

"*You?* You are much too young, surely."

"My family."

"During the war, you mean?"

"Not so much. But 1936, '37, '38, those were Russia's darkest days. My father used to pace up and down the room all night. He couldn't sleep because he never knew when he would be the next to go. I was a small child. I did not know anything of this, and my father would never tell me—he was truly a man, he could not ask for pity. But my mother told me many years later. Every day his friends were disappearing. Every day a friend, a man he knew, a comrade—"

"Where did they disappear to? Jail?"

"We never knew. We could not find out. My father was loyal to his friends. He wrote many letters to the Central Committee asking. But he never received an answer. Ten—twelve of his friends, good friends, disappeared. He was certain that his turn was coming."

"Why did it happen? What had they done?"

"Nothing." Boris sighed deeply and leaned back in his chair. He looked around the pedestrian gaiety of the Metropole restaurant, the people dancing to plodding jazz tunes. "I have already told you so much," he remarked. "We never knew what they had done. Afterwards we tried to guess. We think it must have been because they were all—my father too—Communists from the time of Lenin. Now they were considered a danger—too liberal. Many had traveled, they had met foreigners. Even if the government had sent them and recalled them, they were suspected of foreign influences. We never knew who was responsible. Stalin? Beria? We only knew the terror."

"Aren't they all bitter about it? Aren't *you?*"

Boris smiled like an old man, tired but indulgent. "What am I to do? I am Russian. One friend of my father came back. He was not an important man. A schoolteacher in a small town in the Ukraine. He had no fingers. They had been crushed in a door. One hand, then the other. He was asked, 'Are you an enemy of the party? Are you an enemy of the people? Are you a deviationist?' and he said, 'No,' and 'No,' and 'No!' "

"Well, what had happened? He was falsely accused, but had someone betrayed him?"

"We never knew. Seventeen years afterward he came back. He came to see us. That was two years ago, that was when I saw his hands. I asked him, 'How should I feel?' He said, 'I cannot advise you. My life is gone'— after all, seventeen years, —'but what is the use of living in the past? Bitterness is a—' How do you say this, when something eats, eats metal?"

"Corrosive?"

"Perhaps. Corrosive. 'Bitterness is a corrosive. We must work for the future.' "

"Well, I call that quite inhumanly noble," I said, rather chilled by this moral ending.

"He still believed in Communism, you see. Russia is different now. It is better now. We can talk about those things a little. Khrushchev is a liberal too."

It sounded odd the first time I heard it said. Khrushchev (pronounced *kroosh' chov*) seemed so far from my idea of a liberal, but by the time I left Russia I was convinced that in a Communist context he is, in fact, a liberal, that many of the small acts of liberalism that he has permitted—allowing tourists, permitting a certain contact with foreigners, sanctioning some foreign broadcasts, music, books, cultural exchange of various sorts—will have repercussions among the Russians that are too wide and unexpected for even a totalitarian government to deal with.

"Tell me," I said to Boris, "knowing all this, how can you still be such a loyal worker for the YCL? How can you still support the party?"

"I cannot help it," Boris said, smiling. "I am Russian and I love my country. I cannot hate it only because there are faults. I must work within the party and outside to make my country better and to keep it better."

"But if such things were to happen again, would you protest?"

"Of course."

"Would you take action?"

"If it cost me my life!"

Shura's idea of the kind of theater to see was characteristically different from Boris'. One evening when we had suggested taking him to a play, he had looked at us rather warily. "What kind of play?" he asked.

"What would you like to see?"

"Ah. You mean I should choose?" Reassured and smiling, he said, "Then let us see Raikin. He is here only for another few days."

Raikin is a Leningrad comedian, a singer, quick-change artist, and mime. He was performing in one of the *sad otdykha,* the most popular and the last attraction of the season because soon it would be too cold for audiences to attend the unheated theaters in the parks. It was a chill, drizzling evening when we met Shura at the park gates. He hurried us through the turnstile, insisting that my coat would not be warm enough. "Come along, come along. We have just time enough to get you a blanket for the *inside—*"

At the café next to the theater he ordered vodka for us all. "Here is our blanket," he announced.

With true Leningrad nostalgia the show was called *White Nights,* and was a series of skits on a vast variety of situations ranging from foreign tourists arriving at a Moscow hotel, through a take-off of a pretentious poet battling with his muse, through the social absurdities left by the Revolution, to a sly and telling attack on bureaucracy. Raikin's language was so fast, slangy, and irreverent that Faubion caught only fragments of the monologues, Shura was laughing too hard to be much help, and I understood only the passages of mime which, fortunately, were plentiful.

Afterward, Shura, still laughing said, "What a great man! What a great Russian! Do you know, even Stalin listened to him. Once he ordered Raikin to give a command performance. It was in the days after the war when the fuel shortage was terrible and the winter was one of the most bitter we have known." Raikin's skit was a commentary on this situation. He meets a friend who asks where he is going. "To the Ministry of Fuel," Raikin says, showing his empty sack. "I need wood." In spite of his friend's protests that this is optimism beyond the bounds of reason, Raikin goes off. He returns with a bulging sack over his shoulder. His friend is astonished. "It is amazing! They gave you the wood!"

"Wood?" says Raikin. "This isn't wood. These are just the forms I have to fill out."

"And you got no wood?"

"Well, I got *some* wood." He reaches in his pocket and produces a matchstick.

Shura said, "Believe me, after that the rules were changed."

I had been interested and surprised that Raikin assumed so wide a latitude of comment and criticism of the Revolution and of bureaucracy in the new state. When I asked Shura about this, he leaned across conspiratorially. "He can get away with it," he said, "but still it is dangerous. Do you know why? Do you know the difference between capitalism and socialism?" Smiling broadly, but in a cautious whisper, he said, "Capitalists make social mistakes." He leaned back in his chair, by way of illustration, sticking out his stomach and pretending to pick his teeth with his fingernail. "But socialists make only capital mistakes." He drew his finger across his throat significantly. "Do you understand my meaning?"

"Only too well," Faubion said. "How does Raikin get away with it?"

"The people love him," Shura said promptly. "With people like Raikin, even the government must be careful. Also," he added more thoughtfully, "the Revolution is a long way away. We can be easier about some things. Even laughter."

Later we had several opportunities to see the truth of Shura's remarks demonstrated in the theater. The most popular play in Moscow at the time was Mayakovsky's *Klop* (Bedbug). It is a sharp, funny, and sad spoof of the utopia promised to Russian workers during and after the Revolution and it was running in two theaters simultaneously, both of them packed for each performance. After about twenty years of official disapproval when its bitter-satiric probing of the Communist dream was considered too dangerous for popular entertainment, *Klop* can now be performed—though permission to produce it abroad is still withheld.

A more earnest and more trivial play by a contemporary Soviet dramatist was *Sonnets of Petrarch*. The story revolves around a middle-aged engineer, a good party member, who falls in love with a young librarian to whom he hasn't even spoken. The only things about the play that stay in my memory are a few snatches of dialogue that receive a disproportionate amount of applause. When the old family retainer hears about the hero's troubles with his nagging wife, she says, "In the old days we used to call this a dog's life. Now we call it simply a comrade's life." The audience is plainly delighted.

When the hero's party boss is questioning him about his relations with the young librarian, he says, "I am forced to ask you, where do you sleep nights?"

The hero replies, "I won't talk about my private life. . . . There are some things I can't discuss with the party." More applause.

When the librarian is talking to the hero, she says, "The thing that impresses me most about you is your eyes—there is no party in your eyes." Sympathetic laughter and applause.

Altogether, the sense of a "loosening up" of life and expression in Russia seemed to be present—minor, but noticeable —in the theater as well as in our casual encounters with people.

The Soviet Writers' Union in Moscow has its headquarters in a large house that dates from pre-Revolutionary times. The main rectangular block and the two smaller wings are built on the conventional Moscow pattern, on three sides of a square, enclosing a formal garden and a circular driveway. The fourth side is the street. The property used to belong to a minor prince —it was his city residence—and its chief distinction is that it is the house described by Leo Tolstoy in the early sections of *War and Peace,* the house where the big parties used to be held. In the center of the garden there is now a bust of Tolstoy, a reminder to the writers and their visitors of the Russian considered greatest in their sphere.

I arrived at the Soviet Writers' Union one gray autumn afternoon for one of those semiofficial get-togethers that the Russians like to arrange, where people of similar interests meet and are supposed to exchange views. We had found that all the personal interviews arranged for us by Edward Ivanian were helpful and interesting, but in comparison with our experience of bigger conferences relatively little except a measure of courtesy actually was exchanged. The Russians ask you a few predictable questions about your field or your country, and suggest that you make a brief speech on your impressions of this or that. You, in turn, make some equally predictable comments on the Russian theater (or art, or Soviet literature), ask one or two polite questions, and then everyone has a glass of tea and a cooky and disperses in a cloud of assurances about better mutual understanding in the future. The atmosphere is altogether too genteel to permit either a quarrel or a genuine exchange of views.

I had been invited to the Soviet Writers' Union to suggest some names of Indian writers whom their large and efficient staff of interpreters might translate for the Russian audience. In a pleasant, low-ceilinged room, with comfortable chairs and a long polished table, I met half a dozen women from the Union. They had obviously been carefully selected, because they all spoke adequate English and one of them spoke excellent Hindi. We exchanged formalities, I answered their questions as well as I could. In return I wondered which foreign writers were already popular in Russia. Tagore and Kalidasa from India, I learned, but their real problem was in keeping up with the interests in American literature. Of course, the classics were taught in school in a short course of foreign literature. (The "classics" turned out to be Erskine Caldwell, Theodore Dreiser, especially *An American Tragedy,* Sinclair Lewis, Mark Twain, Jack London, and Upton Sinclair.) Recently they had been encouraged to "experiment" because an edition of Ernest Hemingway's short stories and *A Farewell to Arms* have been so well received. One of the women told me that she went to a bookshop two hours after it opened on the day of publication, and the Hemingway book was already sold out. More recently William Saroyan has been gaining popularity, and soon there will be an edition of early William Faulkner. "I like him myself," one of them said, "but I don't know how the Russian people will react." The only comment that surprised me concerned a writer I had never heard of—Mitchell Wilson—whose books, in their Russian translations, are considered among the "greats."

Altogether it was an uninspired, though friendly, afternoon, and the only thing that made it memorable was that I met Anna Kalma, and eventually was introduced to an aspect of Soviet life I had never before encountered—the life of the Privileged.

All through the meeting I had noticed her with special interest, partly because she was the only one whose questions concerned Indian life rather than Indian writers and partly because she herself seemed (unobtrusively, but still clearly) impatient of the whole affair. Besides, her appearance pleased me. She was a middle-aged woman with graying, short hair that seemed to have had a rather unsuccessful permanent—the ends were too crinkly and the rest too straight—but she was wearing the only well-cut suit I had seen in Russia and her face had an alert expression and a hint of hidden humor that were quite unlike the serious, conscientious, rather withdrawn look I had come to think of as characteristic of Russian women.

After the meeting was over, in the few moments of informal conversation when we were all getting ready to leave, the girl who spoke such good Hindi came over to me and said, "You know, that was Anna Kalma sitting next to you," and when I looked blank, she asked in amazement, "You haven't read any of her books? Some are translated into English." When I apologized for my ignorance, she said, "Sometime you must read them—like many thousands, perhaps millions do here. I studied her books at school. Today she was in a good mood. You should see her in a committee meeting—she can be so severe."

On the outside steps, in the gathering darkness of the early Moscow evening, I found myself next to Anna Kalma again and heard her ask the usual opening question of any conversation, with foreigners or with Russians, in Moscow: What was I doing in Russia?

"Just a tourist," I replied, as usual.

In heavily accented English she asked, "What, for example, are you coming to see?"

"Well, really, just how people live," I said vaguely.

She looked amused. "Perhaps you will take tea with me one day? I can show you a little how a writer lives. That is one part at the least."

I accepted eagerly and suggested a date on the spot, because in spite of the hospitality Russians had shown us in public places I had not yet been invited to a private house in Moscow. One soon becomes familiar with the problems of overcrowded living conditions, apartments shared with other families, the inconveniences of entertaining guests—particularly foreign guests —in a bedroom, so this was a particularly exciting invitation. Still smiling, she wrote down her address and her telephone number—another display of confidence and openness that is rare in Russia. When the tourist bureau car that was to take me back to the hotel drew up, I offered her a ride home, and then she surprised me as I had not been surprised before in Russia. "Thank you, no," she said, "I have my own car here," and swinging the keys on a gloved finger, she strode off down the driveway.

Of course, I knew that some Russians had cars of their own. At diplomatic parties I had seen the lines of shiny black Zims and Zises parked close to the entrance waiting for the top party officials and the scattering of famous actors, singers, writers, scientists who were free to go to such parties. Like other foreigners, I had noticed at the Russian theaters the obvious contrasts between the luxury on stage, the fine clothes and the glitter of jewelry, and the look of the average audience. It seemed clear that the Russians have a hankering for luxury. I had noticed that the most crowded of the plays were usually the most extravagant, and that the spectators particularly enjoyed presentations of their classics, the lives and love stories of the aristocrats and the rich. But I had never had an opportunity to see how the modern Soviet aristocracy lived, how this new class of the Privileged lived in a classless society. Tea with Mrs. Kalma was to prove my first glimpse of that life.

The building where she lived was in a good part of town, on a quiet, wide avenue. It was set back from the street by a strip of city-looking grass, and inside, although the halls were rather cheerless, there was a self-service elevator. A maid in a black dress and white apron opened the door and showed me down a narrow passage to the living room at the end, the most tasteful and charming room I had seen in Russia. Old-fashioned, certainly, but not in the ponderous plush-and-mahogany manner of the hotel rooms; it had a casual, rather worn elegance, like exiled aristocracy.

Anna Kalma sprang up from a tall desk in one corner of the room and walked toward me, both hands outstretched. She had that look of humorous eagerness that had first attracted me and talked in her rapid, clumsy English, cordial and informal.

"Please, do come—you had not trouble finding here? The *gornichnaya* will take your coat—your hands are cold—come in, how can we warm you? The Moscow climate makes you homesick I would not be surprised—"

Actually the room was very well heated and, besides, the pale autumn sunshine was streaming in through the windows, the double windows, as in most Moscow apartments, set with about a foot of space between the inner and the outer panes. The massed flowers on the window ledge caught the light, and so did the dark polish of table tops and chair backs and the warm colors of the Bokhara carpets. I couldn't help commenting on the appearance of the apartment, and Mrs. Kalma (in another good-looking outfit: plaid wool dress and matching jacket, nylons, and high heels), shrugged. "It is an old building. Some people find in this romance, but here we would much rather do without romance and have proper housing."

"I meant the room, the furniture—"

She turned to stare at the desk she had just left. "It looks funny, you think? Typewriter on desk of the eighteenth century. You are interested in furniture? I also. All here is Russian—eighteenth and early nineteenth century—" She moved her arm to indicate the sofa, the brocade-covered chairs, the small tables, the glass-fronted bookcase. "All except this." With affectionate fingers she stroked the surface of an Italian table, intricately inlaid with different colored woods. "I found this four years ago—expensive, but I could not resist." She turned back to me. "During the war we all learn to lose everything. Now when I collect, I feel only it is a loan. I do not become fond. But while I live I like to have near me beautiful things."

They were beautiful, all right, the Russian antiques, the delicate china ornaments, the leather-bound books, most of all the really extraordinary carpet, fine, faded, exquisitely designed, draped over the back of the sofa on which we sat. Beautiful, and beautifully kept. Mrs. Kalma was saying, "My husband also likes such things, but for him it is pictures—always pictures." She made me stand up to look at the painting on the wall above our heads. It looked to me like a Gainsborough. But she said, "Is Russian. We were much influenced by the West in those olden times." She led me to an alcove at the end of the room where rows of oval miniatures hung on the wall. "Members from my husband's family—of course, from olden times." She pointed to one of the smooth, correct little faces, the high collar and curling hair. "His grandfather. . . . But you haven't come to listen about those days. Come, sit. I promised to tell you about a Soviet writer's life. Now, you ask questions—I was for many years journalist, now you shall be journalist and I shall be—shall be, what is the word?"

"Interviewed."

"So. Interviewed. It is a good change-around. Please begin."

"Well . . ." I began, and didn't know how to go on because what I really wanted to ask was "How do you happen to live so well when all the other Russians I've met live so stringently?"

Fortunately she interrupted immediately. "Have you noticed this: writers when they meet always talk about money. Is it true? So, I will tell you." Then she explained to me the rather curious system of payments and royalties in Russian publishing. For your first book you are paid a flat sum of 1,500 rubles per form. A form is 16 pages, so a first novel of average length would bring the writer the equivalent of $3,000 right off. The first edition is always 15,000 copies. When that has been sold out, the writer gets 60 per cent of the original payment for the second edition, 50 per cent for the third edition, and if the book goes into a "mass edition," a paperback printing of 75,000 copies, he again gets 60 per cent of the initial sum. His royalties bear no relation to the cost of the book—some of the paperbacks sell for 20 kopeks (2 cents), and even a book like S. Obrastzov's account of the Chinese classical theater, which is printed on heavy paper, contains over 200 photographs, some of them in color, costs 20 rubles, 75 kopeks ($2.07).

I began to see why Mrs. Kalma lived so well. What it came to was this: if you could get your book published at all, you couldn't help making money, even if it never sold a copy. When I commented on this, Mrs. Kalma's face wrinkled with pleasure. "But of course, yes, naturally! We protect our artists. Do you not see the good advantage? If you are a writer, from the beginning you can live by writing. No need to waste your time doing everything else until at last, perhaps, one day, you are recognized. Or if you are a scholar writing what cannot be popular, then, too, you can be published and live as a writer."

In the course of the afternoon Mrs. Kalma talked a lot about herself and her life and how she started writing. "My childhood was very much protected," she told me, but there was one wonderful disruptive influence in it. The great Vladimir Mayakovsky, poet, painter, journalist, publicist, whose plays *Klop,* *Banya,* and *Misteria Buffe* are still the most popular plays in Moscow, was a friend of her father. He was convinced that young people should learn to stand on their own feet as soon as possible. One day, when she was about twelve years old, he asked her what she could do, and she replied, "I can sew rag dolls." Mayakovsky started to laugh—"You could never forget that laugh—it was the laugh of a crocodile." (She pronounced it "krokodeel.")—"So wide, that laugh, and wicked. I told him, 'Probably I can vaccinate, it looks easy. . . .' Again that krokodeel laugh—the teeth!—so he said, 'Oh, you cost a lot of money!' I was ashamed."

When she was fourteen, Mayakovsky got her a job on the

newspaper for which he worked and there she was put to translating humor because her languages were good. "Jokes," she said, shaking her head, "this, you understand, is the hardest for translation. One I remember even now—I will try again, after so many years, to put it in English. A girl and her fiancé walking past a dwelling house which is not yet finished building. She says, 'One day we might live in such a building.' He blows his nose on his fingers and wipes the fingers on the bricks. She says, 'Oh, to think we shall live in such an unhygienic building!' You see? Nothing. In Russian very funny." Eventually she was moved to the woman's page—"not very interesting, but my pen developed."

Meanwhile she was studying to improve her English, and it was through those lessons that at last she became a writer. She had advertised for an English teacher, and when the applicant appeared, "I was so surprised I nearly fell backwards— she was the first Negro I had ever seen. In our conversation, one day, she said—without intention to impress, you understand —'When my mother was a slave . . .' I couldn't believe!" The mother was Jamaican, eighty years old, and was coming to Moscow to join her daughter, who was an announcer on the Moscow radio foreign broadcasts. Anna Kalma got to know her, and her first book was a fictionalized account of the old woman's story, *Black Sally*. It was published in 1939, is still taught in schools, and is one of the first books given to eight-year-olds.

Since then Anna Kalma has written fifteen books, mostly "romantic biographies," almost all have gone into second and third editions, and some, like her account of her experiences as a major in the Red Army, have become paperbacks. I soon stopped trying to compute in my head how much she has earned in the past fifteen years. Clearly, by Soviet standards, it was a staggering amount. At some point in this flood of information the *gornichnaya* came in to announce tea, addressing Mrs. Kalma with almost pre-Revolutionary formality by her first name and patronymic. I had been used to hearing the usual Soviet *tovarisch*.

Mrs. Kalma led me into the hall, past an open door through which I saw a well-appointed kitchen, into a compact and again beautifully decorated dining room. Flowers and sunshine reflected from the round polished table, cabinets full of old, ornate, gracefully painted china, and the odd but harmonizing accent of the modern Soviet paintings on the walls. It is well known that most contemporary Russian painters strive for Socialist Realism in their art—and you have to hand it to them, Socialist Realism is exactly what they achieve. The possibility that it is still art is hotly defended by Russian critics. Remembering most of the Russian paintings that I had seen, it came as a particular novelty that Mrs. Kalma's pictures looked to me like *art*. She saw me staring at them and said in explanation, "Some of our young painters. We are interested in their work."

"But do the critics approve?"

"Not so much—yet. These things take a little time. Remember it is only forty years."

"But they are still permitted to paint? They are not condemned?"

Mrs. Kalma smiled her slightly satiric smile. "I will tell you. Once I wrote a book that was condemned. *The Diary of Andrei Sazonov*. It was the story of a boy whose father goes to the war. He gives the boy a copybook to write his story. The father is reported missing and Andrei reports what happens to his family with no father, the hardships, how they can manage, wartime. But the father is alive—shell-shocked, all his senses are lost, he is dead-alive. The family decides best to take the father home. Andrei becomes like his nurse, always taking care of him. At the end, the adjutant of the father returns to see him—another shock—all memories of the war are again alive. But this makes the father well again. How this book was criticized! They say, Depressing. Giving youth bad feelings. Even the minister of education made a speech—one-hour speech— condemning my book. I was worried. I like to write for children —it is the most difficult, therefore the most interesting. Do you read Gorki? Once someone ask him how to write for children, he responded, 'The same as for grownups, only better.' I was worried I would no more write for young people—and I was worried about the destiny of my book. But it was not banned. The readers received it well. Many letters come to me. I am alive. I am writing. You see, no one holds a stick over us."

It took me a moment to work out her attitude, and then I asked, "But you would never write a similar book?"

She said, "Only those people do not make blunders who do not work."

"You consider it a blunder? Would you 'confess' it at one of those writers' conferences?"

"The purpose of the conferences is different. Sometimes a critic can point out a flaw that you do not see yourself. Or he can find a solution to some problem of yours. The people that complain, often they are . . . they are White Negroes."

"They are *what?*"

"That is how we say in Russia. Someone who has no grievance who *makes* a grievance—White Negro."

I couldn't help thinking that Mrs. Kalma had come off remarkably lightly from her one brush with official censure. The story of the humiliating apologies that Dudintsev, the author of *Not by Bread Alone,* was compelled to make to various groups in Russia for his "errors" in presenting the seamy side of Soviet bureaucracy is well known both in Russia and abroad.

Or Shostakovich, who was accused of "deviationism and Western tendencies" and had to recant these sins against the people before he could get back in favor with the authorities and rise to his present exalted position of member of the Presidium. I remembered too the story of Peter Leshchenko that Sasha had told us in Leningrad.

When tea was served the tea itself turned out to be the least important part of the meal. There were ham and sausage and pressed black caviar, which many Russians prefer to the more familiar variety. It comes in a solid black lump like a brick of tar, and tastes delicious. There were several different sorts of jam and preserves, there were cake and shortbread, there were black bread, white bread, raisin bread, and toast. There were sliced cucumbers in sour cream, beetroot and a white vegetable somewhere between turnips and horseradish. All of it was served on old florid china in lovely curly shapes and decorated with gold flowers. "A harlequin service," Mrs. Kalma said. "I have collected this china by pieces whenever I could find it. Nothing matches."

"It's a feast," I said.

"Black bread and sausage," Mrs. Kalma said, laughing. "For these a Russian is always homesick. Please try some jam—it comes from our country estate."

As our stay in Russia drew on, I learned that a "country estate" is not quite so bizarre a possession as it sounded that afternoon. The top artists, writers, ballerinas, musicians, actors, directors, scientists—and of course the leading politicians—can have *dachas* (country houses) if they want when they have reached a certain eminence in their field. The way it works is one of those curious Russian compromises between privilege and the System. When the moment comes that through books, performances, or state rewards in the form of cash you have enough money to build a country house, you make your application to the proper government authority for a land grant. You specify the place, the site, the size, and if your application is approved (and if you yourself are persona grata) you are assigned your choice of land. Apart from the few nominal registration fees and such, you don't pay for the land, but you do pay for the building of the house out of your earnings or savings. The design is, to some extent, up to you, but you must remember that your house cannot be "ostentatious."

As it was explained to me, "you cannot build a palace of fifteen rooms." It must be a "suitable" plan and, to ensure that you do not violate the Soviet standards of "suitability," before you build your design must be passed by the council of the village closest to your land to be sure that your house will be about the same size and style as other country houses in the vicinity. After that you're on your own. We were told that recently, because of the difficulties of getting labor and the intractability of the laborers when you get them, a do-it-yourself fervor seems to have gripped the Russian privileged. One of the directors, for instance, of a movie company called Mosfilm, is, like many of his friends, building his own *dacha*. He lives in Moscow, but on weekends he and his family and whatever assistants he can recruit among his colleagues camp at his building site and work on his country house.

Some of the elite, who are not addicted to real country life, prefer to combine space and convenience by leading a kind of exurban life. A particularly fashionable district near Moscow is called Vnukovo Suburb, although strictly speaking it is a bit too far out and not well enough serviced with trains or public conveyances to be really a suburb. You just about have to have a private car to live in Vnukovo Suburb. Gromyko is about the only politician who lives there, the rest are mostly theater people and directors. Alessandrov, one of Russia's most famous movie directors, has the house next to Gromyko, a white Spanish-style villa with a large hall and a couple of reception rooms downstairs, and two or three bedrooms upstairs. He has, besides, a big garden with an orchard, so his weekends, within reach of the city, can still have a faintly country air about them.

Yet other members of this group prefer to live entirely in town, and in that case even they have to be content with relatively cramped quarters. One of the top script writers in Moscow, Mrs. Smirnova, has a "luxurious" flat in one of the best buildings, on the river, near the Kremlin. It has three rooms with a large kitchen-dining room. She shares it with her two daughters.

Oddly enough, the movie stars come in for fewer of the privileges than the directors and writers, or stage actors. They have to be very well established over a number of years before they can claim the advantages of the gilded life. A movie actor doesn't seem to be considered a proper "creative artist" entitled to good living. Oleg Strizhanov, a very handsome and successful young movie hero, one of the most sought-after personalities in Russian films, has not yet been able to get an apartment to himself. Eventually he will probably succeed in getting at least a room or two of his own, possibly in one of the state "dwelling houses" for artists near the airport, where a married couple is permitted two rooms; if they have children, three rooms. But other, less famous apartment hunters wait for years with their names on official lists and pray that the building in which they live will be condemned and torn down for a new block because that way they will get a priority in the eternal search for living accommodations.

In contrast with the usual setup, Mrs. Kalma's apartment looked particularly spacious. Apart from the rooms I had seen, there must have been at least two bedrooms because, as she told me, her maid worked for her full time and lived in. "She prefers it, and it is more convenient for me. Here she has a room, and we provide food. She has been with me many years." I couldn't help contrasting this pleasant arrangement with the problems that members of the diplomatic corps have with their servants who work a strict eight-hour day (with Sundays off) and make it clear that they are doing you a favor if they stay overtime, even if they get paid for it. Some servants—waiters, official chauffeurs, and the like—work sixteen hours a day and get every alternate day off. Servants of any sort are difficult to get in Russia, even for the Russians. In Moscow, as in Leningrad, we saw many cards in windows announcing that help of various sorts was wanted. Mrs. Kalma's maid was an admitted extravagance. "After all," she said, "I pay her two hundred rubles a month—and, of course, presents at New Year and May Day and such occasions." Foreign diplomats, who have to get their servants from the official domestic employment agency, pay anywhere from 900 to 1,200 rubles a month.

When we had finished our tea, Mrs. Kalma called the maid to set out small antique Chinese cups of embossed silver and a cut-crystal decanter of dark-red wine. Again she said, "Please try this wine, it is made from cherries of our estate." It was sweet, and strong and very good, and in the glow of the cherry wine and the sunlight that had turned golden as the afternoon faded, I said, "What a lovely life you seem to have—so different from most of what I've seen."

She nodded seriously. "Yes, we are fortunate, my husband and I. He is the manager of a factory, so he also earns good money. We can spend it all on ourselves. We have no responsibilities—no children, even from my first husband I had no children . . ."

Later, when I met more members of the Privileged (mostly

people in the theatrical world and writers), I learned that almost all of them seemed to have been married twice, and many of them several times. That afternoon with Anna Kalma, however, it was with a bit of a shock that I heard her produce that sturdy Hollywood cliché, "My first husband and I are still good friends. He comes to visit me often."

Divorce—among the elite, at least—is not a complicated matter if both sides agree. I asked Boris about it the next time we met, and he said, "Divorce is easy—but not for some sordid reason like money." You must present your case on some such grounds as "a bad character," or cruelty, or adultery. The divorce court will then ask you to wait a few months, and if at the end of that time there has been no reconciliation your divorce is granted. The man is responsible for the support of the children, but not of the wife.

"What happens," I asked Boris, "if you want to divorce your wife, but she is still in love with you?"

Boris gave me a quick, wary look. "It is not enough reason just to be in love with someone else yourself. Only if your wife is known to be a frivolous person."

"I see," I said as flatly as I could. I felt we were coming uncomfortably close to some complication in Boris' own life.

The phrase "frivolous person" reminded me of the evening we had spent with Nikolai Nikolayevich Svobodin, the young building contractor whom we had met at the Astoria restaurant with Shura. He had conscientiously led us through the Tretyakov galleries, where the ikons were magnificent and the more recent paintings less impressive, and afterward had gone for a drink with us. During this time he had started to talk with unexpected candor about himself. He too, even though he wasn't a member of the elite, was divorced. His wife was a "frivolous person" and he had no trouble proving it because she was having a flagrant affair with another man. She was still living with the other man, though they had not yet married, and in the usual Russian way she had been given custody of their small son. "There was no bond between my wife and me, no understanding," he said, but they had come to an arrangement about the child. He paid for a nanny to take care of the boy while his wife worked, and she agreed to be away from the flat a couple of evenings a week so that he could visit his son without seeing her. "It is the mistake of marrying when you are very young. Since then I haven't met another I would marry. I am still bitter. That is why I like to go alone to restaurants and watch the world."

In contrast, Mrs. Kalma's divorce was apparently quite amicable, and in a way I thought it was probably lucky that she had no children. It is the sons and daughters of the elite who appear to present the severest juvenile problem both to their parents and to the state. They, so one reads in occasional censorious articles in the press, are the pampered, irresponsible youth who have wild parties, drink too much, collect black-market recordings of foreign jazz, drive their parents' cars recklessly, set themselves apart from their hard-working contemporaries in less privileged groups, slack at their college work or pay to have it done for them, and generally forget the primary duty of every Soviet citizen—service to the state. I never met any of them, but occasionally used to see a few in restaurants or hotels. They could be recognized by the superior quality of their clothes, by the fact that they danced a bit more closely than most, ordered food and drink a bit more lavishly, flirted a bit more freely, and certainly got better service from the waiters —but nothing, in my opinion, very outrageous.

However, I was told that one couldn't judge them by these public appearances. For the most part their entertaining is done at home—they are, after all, among the few who *can* entertain at home—and most of their activities are not on view to the foreigner. Even after these youngsters grow up a little, they will continue to present, if not a problem, at least a new element in Soviet society. They will be the first group since the Revolution to look forward to *inheriting* money.

But this aspect of privileged living was not one that I discussed with Mrs. Kalma that afternoon. By the time I left it was already dark, and we had made a date for her and her husband to dine with us at our hotel. At first I had suggested the following weekend, but weekends turned out to be difficult for them because "my husband loves to go to the country for camping." They were driving up to a lake that he was particularly fond of, in the company of a couple of friends (who also had a car of their own) for a weekend of shooting and simple living. Even when we found a date that suited us both, she protested, "But you must come here—you are guests in our country—as you see, our entertainment is very modest, but please—" It took me some time to persuade her. When the maid opened the hall closet to get my coat, I caught a glimpse of several pairs of skis neatly stacked against the back wall.

By chance it was only a few days before I had another opportunity to meet a member of the Privileged, not nearly so sympathetic as Mrs. Kalma, but indubitably one of the elite. Nikolai Nikolayevich had asked us, after we had been to the Tretyakov gallery with him, whether we would like to visit the studio of "one of the most successful Soviet painters." He had an almost missionary zeal about modern Soviet painting and, though I think he deplored our rather tepid view of it, was determined to educate us. Both Faubion and I were touched by Nikolai's kindness to us and his painstaking determination to show us what he considered the best of his city, but neither of us really warmed up to him. His starchy manner and possibly the residue of bitterness left in his nature by his unhappy experiences with his wife made him an uncomfortable person to be with. However, we were pleased at the chance to see the inside of a Russian artist's studio.

Vaguely at the back of my mind was the conventional picture: a bare, drafty, untidy studio which, considering the living conditions in Moscow, might, I thought, for once turn out to be accurate. Surprisingly, we went to one of the most fashionable sections of Moscow, a plaza off the wide shady avenue called Gorki Street in the heart of town. In the center of the plaza was a well-kept garden, and a statue of Prince Dolgoruki, the founder of Moscow, who built a wooden fortress eight hundred years ago on the bank of the Moscow River where the Kremlin now stands.

We went into a large gray stone building that looked a little like one of the older apartment houses on upper Park Avenue. This time there was not only an elevator but a uniformed operator. The door of the studio was opened to us by a large blonde woman who was introduced as the wife of the painter, and when we shook hands I was impressed to see that she wore two diamond rings. She was full of smiles and chatter and wore a black-crepe dress over her tightly corseted figure. As she clicked down the passage ahead of us, I noticed that she too wore nylons and high heels.

The studio was large and airy, with huge windows, but was pleasantly warm and comfortably furnished. Canvases were neatly stacked on shelves specially built for them. Our host was a big, red-faced man with a lot of gray hair, wore tweeds and suède shoes, and stood with his back to an enormous picture on an easel that he had evidently been inspecting. Immediately after greetings and introductions were over, he turned back to it. "This," he said, "will be my offering to the fortieth anniversary of the Revolution. I must finish it before November."

It showed a figure of Lenin, smiling benignly and surrounded by an animated group of people. Beyond them were more people, as though a large crowd were just breaking up, and in the background the towers and walls of the Kremlin. The picture was called "Happy Day" and, so we were told, was intended to show Lenin after his speech in Red Square "when all the people were pleased to talk to him." I thought it a remarkably dull picture.

However, as more and more of the canvases were produced for our inspection, I soon lost all interest in the quality of the art and became absorbed in evidences of one most desirable advantage that the Privileged have over the rest of the Russian people—the possibility of travel. There were sketches of Paris, landscapes from Italy, portraits and studies from the Middle East and various places in Asia.

When we moved across the studio to the long table against the wall, extravagantly set with china and glassware, it did not surprise me to be offered the best Russian wines from Georgia and all kinds of local delicacies, but I hadn't expected to be served French cognac. Our host poured it with gusto, explaining, "I acquired a taste for *this* in Paris—a taste that has never left me!" Apparently, then, it was possible to get imported things in Russia—if you knew the right channels. In shops, restaurants, markets, one never even sees anything that is imported except, possibly, from one of the iron curtain countries. Everything from cars to hairpins is Russian-made. In fact, when any foreign car (always belonging to a diplomat or a tourist) is parked anywhere in Moscow, it is instantly surrounded by a fascinated, wondering crowd.

Conversation over the cognac was almost entirely about Soviet art. I learned gradually, in the course of several encounters with members of the elite, that they are the most relentless shop-talkers. A movie director will spend an hour telling you the exact sequence of shots in a particular film he has made or precisely which themes from which composers provided the background music. An actor will describe in detail the way he built up his conception of a character. And these conversations never seemed to be interspersed with news or gossip, anecdotes, or a casual exchange of opinion. Possibly this was only their manner with foreigners and a cautious approach to "safe" subjects, but it struck me as odd because among the other Russians, the unimportant ones, whom we met the subjects of conversation were quite normally varied—jazz, food, clothes, children, jobs, money, anything except politics, which we discussed only on very rare occasions. Like Sasha or Boris or Shura, they asked countless questions about life in the Western world. The elite talked only about Russia and their work, and sometimes about a trip to one of the "friendly" countries.

That day at the studio I listened to the unavoidable lecture on Soviet painting and wondered in silence whether my host ever worried about being able to keep in line with the dictates of the All-Union Congress of Soviet Artists. In a recent meeting they had condemned, I had read, "naturalism" and "photographism" and had at the same time warned artists to keep away "from purposeless experiments of a formalistic nature." It must be an edgy business being a Soviet artist, full of nervous decisions from year to year as to just what to paint and how to paint it.

When my host asked my opinion of Soviet art, I replied as politely as I could that I found it very realistic. He beamed with pleasure. "Yes, yes! There is only one standard. If the people do not understand a picture, it cannot be art."

Looking around the comfortable room, the upholstered furniture, the fringed lampshades, the loaded table, I wondered whether the almost banal contrast with other Russian rooms didn't occur to my host and hostess, whether they didn't note the sad irony that "the people's art" was increasingly in the hands of people who were entrenching themselves more firmly every day into a thoroughly bourgeois way of life.

I turned to my hostess, and to change the subject asked if she too was an artist. She smiled and said, "Oh, no, I just help my husband." Another item of privilege, I thought. In a country where almost every woman works at a job until she is old enough to retire, the elite, apparently, could have a wife who is simply a wife. Our hostess continued modestly, "My husband has done a very fine portrait of me—in our garden in the country —would you like to see it?"

We all got up from the table and were shown into another room. The walls were covered with rows of framed canvases, and to my astonishment many of them were nudes—I had never seen a painting of a nude in any of the exhibitions of Soviet painting that I had visited. Our hostess said, almost apologetically, "I, too, am sometimes surprised when I come into this room. In Stalinist days we were not permitted to hang them. Sometimes I forget that these are different times."

Beyond this room there was yet another, a kind of study with a large roll-top desk under the window, a couch, bookshelves, and the big, idealized portrait of the artist's wife. "What a nice roomy apartment you have," I remarked.

"This isn't our apartment," she said. "This is just my husband's studio."

Later that week Mrs. Kalma telephoned me at the hotel to say that our dinner date would have to be postponed. She did not have particularly good health, and the doctor had ordered her to stay in bed for some time. When I commiserated with her, she quickly interrupted, "No, no. Please do not concern. The Writers' Union takes care of all this."

Judging from the array in her apartment, I thought that Mrs. Kalma must be fond of flowers, and decided to send her some—and then discovered what an extravagance those flowers represented. I was directed to a shop with a delivery service, one of the few in Moscow, and found that a bunch of chrysanthemums cost 90 rubles ($9). The delivery service cost an extra 20 rubles.

Afterward when I talked to Mrs. Kalma about her illness, I learned that the Writers' Union does much more than take care of doctors and hospitalization. If, for instance, as a Privileged Person belonging to any one of the unions in your field, you find that your home conditions are too crowded to make work possible; or the children get in your way; or, unlike Mrs. Kalma, you haven't a room to yourself in which to work; or you haven't a servant and housework takes up too much of your time; or you just need a change and a different atmosphere—you can apply for a stay in one of the Houses of Creation, a sort of cross between a hotel and a club. As a scenario writer, for instance, even though you get 60,000 to 90,000 rubles for a script and a bonus that can go as high as 150 per cent of the original payment, depending on the success of the film, still you may find it impossible to work at home and may need to have a quiet, uncomplicated life in the country for a while. A playwright, who gets 4 per cent of the take on every performance of his play, may find himself in the same fix. In that case, the writer can go to his particular organization and make arrangements to stay at one of the Houses of Creation and there find the peace necessary to get his work done.

At the House of Creation, according to various people I met

who had done just that, you are given a room to yourself and a bath. Meals are provided either in your room or in a public dining room. The food, on the whole, has the reputation of being better than it is in the cities because it is all "country food"—local produce. A permanent staff of servants takes care of the housework. There are lounges for relaxation in the company of people who are supposed to be compatible since they are all either acquaintances or members of the same profession. And then there is the vast Russian countryside in which to take walks, think, fish, hunt, or whatever the locality offers. The Writers' House of Creation near Moscow is, according to Mrs. Kalma, "literally a palace," converted from one of the princely estates of the old days. "There is walks in pretty country. Walks and quiet and the birch woods."

I asked her whether she would be going to one of the Houses of Creation to recuperate from her illness, but she said that this time she thought a trip abroad would be the best thing for her. Even after my visit to the artist's studio this casual acceptance of the right to travel sounded strange in the Soviet context. Most of the Russians, I knew, had considerable trouble arranging even a few days in a nearby town. Among the elite too it is a recent privilege. These days, for instance, it has become fashionable for members of the elite to send their children abroad to boarding schools. Yugoslavia and Czechoslovakia, which are supposed to have particularly good schools, are the most favored.

Travel for pleasure is a bit more restricted, but still possible, largely in the Communist countries of Eastern Europe and in China. Occasionally one or another of the Privileged talks about a holiday in the Carpathians, where the scenery is so beautiful, or a trip to Finland, where the clothes are so good and, relatively, so cheap. Anna Kalma herself had told me how much she liked to travel. "In Russian we say, 'It is easy for me to get up and leave.' Anyone suggests, and I will get up and go there."

This time, if she wanted a trip, Italy was the logical choice. She had been asked by her publisher to write a biography of Garibaldi. In the course of her preliminary research she came upon some quite obscure material about Russians who were connected with Garibaldi's movement and had half decided to change the focus of her book to those Russians. If she wanted to she could almost certainly take a trip to Italy to uncover more material about them.

I asked her, since she was so fond of travel, whether she had ever considered going to America and, recalling our first conversation, added, "Just to see how people live."

"It would be interesting," she said, and then in that shrewd, amused voice of hers added, "But I am not sure that I am so anxious to travel as that much. After all, I have a very good life here."

Moscow: Part II

ABOUT THE MIDDLE of October, when we had been in Moscow a month or so, I felt our lives begin to shift almost imperceptibly from the usual tourist routine to a more complex, more intimate, and more puzzling concern with the city, its activities, and its people. For one thing we had begun to feel pretty much at home in Moscow, and, as if this feeling somehow communicated itself to the people we knew, one or two of them at least stopped being merely chance acquaintances and became something a little closer to friends. Boris, for instance, announced one day that he would like to bring his wife to see us.

Whenever we went into the office of the tourist bureau in the Metropole lobby, to order a car or to make theater reservations, the people there no longer asked us with bewildered politeness whether we were *sure* we didn't want to see something of Russia besides Moscow. They had stopped suggesting informative trips to Kharkov, Rostov, Stalingrad, Kiev, Yalta, or any of the other towns that are open to tourists. They had accepted the idea that Faubion and I were firm in our decision *not* to be dragged through industrial centers, or to trail around collective farms, or to visit health resorts. Of the two journeys we had wanted to make, one—a river boat down the Volga, stopping off at various towns and ending in Astrakhan on the Caspian Sea—turned out to be impossible. The tourist official said, "I am sorry. There are no arrangements for tourists in Astrakhan."

"We don't mind where we stay—a *pension,* some small hotel —there must be something of the sort in a city the size of Astrakhan."

"I'm sorry. There are no arrangements for tourists in Astrakhan."

"But where do visiting Russians stay?"

"I'm sorry. Perhaps next year."

"But we won't be here next year."

"I'm sorry."

Since all one's travel arrangements have to be made through Intourist, that ended the matter.

The other place we wanted to go was Samarkand, because it sounded romantic. That trip turned out to be possible, but we decided to leave it until the end of our Russian visit, and meanwhile we settled in for another month in Moscow with the general conviction that people are usually more interesting than places and the knowledge that in Moscow we had, at least, made a start on knowing a few of them.

Another reason why I had a sense of our changing life in the city was that from the middle of October the pace of Moscow itself altered, and there is something about watching the turn of the season or the arrival of a familiar, annual moment in a city's life that gives a feeling of participation, of closeness with a place, with a foreign world. The Bolshoi, which started late that year because of the performances the company had given for the Youth Festival during the summer holidays, was almost the official opening of the Moscow Season. Embassy people had come back from tours and holidays and the round of diplomatic parties that is a part of any capital had begun. The university had opened and now we saw Boris and Shura only on weekends and very occasionally, after a good deal of organization, on a weekday evening. The first snow had fallen about a week before. It had melted at once, but coming out of the theater at night we had for a moment seen the city filmed with white and felt the grip of the cold on our faces.

Also, it was mushroom-hunting season, a sure sign of late autumn in Moscow. In buses and suburban trains, Muscovites would find their way to the outskirts of town and then walk to the famous silver-birch woods that surround the city. The trees are a pale, delicate green even in midsummer, and in autumn they change from a gilded yellow to brown (no flamboyant reds and oranges here). It is the best mushroom-picking season, and every weekend families, groups of children, pairs of lovers wander through the cool, freckled light of the Moscow woods hunting out their favorites—rusties, fox mushrooms, birch mushrooms, stump mushrooms, not just the one or two familiar varieties one gets in Western Europe. Once when I asked why, in spite of this dedicated pursuit of the mushroom, no Moscow restaurant that I had been in served them, I was told, "But the whole point is lost if you buy them or could order them in a restaurant. Someone else has had the enjoyment by then." Someone else, that is, had got up early in the morning, packed a picnic lunch (black bread and sausage and fruit) in a carpetbag for the family and managed to reach the woods while the mists of morning were still on them and the smell of autumn was in the air.

Sometimes, late on a Sunday evening, we would see mushroom pickers walking home from stations or bus stops, baskets of mushrooms on their arms, quiet, tired, and with that bemused, disheveled look of a strenuous day spent in the country. Sometimes when you wanted to make a date with a Muscovite for a Saturday or Sunday, you would get some answer like this: "It is autumn—I've promised the children to go mushroom gathering." This excuse takes precedence over practically anything else.

As winter approached, everyone in Moscow seemed busier and more energetic and there was an added electricity in the air as the year was moving toward November 7, the anniversary of the Revolution, the biggest celebration on the Russian calendar, and this year particularly exciting because it would mark exactly forty years of Soviet rule.

Edward Ivanian had called to ask us whether we needed any help in getting tickets for the Bolshoi. He had suggested, and Faubion had instantly agreed, that the best way to get an idea of the range, the experience, and the atmosphere of Russia's greatest theater was to go to the Bolshoi every night for at least a week, and only after that to pick and choose among the productions in the balance of its repertoire.

The Bolshoi was packed almost every night with tourists, diplomats, and hundreds and hundreds of Russians—students, officials, visitors, the famous and privileged as well as "simple workers"—even though the theater holds nearly three thousand people and the tickets are more than double the price of any of the other theaters. For the opening night of the almost legendary Bolshoi, certainly the most important theatrical occasion of the Moscow season, I wore the very grandest sari I had brought with me to Russia but had never so far had an opportunity to wear.

At a quarter past seven Faubion and I walked from the Metropole across Sverdlov Square to the Bolshoi. On our way we paused for a moment in the cold night air to stare at the floodlit portico of the theater, the eight immense white pillars rising to the pediment of the porch topped by a figure in a chariot drawn by four rearing horses. The great bank of steps below the columns was crowded with people, some smoking, talking, waiting for friends, others hopefully inquiring of each new arrival whether he would sell his ticket, yet others simply watching each big car as it swept up and peering at its occupants to spot celebrities.

Inside the brilliantly lit white-marble lobby the crowd was even thicker and the atmosphere was sparked with the special exhilaration of an opening night. I looked around carefully at people's clothes and found once again that I was embarrassingly overdressed. There were a few women in evening dresses and a few more in short dresses of silk or satin or taffeta, and even some with a low décolletage or bare shoulders, but by then I had picked up the Russian trick of spotting foreigners by their clothes and could see at once that they were mostly tourists and diplomats. The Russians, slightly more extravagantly dressed than usual but still far more modestly than a comparable crowd anywhere else, were in short, dark-colored dresses occasionally made noticeable by a string of small pearls, a jeweled clip, high heels, or the good material of the dress itself. They presented a typical but disappointingly subdued appearance. It is a tradition at the Bolshoi that before the performance and during each interval the members of the audience join in an informal parade in the lobby. In twos and threes, girls on the arms of their escorts, pairs of men walking almost silently, clusters of women talking with animation, pace slowly around the lobby, moving in a changing circle to look at one another's clothes, to nod to friends, to get the feel of the audience. I found it rather tragic that this tradition is still meticulously maintained even though its point is lost. Once there must have been great glamour and visual excitement in the stylish, coquettish, malicious, and admiring moments of the parade. It is now entirely absent.

The interior of the Bolshoi Theater is a most satisfactory splash of crimson and gold. The tiers of balconies and boxes are draped in crimson damask, the balustrades encrusted with gilt moldings. The ceiling is painted with pastel figures holding musical instruments and masks, and in the center hangs the massive, famous chandelier, a glittering cloud of crystal and lights, marvelous from the main floor but a torment to the people in the top balconies, who see the stage in frustrating glimpses through its flashing net. As a focus for the attention of the gathering audience is the great curtain covering one of the biggest proscenium arches in the world, an elaborate brocade in red and bronze and gold, thoroughly in keeping with the magnificence of the Tsarist Bolshoi but woven with designs of hammers and sickles, of red stars and wheat stalks, all interspersed with the letters CCCP, the Russian script for U.S.S.R., all symbolic of the new Soviet society.

On opening night the Russian national anthem is played before the performance starts. It was the only time during our stay in Russia that I heard it. Opening night at the Bolshoi is also the one occasion on which one can be certain of seeing Khrushchev. The box nearest the stage on the left of the auditorium is permanently reserved for the party heads and on nights when they do not appear it remains empty even if the house is filled to capacity and people are queueing for standing room.

Khrushchev and Bulganin arrived at the theater during the interval after the first act. A subdued whispering and excitement in the audience just as the lights were going down made us stare with them at the quiet, straight figure with the neat gray beard and at the round, rumpled, bald pink face—both so familiar from photographs. The box immediately above them was filled with security personnel and the one next to them remained empty. There is a rumor that the anteroom behind the stage box is permanently stocked with vodka and cognac and sandwiches for refreshment during the intervals. Vodka can't be bought anywhere in the Bolshoi. It is not considered a "refined" drink. The cafés and bars in the theater serve anything from beer to champagne, but not vodka.

The opening performance at the Bolshoi is always a long, patriotic opera by Glinka (the "father of Russian Music," of course), called *Ivan Susanin*. It used to be known as *A Life for the Tsar* but the name was changed after the Revolution, for obvious reasons. It tells the story of a heroic Russian, Ivan Susanin, who is determined to help the Russian armies withstand the invasion of the Poles. This action takes place in 1612 when the Poles have reached the small town where Ivan Susanin is a respected citizen. He pretends to accept the Polish bribes and promises to lead them to the Russian encampment deep in the snowy forests. Instead, he guides the band of Poles farther and farther away from the Russian stockade and hopelessly lost in the winter wilderness, Ivan Susanin freezes to death along with the Poles, thus saving Russia.

The opera ends with a victory celebration in Moscow's Red Square. The Kremlin bells ring. The huge chorus sings "Glory, Glory to you, Russia! Glory to our Russian land!" Through enormous gates stream the triumphal processions carrying flags and ikons. The Tsar's guards appear on horseback. There is a full brass band on stage. People jam every inch of the steps, monuments, and walls. The sound of the massed singing punctuated by bells is almost deafening. I don't think I have ever seen such a wildly extravagant tableau on stage for a final curtain.

During the intervals between the five acts, Faubion and I did all the proper Bolshoi things. We stood in the lobby to watch the people parading. We found our way to the "high-class" café, where everything is neat and white, where there are tables and chairs and waitresses to bring you a drink and a snack and where you buy champagne (Russian champagne, naturally) by the bottle. We also explored the "lower-class" bar, where there is only a long counter at which you line up to give your order to the bar attendants, then take your drink to one of the high, marble-topped tables at which you stand (no chairs) and perhaps talk to the other people clustered round it while you finish your drinks. At this bar also you can order champagne—by the glass.

Although the atmosphere and activity of the Bolshoi were wonderfully exotic to me that first evening, and although I was deeply impressed with the skill and the lavishness of the production, I find that in retrospect it is the small things about the opera that I remember best, the insignificant details, faithfully reproduced on stage, of the life of such a distant era of Russian history. The betrothal party, for instance, of Ivan Susanin's daughter, at which the chief ceremony is the presentation of both bread and salt to the young couple, and the gifts from the villagers are always of food and cloth. Or the interior of a village hut which, even on the enormous scale that the size of the Bolshoi stage demands, still managed to produce an odd dual impression of spartan living and coziness. The low beams and the big stove, the bare wooden furniture, and the bustling women cooking and baking and making the kitchen the most active and most important room in the house.

But perhaps the most haunting moment of all is when the singers and dancers come out in front of the curtain to take their bows. In costumes and decorations and jewelry dating from the old, the vanished Russia, they bow to the boxes where the Russian royalty and nobility used to sit, they acknowledge the deafening applause from the floor of the house with traditional curtsies, and all the time, behind them, the lights pick

out the hammers and sickles and the letters CCCP on the great
Bolshoi curtain.

Throughout the week we went to the Bolshoi every night and
saw, alternately, operas and ballets. Even the names of the
programs held a kind of remote and foreign magic—*The Fountain of Bakhchisarai, Russlan and Ludmilla, Prince Igor, Eugene Onegin, Gayane*—stories, legends, moments of history that
were almost all entirely unfamiliar to me. By the end of the
week we began to have a less dazzled view of the Bolshoi. We
continued to admire the astounding skill and virtuosity of every
performance, but began imperceptibly to take it for granted
and to wish for a bit more heart. The clear and literal presentation of each new production was still impressive, but we
began to look for ideas instead of stories. Possibly this was
because we were getting too intensive a view of the Bolshoi,
and certainly I never doubted that its range and incredibly high
standard of performance made the Bolshoi just about the
greatest theater in the world. The only exception that I could
think of was the Kabuki-za in Tokyo.

One other aspect of the Bolshoi performances struck me as
interesting, even significant. Like a recurrent theme through
many of the stories and much of the music ran the reminder of
the place of Asia and Asians in Russian history and legend.
Once I thought about it, this refrain didn't seem so very sur-
prising—after all, most of Russia is Asia. All the same, I began
to grasp how much adjustment and blending and welding it
must have taken to make one nation out of such diverse ele-
ments. In a sense it is comparable to the American process of
molding people of many different countries and backgrounds
into one nation. The differences, however, are equally obvious,
both in the methods that America and Russia use and in the

initial situations. Foreigners come to America, an already established country, leaving behind them homes and nationalities. They can, therefore, more easily accept the idea of "Americanism" ahead of past loyalties. The Russian government must deal with people entirely different in race, religion, background, culture, who are settled in homes that have been theirs for generations—people who, quite frequently, have been historic enemies of the Western Russians with an equal claim to Russian land. Consequently, with a mixture of care and ruthlessness the Russians have coped with a tricky problem by making a great point of provincial loyalties, by making their country a union of different republics rather than a consolidated national entity.

This sense of Asia appears again and again in the great operas and ballets of the Bolshoi. In the program notes for *Ivan Susanin* you are reminded that Glinka traveled widely in the south of Russia where he was so impressed by the Oriental music that Asian and Middle Eastern themes were continually threaded through his later works. In *The Fountain of Bakhchiserai* the beautiful, blonde Maria is captured by a Tartar chieftain and carried off to his palace in the south. There, to heavily "Oriental" music by Asafiev, the women of the harem dance, and the full complement of accessories for an *Arabian Nights* kind of court is produced—eunuchs, slave girls, concubines, dancers. The concubine who used to be the favorite of the Tartar Khan kills Maria in a jealous rage, and the Khan, about to take his revenge, stops himself at the last moment with the memory of the gentle Maria. In the last act the music gets even wilder as the Tartar warriors perform their whirling sword dances partly to divert their grieving Khan and partly to prepare for yet another battle against the northern Russians.

In Glinka's *Russlan and Ludmilla,* based on Pushkin's fairy-tale poem, there are again echoes of Oriental themes. At the celebration of Ludmilla's betrothal in her father's Kiev palace the rejected suitors are a Tartar, a "Varangian knight" and a turbaned "Khazar prince." Even after Ludmilla is mysteriously kidnaped by the wicked wizard, the refrains continue. Russlan, in his search for his beloved Ludmilla, finds himself in an enchanted world where he is tempted by dancing girls, bemused by Oriental splendor and luxury, and rides on a flying carpet. Eventually, of course, he defeats his rivals, brings Ludmilla back to Kiev and establishes his right to marry her.

Both the music and the dancing of *Prince Igor* and *Gayane* are even better known for their Eastern character. Altogether there seemed to be a continual consciousness of the flow and influence—and danger—from the east and the south into Russia proper. I couldn't help contrasting the moods and moments of these Russian stories with the history of my own country. India, too, has over the centuries been invaded by countless foreigners—by Phoenicians, Scythians, Persians, by the armies of Alexander the Great, by Tamburlaine, by Kublai Khan, by the Moghuls, and at last by the British. But our stories end rather differently. India never really fought a successful war and managed to hold back almost none of the invaders. For the most part we absorbed our conquerors, accepted some changes from them, and in turn made them into Indians. Only the British didn't melt into the Indian landscape, and in the end they retreated. Possibly it is in some measure due to this aspect of our history that the Indian view of foreigners is fairly relaxed on the whole, while the Russians seem to feel continually threatened from outside. Russian capitals and cities have frequently been attacked, sometimes destroyed, occasionally captured, but the Russians' urge has always been to drive the invaders out, to guard their frontiers, to preserve the in-

tegrity of "our beloved land." At the very beginning of the
first act of *Ivan Susanin* this conviction is triumphantly sung
out, "He who dares to attack Russia shall be overtaken by
death!" And I thought of the Bible saying which Russians have
adapted as a proverb: "He who comes [to Russia] with a
sword will perish by the sword."

Every night after the Bolshoi Faubion and I would come back
to the Metropole for a late supper in the restaurant, and on
those evenings we had a number of weird encounters with
people at neighboring tables. The Bolshoi productions are almost all very long. Not only does the company believe in putting on uncut versions of all ballets and operas but the long
intervals necessary for changing the elaborate, no-expense-
spared sets add to the making of lengthy performances. As a
result we used to get back to the Metropole only just in time
to order something to eat before the restaurant closed. The
other guests had been settled at the Metropole for hours, drinking and eating. Many of them were usually pretty drunk by the
time we got there.

One night a man came staggering up to our table, bowed to
me, and even through his thickened speech I could recognize
the familiar *"Hindi-Russki bhai-bhai."* Beyond that I couldn't
understand a word and turned helplessly to Faubion for a translation. The man had asked, "Who is this person with you?"

I replied, "My husband. He is American."

Without a sign of interest he promptly started using Faubion
as an interpreter. "India and Russia! We understand each
other. Our side of the world is civilized—we are cultured and
we want peace." He waited for Faubion to translate this, and
then continued, "The Americans—they are animals!" Faubion
hesitated a bit, but the man insisted, "Tell her! The Americans
are animals! They only want war! Animals!"

Faubion dutifully translated, and the man, never grasping the absurdity of the position, continued the tirade. "Why do they threaten all the time? Have they no thought for their children?"

Faubion was getting angry. He turned away from the man, but the drunk tapped him on the shoulder. "No, no. This is important for me to say—this sari means peace and a good future to us. Jawaharlal Nehru" (perfectly pronounced) "understands the great wish of us all—NO MORE WAR!" Addressing me again, he said, "Forgive me, but you in your sari are like a mother to me—don't be offended—it is mothers that understand peace—"

One of the Metropole waiters (who had come to think of us as almost permanent fixtures in the hotel and had developed a certain protectiveness) came over to tell the man quietly, but firmly, that he must either return to his table or leave the restaurant. He allowed himself to be led away from our table, and only turned back twice to shout, "Animals! No civilization!"

Another evening it was a young man who came up to our table. He was quiet and modest and not at all drunk. He had chosen to sit with us because he wanted to buy Faubion's suit. This request startled me—the boy was so straightforward and unembarrassed about it. He asked, first in German, if Faubion were German. Then in French if he were French. Finally in English if he were English. At the word "American" he sat up more alertly, but when we tried to pursue the conversation in English it became clear that those few phrases were all he knew. He must have hoped to conduct his transaction in a few words of broken English and a great deal of sign language, and he lapsed into Russian with relief when he found that Faubion could speak it adequately. "I very much wish to know," he said politely, "how much you would ask for the suit you are wearing."

Faubion, rather agitated, said, "But I don't want to sell it. I haven't enough clothes as it is."

"When you leave Russia you can buy more clothes. Will you sell it to me when you are leaving Moscow?"

Faubion said, "No, no!" (For some reason the idea rather shocked me too.) "Anyway, it is a very old suit. It would not be worth anything you pay for it."

"To me it would be worth the price. I will pay you the same that you paid for the suit when it was new."

In fact the suit had cost about $60 at Bloomingdale's six years before. Faubion looked very uncomfortable and repeated, "No, no. I cannot sell my old clothes."

I think the young man thought we were trying to bargain. He said, "If you are worried about having too many rubles, I will pay in dollars."

Here my curiosity got the better of me and I had to ask how he would be able to get $60 in dollars. Russians are not permitted to have foreign currency, and all transactions in foreign exchange have to be made through the state bank after the proper documents and authorizations have been shown. The young man looked a bit bored but explained the system. First he made whatever contacts with foreigners, tourists mostly, that he could manage to reach in Moscow. Then he would offer to exchange their foreign currency for them at a much higher rate than they would get at the bank. The advantages on both sides are obvious. For instance, an American tourist pays for his hotel accommodations, his food, and his transport before he ever comes to Russia, and he pays in his own currency at the official rate of four rubles to the dollar. In exchange, Intourist gives him various books of coupons which he presents as the occasion arises during his stay in Russia. Once he is in the Soviet Union he can exchange his traveler's checks at the special tourist rate of ten rubles to the dollar—he will need the rubles for theater tickets, liquor, and anything he wants to buy that is not covered by his coupons—or he can buy gold here in rubles and take the gold out—including meals in restaurants and hotels that are not specifically run for tourists. Our young acquaintance at the Metropole assured us, however, that the rate he would give to such a tourist would be thirty rubles to the dollar. Gradually, in this way, he would accumulate a supply of dollars (or pounds, or francs, or marks, etc.) with which he could then buy things from other tourists. In a completely matter-of-fact tone he added, "We very well understand that rubles are of no use to you. When a tourist is in Moscow for only a few days, what will he do with sixty dollars in rubles?"

"But where do you get enough rubles in the first place?" I asked, and only then realized that this was quite unwarranted rudeness.

The young man didn't seem offended. "I join with several of my friends in this. Together we manage to collect enough."

Even after we had persuaded him that we really didn't want to sell clothes, or any of the other items he suggested—fountain pens, watches, cigarette lighters, shoes, stockings, and so on—he continued to sit at our table. I dare say that so late in the evening there were no other prospects in the Metropole restaurant. We talked in the usual way of life in America and life in Russia, and I found that by then I was quite familiar with the questions and the comments. "We have a good life here. It is much better than it was, and things will get better still."

"You prefer this government to the last one?"

"You mean Stalin? Oh, yes. For the young people it is better. But my mother—she wept for three days when Stalin died. She cannot believe all what we are told now. For so many years he was a hero—our greatest hero—for her it is very difficult to forget all that. For me it is easier. I am young."

"Do you ever think of leaving Russia, of traveling, of seeing for yourself what life in other places is like?"

"Leave Russia? Never. I am a Muscovite." He sounded astonished. "I *live* in Moscow. I could not wish to leave."

Once again I was aware of the obsessive place Moscow occupies in the minds and hearts of Russians. Every evening the orchestra at the Metropole (or any other restaurant) played *Moscow Nights* with its refrain, "If you knew how dear you are, Moscow nights . . ." Every evening *Good Night, Muscovites* was the last tune. Often we heard the hit tune, *Green Lights of the Taxis,* which is a sentimental song about lovers in Moscow watching the taxis cruising by (showing a green light in the windshield when they are unoccupied). Of course, its chorus is about Moscow: "While the city sleeps, we meet, and we watch the green lights of the taxis." Magazines and newspapers are eternally studded with features about "Our Moscow," the city that Gorki called "both the brains and the broad heart of Russia." It is not a new love—probably the best-known line from Chekhov is the yearning, "To Moscow! To Moscow!" from *The Three Sisters.*

As the young man talked it seemed to me that Moscow had a particularly powerful kind of magic. After all, here was a boy trying to make an illicit deal to get an ordinary enough item of clothing, but entirely without self-pity or a sense of the pathos of his position because he was privileged to live in Moscow.

It occurred to me, too, that he was what Shura had described to us as a "beeznessman," a spiv, concerned with small-time shady enterprises, but he seemed so well mannered that I wondered if, perhaps, he had a proper job as well and used "beezness" only to supplement his income. His parting words to us were, "I shall see you again; perhaps before you leave you will find something that you wish to sell. Perhaps, also, I can help you with something in Moscow. I am at your service."

We did not make an appointment, and since he didn't know our name—or we his—I didn't see how we could meet, but I rather hoped that somehow we would.

On yet another evening we returned to the Metropole, this time with an English friend, Caryl Doncaster, with whom we had been to the ballet. Caryl is a young and pretty woman who is a producer for Independent Television in England and was in Russia making a film of Russian family life. Quite apart from her looks and talent, what made her really outstanding in the Metropole restaurant was the fact that she dresses very stylishly. It was only a matter of moments before a Red Army officer came up to our table and asked formal permission to join us. He had his eyes riveted on Caryl.

Soon we learned that he was a captain, that he was in Moscow on leave, that he came from Brest. "I guard the frontier," he told us, "but I would never cross it. Only if the government ordered me to."

To begin with, our talk was quite amicable and quite dull. I scarcely listened when we came to the inevitable question: "Don't you think the life in Russia is very good?"

It was Caryl who answered politely, "Yes, very."

"Much better than America," the captain announced.

"Well, I wouldn't say that," Caryl remarked, and Faubion, from force of habit, translated this. It seemed to irritate the captain.

"America is very bad to workers," he said sharply.

"Oh, no," Caryl replied equally sharply. "Very good."

"You must have been listening to American propaganda."

"No. I've been there, and I traveled a lot—"

"But you only saw the outsides of the houses. The streets. It is all for show. Fifth Avenue. I have heard of Fifth Avenue—that is just for visitors to see."

"On the contrary—"

Almost indulgently he interrupted her. "There are two Americas," he explained. "A fine life for the capitalists, but misery and starvation for the workers. How sad to see so many unemployed, so many starving! If you had looked the other side of Fifth Avenue you would have seen them."

"You are wrong," Caryl said firmly, and in spite of his attempts to cut her short, she insisted on listing some of the benefits of American workers and describing the lives of a few ordinary Americans as she had seen them during her visits there. Frequently she turned to me for confirmation and Faubion continued solemnly to translate. The officer scarcely looked at him and seemed to find nothing odd about the fact that an Englishwoman and an Indian were speaking for America. He never turned to Faubion for confirmation or to express a doubt. At the end of Caryl's long, impassioned speech he merely said, quite flatly, "I don't believe you."

Caryl, by now quite angry, said, "I don't care what you believe, it's true!"

I suppose we should have expected the next question. The first Russian sputnik had been announced a few days before and, naturally, had caused considerable excitement in Moscow, though less than I would have guessed. Inevitably the Russian captain asked triumphantly, "If America is so good, why did it not launch the sputnik?"

Very briskly Caryl replied, "Because it spends its money on its workers."

Inexplicably, the officer suddenly asked Caryl to dance. She refused, and he accepted the refusal quite without rancor. "I think you do not like Russian army officers," he said.

"I don't like uniforms. Or what they stand for."

This seemed to make him angry all over again. In a very loud voice he said, "Russian officers are respected all over the world. They are the strongest people, just as their country is the strongest."

"Nonsense!"

"You do not know!" Perhaps he decided to educate us rather than argue because, apropos of nothing, he asked, "Do you know Lenin?"

Rather flippantly Caryl replied, "Not personally, I'm afraid. I believe he's dead?"

The officer's decision must have ended abruptly. In a fury he said, "Why do you laugh? I am not used to being laughed at!"

Caryl said, "Well, it's time you learned."

This ended the conversation. The captain stood up. He bowed to all of us. To Caryl he said, "I am sure you are a good woman. But you are very misguided. Good night."

Afterward we had to remind ourselves that he was probably pretty drunk, that one meets bigots and misinformed people in any country, that the captain was vastly outnumbered by the Russians we met under similar circumstances who were genuinely interested in the rest of the world, willing to listen to another point of view, and eager to be friendly. Still, it was a disturbing encounter.

Often during those after-theater evenings we would talk to one or another of the Metropole waiters, as it was a relatively slack time for them. They weren't supposed to drink on duty, but usually they would accept a surreptitious glass of vodka and be eager to discuss the opera or ballet we had just seen or to talk about their life in general. They worked long hours—

9 A.M. to one o'clock the following morning—but they had every alternate day off, or, as they described it, "one day working, one day walking about." When Faubion asked what they meant by "walking about," the usual reply was a shrug of the shoulders meaning "nothing much." They would walk about the city, meeting friends at street corners, walking about some more with them, hoping for something to turn up. Home life was too crowded to be very appealing, entertainments too expensive (and too repetitive) for them, sports seemed to involve belonging to a club and working almost as hard as a professional sportsman. As one of them put it to us, "The curse of Russia is boredom."

One of the waiters, however, had a burning interest in literature and continually found opportunities to stand at our table and question Faubion about American writers. He was cautious in front of the other waiters but in whispered conversations and scribbled notes managed to learn the names of the Western writers whom we admired. He had heard of practically none of them. He had, he said, a friend in Finland who might be able to smuggle some of their books through to him.

We, in turn, asked him about Russian writers. "My favorite," he said, "is Turgenev—he is the most subtle. Though I read Pushkin with pleasure and Tolstoy with admiration."

"I meant, among Soviet writers?"

He made a scornful face. "We have no writers. Not real *writers*. Simonov I accept, but I do not like to read him. Ehrenburg? Too dull. Alexei Tolstoy? It was done better by the classics. Sholokhov? Yes, he is all right—but no more, only all right. But I will tell you the poet I love—Valery Bryusov. This poet is my god."

"Well, we must buy his poetry and read it."

"That will be difficult. You see, he is," his voice dropped as though about to say a bad word, "he is a *symbolist*."

The same waiter also told us, on another evening, that the Youth Festival of a few months before had changed his whole view of Americans. "I had been instructed never to call an American 'my friend' or 'comrade,' because they would be insulted, because they have a strong feeling of class. But I found it is not so. I found that *they* call *me* 'friend' first. Now I wonder what other lies I have been told."

Between these spasmodic or unexpected conversations we used to watch the rest of the Metropole clientele. We soon got used to the frequent coming and going of foreign delegations and to the sight of provincial Russians on holiday in the big city. Occasionally, late in the evening, some dark young man would get up from his table, grip the hand of a plump, pink, smiling girl and drag her to the dance floor. She would usually be wearing a shapeless short dress, often of flowered rayon, and her partner would be in dark slacks and an open shirt. He would clap twice, then, with one hand at his waist and the other snapping briskly above his head, he would begin a whirling, energetic dance. She would follow him more modestly, giggling and shy, but keeping up with his rapid springs and turns. At first the music of the conscientious Metropole orchestra would be quite out of mood with their dance, but soon most of the people in the room would be watching the couple and clapping in time. The band would pause for a few seconds, and then take up a cheerful country tune, gradually the dance floor would clear and the girl in her short socks and sneakers and her partner with his lively gestures would bounce around the room with a fine abandon.

Once a waiter standing near our table watching such a couple remarked, "There, you see—*they* know how to enjoy themselves. What do these others know about pleasure?"

We asked where the couple might come from—obviously they were not Muscovites.

"Somewhere in the south," he replied. "I expect they are workers from some collective farm, in Moscow for a conference or as part of a tourist group. I was brought up in the country and I know how they must feel seeing all this." He made a slight gesture with his hand toward the city clientele. "First they are excited by the idea of the capital. Then they get lonely and depressed. And homesick—no wonder they want to dance their own dances."

I thought his explanation was probably quite accurate because only a few days before I had seen a comparable example of the provincial Russian's need to carry something of his own atmosphere with him, even on holiday.

The U.S.S.R. Agricultural Exhibition, which we had visited one afternoon, is a permanent exhibition occupying a massive tract of land on the outskirts of Moscow. It is a favorite place for Russian tourists. There they can walk through the orchards and along the avenues, pause by the artificial lakes, wander through the "monumental palace-like pavilions" (as the guidebook describes them), one for each of the Soviet republics, built in the style characteristic of the region and displaying the agricultural products of the province. "Thousands of talented architects, artists and sculptors worked to adorn it," the guidebook says.

The result of their efforts is, in my opinion, something less than beautiful, but there is no question that Russian sightseers love to stare at the central fountain with its huge gilded figures of women (one for every Soviet republic), each holding the grain characteristic of her province. Or they stand astonished before the famous, much-copied, and absolutely monumental statues of the Soviet boy and girl, chin up, marching bravely into the future, and, I suppose, feel proud of Soviet achievement in what they see around them. The moment at which the homesickness can be noticed comes when it is time to eat.

Of the many restaurants scattered about the exhibition grounds, the provincial visitors always seem to choose the one that provides their own local dishes. In the Kazak restaurant, for instance, sunburned Muslims in belted coats, boots and lambskin hats can be seen sitting on carpets spread over low platforms, eating skewered mutton with fresh lemon and raw onion, soaking big discs of bread in bowls of meat-and-rice soup, and drinking green tea for hours afterward.

The afternoon that we were there a group of just such Kazak tourists, farm workers who had been rewarded with a trip to Moscow for exceptional crop production, had apparently looked around the cold, grandiose display of the exhibition and decided that they wanted a respite of their own kind of gaiety. On the steps of the Kazak pavilion, a man with a drum and another with a flute began to play. A couple of the girls in the party began to dance, sometimes their own rhythmic country dances and sometimes something more sinuous copied from Indian movies, which are very popular in Russia. Soon a crowd collected and began to clap and encourage them. For a while the whole atmosphere of that section of the exhibition changed. Nobody bothered to go into the pavilion to gaze solemnly at the hills of fruit and vegetables and grain, for on the steps an outing was ending as an outing *should* end, with music and dancing and people joining in.

Such displays were, however, rare at the Metropole in the late evenings. Mostly the strangers who attracted the attention of Russians coming to the restaurant were the scattered American tourists, the Western journalists assembling for the fortieth anniversary celebrations. The Eastern European circus people who had arrived to participate in the great "international" performances that were to be part of the festivities also were a focus of interest. With the special, raffish exuberance of any circus people, they would suddenly execute conjuring tricks at the table, or leap into acrobatic dances, or chatter and joke in loud, uninhibited voices. It was all, evidently, an enthralling sight for the usually staid and quiet Russian customers of the Metropole restaurant—it was for us too.

The day Boris brought his wife to see us I had decided that we had better meet in our rooms at the hotel because, I felt, we would be able to talk more freely there than among the distractions of a public place. Yelena turned out to be a plumpish girl with long, light-brown hair that she wore in a bun. She was dressed in an uninteresting brown suit. Except for her habitually disapproving expression, she could have been good looking, but she did nothing to encourage this possibility. To Russians I suppose she was far above average in looks and her mass of soft hair must have been her most-admired feature.

Shura, who was my authority on such matters, had assured me that Russian men are fussy about the hair style of the girl they take out. The gamine look, the Gina Lollobrigida coiffure, the short curls, are not admired at all—in fact, these are locally known as the "after-typhus haircut" because they remind Russians of the distressing period when the hair is growing again after the head has been shaved during a bout of typhus. A "special" girl, to elicit admiration from young men, should have plenty of hair, preferably softly wavy, preferably long, which she can wear in a loose bun with just a couple of tendrils seductively escaping on her forehead or ear. She should wear no make-up during the day and only a hint of lipstick and some unobtrusive face powder in the evening. She shouldn't go in for giddy experiments with her hair and make-up— she'd have trouble doing it anyway since there are no beauty parlors as we think of them. The hairdresser will give her a permanent or wash and cut her hair for her but will not "style" it. The girl should dress simply and modestly in dark clothes and wear high heels only occasionally. Above all, she should be "sincere." In fact, she should be very like Yelena. I began to be even more curious about the faint discontent I had sensed in Boris about his marriage.

Our conversation was absolutely formal and totally uninteresting. We were all careful, polite, constrained and I, for one, felt as though I was being put through some test. The only information Yelena gave us was that she, too, was a student, that her special field was engineering, and that she hoped, eventually, to get a job in the post and telegraph service. Most of the rest of her time, she explained, was spent in YCL work.

"I suppose," I said, "that doesn't leave you much time for family life."

Boris rattled something off to her in Russian, and she replied sternly, "There are more important considerations."

Rather nettled, I said, "Well, in any case, under the present living conditions in Moscow, I don't suppose you would have much privacy with your husband even if you weren't so busy."

Again she listened carefully to the translation, and then said, "Housing will soon be improved in Moscow." She then pointed out that even the present state of housing was not without its advantages, particularly for the young and the unmarried. Her view seemed to be that these external conditions, perhaps fortuitously, discouraged self-indulgence. With a prudishness that was typical of YCL members whom I met and an air of distaste that was her own, she remarked, "If we are to work well for the Party we cannot lead loose private lives. We are supposed to set a standard, you know."

As she talked I could see how easily she could be a pretty girl. She was surely speaking from conviction, not from a lack of opportunity, past or present, and I couldn't help dimly regretting the early days of Communism that I had read about, the inflammatory talk of Free Love and the scorn of bourgeois convention. In Yelena's unexploited good looks, her severe view of her place in life, her neat bourgeois personality, something more than a political system seemed to have been irretrievably lost.

I think that Boris more than the rest of us was conscious of the strained atmosphere in our first meeting with Yelena. When after a relatively short time she said that they must go, he made no protest, though usually he was quite happy to talk for hours. We all stood up, shook hands, said good-by in Russian and English, and parted with no suggestion of future meetings.

The next day Boris appeared at the Metropole, unexpected and unannounced. He seemed nervous and ill at ease and wandered about our living room fidgeting with things. His blond hair, which was always untidy, flopped over his forehead in even greater disarray and gave him quite a distracted look. "You are busy?" he asked rapidly. "You wish to go out? You have invited people?"

We assured him that we were doing nothing. He gave a deep sigh and sat down on the sofa under the hideous, murky painting of a wooden house surrounded by brooding trees, all executed in the most painstaking detail. He pushed his hair back and said glumly, "So. Yes . . . Well, how did you like Yelena?"

"She seemed very nice," I said.

"And good-looking," Faubion supplied.

Boris stared out through the French doors to the balcony. "Yes, yes, yes. She is a good girl. Very good. Also very serious. I am lucky to be married to her. So all my friends tell me."

"How old is she?" I asked.

"Twenty years."

"Very young."

"Yes. Young." After a moment he said timidly, "Enough young that for her is possibility of change?"

"I should think so. Do you want her to change?"

Boris sprang up and began to walk about the room again, adjusting the bits of lace on the chairs, aligning the crystal decanter with the little vodka glasses. "This is the trouble. *I* have changed. It is two years that we are married. Also I was very young. I thought, 'I love her. She is good.' I thought, 'Like this is always marriage. Like we live. Like I admire her.' It is right."

"Now do you think marriage should be something else?"

"Now I know I do not love her. Still she is good. But I do not love her. I think, maybe, *I* am not serious. If I am serious I will be happy to be married to Yelena."

Poor Boris, guilty and upset, I could very well see the problem that Yelena presented in his life—the whole Soviet attitude seemed to be on her side and in favor of girls like her. The girl who is casual and fun to be with elicits a certain distrust. The concept of the "popular girl," the one who is pretty and gay and entertaining with men, even if she is not a flirt, is not much in evidence in Russia. It is assumed that such a girl can't be "sincere."

From reading stories and articles in popular Russian magazines—ones that have an English edition—I had managed to get a fairly clear idea of the Perfect Girl in Soviet society, and even of the desirable course of a romance or a marriage. In one magazine I found a reproduction of the painting called "After the Parting." It showed a girl sitting alone at a café table. From the disarrangement of the china on the table and the pushed-away chair at the side it is clear that her date has left in a far from calm mood. Under the picture was the artist's explanation of the situation. The girl, it turned out, "is not the negative type. Indeed, she is fundamentally a good girl. Only she had taken a more light-minded attitude toward life than others of her age . . ." In short, the artist plainly felt that she deserved to be deserted, but he also assured the magazine readers that she was not beyond hope because "she will leave the café a changed person, capable of recasting her life . . . along different lines. She too will find happiness." Presumably by becoming heavy-minded.

I read a love story in which the perfect, sincere girl is a biologist. I spotted her at once as the heroine because she is described as having "a serious intellectual friendship" with another woman. She has the pleasantly complicated problem of choosing between a physicist and, more vaguely, a scientist who makes "an important scientific discovery." She, too, makes the properly serious decision and stays with her husband even though her marriage is far from satisfactory. This solid concentration on science came as no particular surprise because Shura had told me that scientists and artists (preferably performing artists) are the most enviable dates for a girl. They are, for the most part, untouched by politics and can often get unusual privileges in living quarters, holidays, and permission to travel. Army officers come a poor third because, although the pay is good and they start at a higher salary than most, it's not much of a life in the lower echelons and uncomfortably involved in politics in the higher.

Another story I came across concerned a woman who had been wonderfully happy with her husband and child, but during the war she got word that her husband had been killed. She then decided to become a chemist and found the work so engrossing that at one point her young son asked, "Weren't you lonesome for your chemistry when you lived with my father?"

Eventually they learned that the father was not dead but had left the mother for the woman who nursed him back to health after he had been seriously wounded. He tried to reclaim his son, and explained in a letter, "Your mother was always the delight of my life. . . . But to this other woman I was bound by sorrow and suffering, and such ties are stronger." The son, however, decided to remain with the chemist.

In yet another issue an account of a romance—a story of love at first sight—was told by a worker in a tobacco factory:

"One day the word was passed around the shop that we had got a new shift superintendent. I paid no more attention to it and having finished adjusting a machine sat down on a window sill to leaf through a magazine.

" 'Got nothing to do, comrade?' I suddenly heard a woman's voice next to me. 'If your own work is done, you could give some pointers to new workers.' I turned and found myself looking into a pair of gray eyes . . . Nina entered my life as suddenly and as simply as she had entered the factory." His mother is pleased and remarks, "She's a pretty girl and with a position, too." However, male vanity is still an operative factor, and he is worried by the fact that Nina is his superior. He decides to catch up with her educationally by taking a "technical correspondence course." They marry and live happily ever after.

However, all this background information didn't help us very much in trying to comfort Boris. Faubion was gazing vaguely into his vodka glass and saying nothing, so at last I said as convincingly as I could, "Don't be too distressed, Boris. This may only be a passing phase." And then, remembering a good old stand-by of women's magazines, I added, "Perhaps you will come to love her again, in a different way."

Boris reacted rather violently. He whirled around, almost

knocking over a chair. "No, no, no, no!" He said. "You see, I have *found* the girl I love. For that I know the other is not right. It was not love before. Now it is real—but what can I do?"

"Divorce?" I suggested hesitantly.

"Impossible. Yelena would never allow."

"And you couldn't get a divorce without her consent?"

"Divorce for what? If *only* she were known to be a frivolous person . . ."

"You might try explaining to her . . ."

Boris looked horrified. "Never! She could report me to the YCL!"

"Well, what if she does?"

Very sadly he said, "I have not great ambition. But when I am old enough I hope I may become a party member. I wish to advance in my work, you see. I must not, so young, acquire things against me—how do you say that? Bad reports of me?"

"Black marks against me?"

"So. Black marks."

"And you think Yelena would be vindictive?"

"She would be doing the right thing."

"And what about your other girl?"

"Ah, Maya . . ." Boris said softly. "She is—she is different. One day you will meet her."

Boris seemed in much better spirits after this, either at the thought of Maya or from relief at having talked to someone about his problem. We all felt rather excited and talkative, as though we had just been through a dangerous moment together. Boris came out with us to an unexpectedly cheerful dinner at the Armenian restaurant that Edward Ivanian had recommended. There we talked and laughed immoderately about nothing much, and Boris sang us snatches of songs in a carefree way that was quite unlike the earnest young student we had first known. At last he pushed his plate away and said, "I am full—full of love."

On one of those days Shura called up to ask when I wanted Irina to go shopping with me and show me around the stores. I was pleased that she had remembered our tentative date—one soon gets into the habit of uncritical delight at having a Russian follow up a first meeting. We arranged to meet at the Metropole the next Sunday.

Faubion, as always, refused to go on any shopping expeditions, and Shura promptly decided to stay with him at the Metropole restaurant, which he liked so much. We left them sitting at a conspicuous table from which Shura could watch the people come and go. I asked one of the Intourist interpreters to accompany Irina and me, and the three of us set out first to the Red Square.

It was by then nearing the end of October, only a matter of days before the fortieth anniversary of the Bolshevik Revolution. There was a feeling of festivity and expectation in the Moscow air, the shops were decorated and filled with souvenirs and special merchandise brought out for the occasion, so it was a good time to go shopping. By American standards, or just about any foreign standards, Russia is notoriously short of consumers' goods, but still the shops are filled with rather expensive, rather shoddy merchandise. Day-to-day shopping in Moscow is almost always a crowded, long-drawn-out bore, but shopping for pleasure (of a sort) is possible in the department stores and the small specialty shops—antique shops, "Houses of Modes," and the like.

Irina led us first to the enormous railway terminus of a building that houses GUM's department store. The tiers of galleries that run around the vast central well of the building were alive with shoppers, so were the individual shops that open off the galleries, where one can buy anything, short of a car, that is made in Russia. Women carrying parcels and baskets jammed the counters where there was a sale of rayon slips and of enamel kitchenware. The whole place was decorated with strips of red bunting, with stars and slogans. It took me a moment or two to realize that, except for the pictures of Lenin and the hammer and sickle on the flags, the feeling was very much that of the days immediately before Christmas in New York.

Only that morning, on the building across the street from our hotel rooms, large painted signs had gone up saying, *"Miru mir"* (Peace on Earth) and "Good will to men" (or, more exactly, "Brotherly greetings to all people struggling for peace"). In GUM's there was the same mixture of celebration and frayed nerves. I could imagine any one of those women muttering to herself, ". . . and a plaid scarf for Anna . . . no, no, I gave her that last year. A bottle of perfume, perhaps? That's always safe . . ." and hurrying to the perfume counter to buy a crystal bottle the shape of one of the Kremlin towers filled with a sweet, rather heavy perfume called "Kremlin"—the best, Irina said.

Watching the crowds at the counters I noticed that the sales-girls seemed harassed and short tempered but that any foreigner got instant attention regardless of how long others had been waiting. I remembered being told a story about a foreigner who had seen a diamond ring in a Moscow shop and had been so impressed at the low price that he had asked to buy it. The salesgirl had insisted on fetching a magnifying glass to point out the small flaw in the stone that accounted for its relative cheapness. The point of the story had been that when no in-dividual profit motive is involved there is a much higher stand-

ard of honesty and courtesy from salespeople and shop mana-
gers. Judging from GUM's that day, this principle did not extend to the Russian customers.

Irina took us to the top floor, past displays and counters of
cameras, radios, TV sets, past blouses, lingerie, stockings, costume jewelry and all the rest. A quick look at the prices told me
that cameras and radios were relatively cheap, anything made of
nylon wickedly expensive. At last we came to a filled, but fairly
quiet salon where a fashion show was in progress. As we settled
ourselves in chairs at the side of the room, for the first time
I saw Irina smile with pleasurable anticipation. "I would very
much like to be a dress designer," she said, "and there is a
future for that in Russia—now." However, I think she still felt
a little guilty about being interested in anything as frivolous
as nice clothes, though perhaps that was constraint brought on
by the presence of the interpreter and the semiofficial air she
gave to our excursion.

The models came out between curtains of a decorated stage,
walked slowly down a long, brightly lit ramp, turned a couple
of times, and then walked back. Meanwhile the clear, rather
severe tones of a mistress of ceremonies came over the loudspeaker, explaining each dress and when it should be worn,
giving the price and the name of the designer. The whole show
was accompanied by music from a small string orchestra. Each
dress was accorded a tune "appropriate to its style"—*Deep
Purple* for a cocktail dress, *Sandman* for an evening dress, and,
rather to my surprise, *Mack the Knife* from *The Threepenny
Opera* for a rather dizzy short evening dress in blue taffeta. The
most daring item of the collection, eliciting a subdued gasp
from the audience, was made of plain black velvet, but when
the mannequin took off her silver fox stole, we all saw that the
dress was *off the shoulders*. I had certainly never seen anyone

in Russia wear a dress even remotely like it. The orchestra, too, gave it special attention with a very sultry performance of *Night and Day*.

It is well known that Russian clothes are notably lacking in style, and on the whole the ones displayed by GUM were no exception. Still I was interested to see some rather well-cut slacks and ski clothes. I have never seen a Russian woman in slacks, except for the baggy trousers, caught at the ankle, that school girls wear for gym and sports and some of the poorer workers (such as street cleaners) wear for the messier jobs. A friend of mine from the Indian Embassy, a girl who was studying Russian at Moscow University, used to wear slacks to her classes because she found the cold of a Moscow winter altogether too piercing for either saris or dresses. But whenever she wore slacks she would have to brace herself against the reproving murmur of *"Styliaga, styliaga"* that would follow her as she walked down the university corridors or across the grounds. Evidently some kind of liberalization of taste was being promoted in the Moscow fashion shows.

For some reason, at GUM's, I felt quite embarrassed at the arrival of the male models showing men's business suits, tweeds, and topcoats. They were all plump and natty and stiff. I looked around quickly to see if there were any men in the salon. There weren't. But I also found a rather chilly fascination in the unemotional voice of the mistress of ceremonies making comments that would be impossible in an American fashion show. "This model," she would announce calmly, with no attempt to sugar the pill, "is not recommended for fat women." Or, "This material will stand a lot of hard wear. It is recommended for women who haven't the money for many clothes."

Irina, however, was delighted. Afterward she told me that it was an exceptionally good show, a special effort for the holidays.

"What other days do you celebrate so lavishly?" I asked, because it was a question that had never occurred to me before.

"May Day. New Year's. Birthdays. The anniversary of the Revolution, of course . . ." When religious festivals are cut out the days of gaiety and celebration seem pitifully few.

"And what do you do on those days?"

Irina looked vague. "Some days we give presents. Some people have evening parties . . . eat and drink . . ."

"With your family?"

"Yes. Or several families together. Because there is much cooking."

Recently the magazines had been full of recipes "For the Holiday Table." Jellied pike perch, boiled sturgeon, roast suckling pig, Moscow dumpling, Moldavian chestnut cake, Byelorussian poppy-seed roll. It was easy to see that when a kitchen is shared with other families, the cooking of such extravagant dishes can be simplified by making a joint venture of the whole occasion.

After GUM's we had only time enough to go to a small shop called Dom Modeli which dealt exclusively in dresses, both ready-made and custom-made. Here too a fashion show was about to begin. The salon was smaller than the one at GUM's but more elegantly decorated in white and pale green and gilt, with white-covered chairs set between the marble pillars. Before the show started we were given a short lecture by the mistress of ceremonies on the season's styles. She, too, was a firmly corseted woman in brown crepe, with the assured, informative air of a headmistress. All the styles, she told us, were changing this season. This year we would wear dresses with loose sleeves. Our suits would have shorter jackets and sometimes an over-blouse instead of a jacket, which could be worn belted or loose. We would go in for matching dress and jacket combinations.

Male fashions would have more tapering trousers, in the Italian manner. And so on. She ended triumphantly with the announcement: "This is the fashion show of the 1957-58 winter season!"

The clothes were not much better or more stylish than those at GUM's, and many of them were clearly designed for, and modeled by, portly middle-aged women. "This," said the mistress of ceremonies, about a fussy suit in oatmeal-colored wool, "is very good for concerts. The material does not crease easily and the skirt will hold its shape even when you sit a long time."

I asked Irina why most of the mannequins were so much older than those at GUM's—the others had seemed to me both pretty and, by Russian standards, quite slender.

Irina said, "This is a very exclusive shop. Women with money come here. Most of their clothes are made to order."

I had a sudden picture of the clientele, the stout wives of successful politicians and other members of the Privileged. Naturally there would be few young people able to indulge a taste for the luxuries of Soviet life.

When we returned to the Metropole, thanked the interpreter, and left to join Shura and Faubion in the restaurant we found them deep in what appeared to be a hilarious conversation. As soon as he saw us Shura sprang up, dragged up chairs for us, beckoned the waiter, and asked very seriously, "How were the models?"

"Rather pretty, I thought. At least the ones at GUM's. The others were too fat. The GUM models had very good figures."

"That is a city taste," Shura said. "In Moscow they like them thin. In the country they like them fat."

"How do you like them?" Faubion asked.

"I?" Shura said, smiling wickedly. "I am a city boy—who could live in the country . . ." Even Irina looked amused.

"What were you laughing about when we came in?" I asked Faubion.

"Shura was telling me jokes."

Some of Shura's jokes I had heard before, like the one about the American who came to the Soviet Union and complained to a Russian that there was no freedom of speech in Russia. In America, he said, if a man stood outside the White House and yelled out that Eisenhower was a fool, nothing would happen to him. "We have just as much freedom of speech," the Russian replies. "If any Russian stood outside the Kremlin and yelled out that Eisenhower was a fool, nothing would happen to him either."

But some were quite new to me, like the one that consists almost entirely of gestures. It is a commentary on the progress of Communism in Russia. Shura tucked his thumbs behind the lapels of his jacket, leaving his fingers showing. "Lenin," he said. "You understand? He always used to stand like this. Two leaders," he flipped his thumbs out from behind his lapels, "and eight people." He wiggled his fingers. Then he dropped one hand to his side, leaving the other in place. "Stalin. He always stood like this. One leader, four people." Then he locked his fingers across his stomach, with his thumbs sticking up. "Khrushchev. This is how he stands. Two leaders," he wiggled his thumbs, "but where are the people?"

We all noticed that Irina was beginning to look uncomfortable, glancing around nervously to see if waiters or people at the neighboring tables could overhear. Actually Shura, even with his carefree manner, was quite discreet himself. He always stopped talking or changed the subject when the waiter was serving us, and usually used the orchestra or noisy nearby conversations as a cover for his more irreverent comments and jokes. But we changed the conversation anyway, to set Irina's mind at rest.

It was on an evening a few days later—without Irina—that Shura had arranged to take us to a theater of his choosing. "You like plays, you like music," he had said to Faubion. "Very well, you shall see both together at the *Savoy Ball*—the best new musical in Moscow. But the critics disapprove very much."

Savoy Ball was so crowded that we had to get tickets through Intourist, which always has priority for seats for tourists, but Shura insisted on paying. I was pleased that Shura had suggested it, partly because *Savoy Ball* was my first Russian musical, and partly because it was closed down soon after as "unsuitable." I could never understand why it had received such fierce official attention. It was frivolous certainly, and by the standard of American musicals hopelessly old-fashioned—a silly operetta with an involved plot set in the south of France—but entirely innocuous. Shura, like the rest of the very young, very eager audience of students and soldiers and youthful workers and their girls, loved it without qualification.

Afterward, when we asked him what he found so appealing about the show, he replied, "I like to laugh. I like gaiety. You will say it means nothing—but that is what I like. You see I will never be a member of the YCL."

"No gaiety allowed in the YCL?"

"Only the YCL kind of gaiety." Shura turned down the corners of his mouth. "You know? Sing together while you help to dig the subway—volunteer work, of course. So you are gay."

Shura's words gave me a clear picture. A friend of mine who lived in the Ukraina Hotel had told me a story about the construction of the garden in the square in front of the hotel. The Ukraina was very new, completed only weeks before thousands of students from all over the world poured into Moscow for the Youth Festival. Guests were allowed to move in, but the approach to the hotel was still the muddy wasteland that the builders had left. My friend, watching from her window, had been deeply impressed by the groups of YCL members, the Young Pioneers with their red scarves, the volunteer workers, coming to the Ukraina after school or college or jobs. Full-grown shrubs, flowers, small trees were planted, turf was laid down, paths graveled. In two weeks the whole garden was complete—in time for the Festival. "It wasn't just the community spirit that struck me," she said, "it was the jolly way that they set about saving the face of their district before the foreigners."

When Faubion translated all this, Shura just gave us a cynical look. "Yes, yes, yes, yes. That is how to get ahead in the YCL. When you first join you have to write down your ambitions—'I want to help my country,' that sort of thing. Afterward they hold you to it. You must be a leader in community activities, and you must get others to work too. And, then, you might as well be cheerful about it." In an unexpectedly serious voice he added, "There are so many difficulties in Russian life, perhaps it is best to learn to enjoy the difficulties."

"You have never thought of joining the YCL?" Faubion asked.

Shura again smiled in his carefree, slightly naughty way. "Once Boris tried to persuade me, but it was no good. One of the boys reported me for gambling."

"What kind of gambling?"

"A card game called preference." As Shura described it, preference is played by three people. They use only 32 cards, the top eight of each suit, and in Russia the order of strength is spades, clubs, diamonds, and finally hearts. Each player is dealt ten cards, the extra two remain hidden, and then bidding proceeds much as it would in cutthroat bridge. A basic bid means that the player must get six tricks, each successive bid means winning an extra trick above the six. Whoever wins the bid is permitted to discard the two worst cards in his hand and take the two hidden ones. After this, he tries to make his bid.

"Was the boy right?" Faubion asked. "Were you actually gambling, or just playing for fun?"

"Of course I was gambling. But it wasn't a bad thing. The boy did not know that I am a very good preference player, and I used to give most of my winnings to my mother."

That was the first and only time that Shura mentioned his mother to us.

The 7th of November drew closer, the children's entertainment in Moscow became even more lavish and varied than it normally is. At any time of the year there is a circus playing somewhere in the city. There is even a school that concentrates only on the training of clowns. For the holidays there was a special international circus in Moscow. A circus, that is, with representatives from all the Communist countries. Throughout the season, from September to June, there is at least one and usually two puppet theaters in operation. Every weekend there are children's ballets, operas, concerts, and a children's theater that puts on dramatic plays. To these was added an enchanting animal theater dating from Tsarist times where variety shows are put on and the actors are all animals. All this besides the more familiar pleasures—zoos, amusement parks, playgrounds. Every weekend we took Jai to one or another of these entertainments. At none of them did he have to pay for a ticket.

Two aspects of the surging life of the Russian children's entertainment world interested me particularly. One was that no concessions in production, taste, professional skill, or artistic attainment are made for the children. Only the themes and the timing of the shows are specifically geared for children. One charming ballet to which I took Jai began at noon and had a long intermission at midafternoon for sandwiches and *limonad* in the theater café. It was called *Doktor Aibolit* (roughly translated Dr. Ouch-it-hurts) and was composed of a wonderful mixture of animals, pirates, resourceful children, and fantastic settings designed to please any small child.

Dr. Aibolit, a kindly old man, lives in the forest and sick animals come to him to be cured (special applause for the comic bear with a sore paw, delighted laughter when the cat and dog start fighting). Next to him, in two little huts, live a boy and a girl who help the doctor in his work. The doctor is called away to an unspecified jungle in the tropics to deal with an epidemic among the monkeys, and the children stow away on the ship. In the exotic setting of the jungle the mother monkeys bring their babies to the doctor for treatment (commiserating groans and laughter as each monkey gets his injection), but then the doctor and his two friends are captured by brigands and taken off to certain death. The children, however, think of an excellent plan. They pour the doctor's ether over bunches of flowers which they then present to each brigand, and as the brigands go to sleep, they escape. Then comes a splendid chase, ending at a shaky palm-tree bridge over a river full of crocodiles. The doctor and the children just manage to get across, but the bridge collapses under the brigands. They are rather realistically eaten by the crocodiles (horrified excitement when one of the crocodiles spits out a shoe).

When the party at last gets home to the forest, they find that a wicked animal trainer has taken over the doctor's house and has beaten all the animals into serving him. Naturally, the ballet ends satisfactorily: the evil trainer gets locked up in his own cage, there is a joyful dance by the freed animals, and the doctor and the children are happy at seeing their friends again.

All of this, however, was produced with a meticulous eye

for quality. It was held in one of Moscow's best theaters, the Musical Theater, and the performers (all adults) were among the best dancers and actors. The scenic effects—too elaborate for modern Western taste, but much admired in Russia—were just as grand and detailed as for any adult production. And this was not for one isolated show (as one might describe Mary Martin's *Peter Pan* in New York), but part of a regular and continuing children's theater world.

The uncanny virtuosity of the puppets and the highly trained puppeteers of the famous Obraztsov troupe are another case in point. During the week this company puts on plays and satires for grownups—puppets are, in any case, considered perfectly acceptable adult entertainment—but for weekends the same people alter their programs to include revues and stories suitable for children.

The other aspect of children's entertainment that seemed to me worth noting was the content of indoctrination. It is easy to make too much of this because one is rather apt to look for propaganda in Russia while one forgets comparable instances in other countries. Still, certain moments impressed me strongly, and in a general way there seemed always to be a gentle but pervasive forming of attitudes in the young. Kings and queens, for example (or tsars and princes), are always wicked. In a splendid opera, *The Miraculous Bird,* that I went to with my son, the heroine is a peasant, Marya. The villain is the son of the Tsar, who is acted throughout as a gross and grasping buffoon who demands Marya for himself. He sends her husband off on a series of dangerous journeys, but Marya remains faithful. In the last act the husband arrives just in time to save Marya from being thrown to the wolves for her stubbornness, and the peasants throw the Tsar and his family to the wolves instead. Roughly this type of plot appeared so often that after a while, whenever Jai heard a tsar mentioned, his immediate question was "And how was *he* killed?"

As one might expect, there seemed to be a quota of anti-American cracks and comments for many of the shows. The one, in my experience, that drew the biggest response was in the international circus that was performing in Moscow as part of the celebrations for the fortieth anniversary of the Revolution. At one moment the master of ceremonies announced, "And now we will play for you the most beautiful song ever heard." A spotlight moved slowly across the roof, and over the microphone came the much-publicized "beep-beep" of the first sputnik. When the lights went up, a lonely clown was wandering around the arena patting a balloon into the air until it burst. The master of ceremonies shouted, "Who are you and what are you doing? Can't you see you have no place in this show?"

The clown said, "But I am an American and I'm trying to launch my sputnik."

In a puppet variety show called *The Extraordinary Concert,* one of the acts consisted of songs by "a transatlantic star." The puppet who appeared had platinum-blond hair and a low-cut dress (both very much frowned on in Russia). She sang a blues and then broke into hot jazz accompanied by a rather strange solo jitterbug. Blues are disapproved of because they are considered "depressing" and bad for morale, and the official verdict on jazz is that "good" jazz is acceptable (meaning anything sweet and sentimental) but hot jazz is at best ridiculous and at worst an American corrupting influence. Clearly the whole turn was intended as satire and received enthusiastic applause from the audience of children, but whether they were delighted with the satire or with the chance to hear American jazz, I couldn't decide. Anyway, the puppet had to give an encore.

A popular theme for many of the shows concerns some incident in what Jai described as "the fight between the Reds and the Whites." Sometimes the hero is a small boy who carries medicines through the lines to wounded Red soldiers, sometimes other, similar individual acts of heroism are celebrated. The fight between Reds and Whites soon replaced cops and robbers and cowboys and Indians in our games, with Jai always insisting on being a Red.

Children are, of course, strongly predisposed to like the winning side, but in other countries one does occasionally find instances (Cavaliers and Roundheads in England are one) in which the glamour and romance of the losing side outweigh the advantages of being victors. In Russia, I felt that such a point of view would be impossible among the children.

In schools, as one might expect, the indoctrination is more obvious and more insistent. Even an advanced music or ballet student has to put in a certain number of hours a week on "dia-mat" (dialectical materialism), and in the lower grades it is constantly present in textbooks and teaching. But still there is no doubt that a child of Jai's age can have a very good time in Russia, better than at any other period of his life. A lot of attention is focused on him and his needs and pleasures are a constant consideration.

A Russian childhood covers only a short period, however. Judging from young Valery and from what Boris and Shura and others told us about their upbringing, Russian children seem to grow up very soon. There appears to be no distinct teen-age life. You are a child, and then you are an adult. By the time you are a couple of years into your secondary school, the other pressures of Soviet life have begun to operate. You are already in the academic race, and the pace will get more intense as you get to college. Then you are in the managingto-stay-away-from-deadly-jobs-in-the-provinces race, which you win only by getting very good grades. Boris had told us it was one of the dreads of the college student that if his marks weren't good enough he might be sent as a schoolteacher to some remote village or to work in a factory or development in Siberia. "For intellectuals," he had said moderately, "it is very difficult. We hear many cases of mental breakdown. No one to talk to. Nothing to do. Where to go? Everything is so far away."

But even if you stay in Moscow by brains or talent or influence you still have to face the driving exigencies of day-to-day living in the city—housing, and clothes, and where to put the new baby. From fourteen on, you start a story as Valery used to, casually and realistically, with the phrase, "When I was young . . ." From the uncertain vantage point of maturity, these adult children can look back and say with some nostalgia, as Valery did on Jai's birthday, "But for a child everything must be done."

At the end of October a friend of ours, Ambassador Malalasekara of Ceylon, asked us if we would like to accompany him and his wife on an excursion to a place called Zagorsk. He is, apart from his diplomatic attainments, a Buddhist scholar, so he was particularly interested in seeing Russia's largest religious center—even if it is described by the tourist bureau as a "National Historical-Artistic Museum," where you can see "an interesting architectural ensemble, which gives an idea of Russian architecture in the fifteenth-eighteenth centuries." We were naturally delighted with an opportunity to visit Zagorsk and appreciated the organization involved in arranging the trip. Even diplomats are not allowed to travel more than forty kilometers outside Moscow without special permission, and Zagorsk is almost twice that distance. For the tourist some trips (Zagorsk among them) are much easier because the arrangements are made by Intourist and, in any case, he travels under its auspices. But he must return the same day even if he has, as an American friend of ours had, an invitation to spend the night.

After so many weeks in Moscow I had completely lost a sense of the Russian countryside and its life that encircled the city. To me the journey to Zagorsk was a sobering experience, a glimpse of life in the country, a small but memorable explanation of the Muscovite's fear of being exiled from his city.

As we drove out of Moscow that morning, through the gloomy industrial suburbs, through the thinning housing projects, to reach the Zagorsk road, we were full of talk and comment. Gradually, as we reached proper country, we began to fall silent. After we passed the Moscow outskirts we saw very few cars, even though the road was first rate, the country a gentle and beautiful succession of birch and pine woods, low hills and farmland, and the day sunny. Most of the traffic seemed to consist of trucks carrying wood and vegetables to Moscow, so it was understandable that we didn't see any hitchhikers either. Nor did we see a single bus.

At long intervals we would come upon a small village along the side of the road, no more than a scattering of wooden huts, really, crooked, half sinking into the soft ground, patched, pitiful. At last one of us commented on the warped look these shacks gave to any village, and Mrs. Malalasekara, a gentle, charming woman, said hesitantly, "I didn't like to remark on it. I thought there was something wrong with my eyes. Everything looks out of alignment."

Of course, all of us were used to seeing poverty in Asia, but poverty is much grimmer in the cold. Warmth—human or climatic—is needed to make it bearable. In Asia there is both,

and a sense of life and activity as well. Children playing
in the dirt, women gossiping at the well, animals wandering
about, a village storyteller holding a small crowd fascinated
under a tree, a sense of crowded but easygoing humanity.

But in Russia the villages seemed oddly deserted. We saw
few people or animals. The sense of isolation was everywhere.
Whatever do the villagers do in winter? I wondered. I was
sharply aware of their lack of mobility. Unless they are prepared to walk for half a day (almost impossible in winter,
anyway), how do they get out of their villages? The television
aerials on the rooftops had disappeared soon after we left the
Moscow environs. We didn't see a single movie house. There
weren't any shops. The only centers that might have provided
some recreation or amusement seemed to be the occasional
wooden hut in a village labeled "Club House" or "Komsomol
Club" (the name of the Young Communist League). Yet by
then, halfway through our journey, we were scarcely more than
an hour out of Moscow. Suddenly the terrible boredom of village life in Russia became real to me. It has often been described. It can be read about in Turgenev, seen in Chekhov, heard
in the conversation of Muscovites, jealous of their city life. And
even those descriptions assume a level of living, an assumption
of privileges, that seemed to me nowhere apparent in the villages we passed. The boredom of the rich (or the relatively
rich) can be far more articulate and moving than the boredom
of the poor. But it hasn't that frightening air of finality. The
whole picture was surrounded in my mind with a sense of the
Russian climate, when the ground is frozen solid half the year
and even work is impossible. Every now and again we would
see a Russian village woman trudging down the street, carrying
a basket, and she would be stamped with the look of the Russian poor—wool scarf over her head and dark, shabby coat

(too tight across the back, too short in the sleeves) over a dark, shabby dress. Woolen stockings. Men's shoes. We passed shacks with straw piled against them, held close to the wooden walls with thin laths. To me, on that sunny, pleasant day, it was all part of a picture of the Russian winter.

Zagorsk, however, we found crowded with people. The Troitse-Sergiev Monastery and the surrounding cluster of churches and monuments, all enclosed like a fortress by their high white wall, were busy with Russians who had come in from villages within walking distance. A small market was in progress in the town square, but we were told by our driver that most of the people had come in for the eleven-o'clock Mass in the winter cathedral. The summer cathedral is larger, but too cold for use after about the middle of October.

We reached the buildings through the deep arch cut in the protective wall. This arch leads from the town plaza into the religious compound and is painted with scenes from the lives of the saints, stiff, haloed figures in bright colors. When we entered the gardens we saw around us the several buildings that make up the Zagorsk center—the religious college, the three cathedrals, the bell tower, the shrines, the houses of the priests—and when we looked up we could see the blue domes of the churches, mottled with gold stars, exotic and wonderful against the pale northern sky.

Inside the archway a young bearded priest was waiting for us. He was dressed in the black habit and distinctive black cylindrical hat, draped in black crape, of the Russian Orthodox Church. He spoke a little English, was still studying it, so he had been assigned to show us around. He took us first to a seventeenth-century cathedral, a fantasy of pale-green plaster with intricate moldings of grapevines twining around each pillar. He led us in, through packed rows of worshipers, to where the Mass was already in progress.

Under the immense dark paintings of ceilings and walls, in front of the gilded wooden lace screens that enclosed the altar, a huge congregation was gathered. We had been told that most of the people in Russia who were still actively religious belong to older generations unable to shake off the long training of their youth. In the Zagorsk cathedral, however, we saw plenty of young people—men and women—many of them with their small children or babies in arms. They stood through the service (no pews in Russian churches), the women in shawls with bundles and baskets beside them on the floor, occasionally pushing down on the shoulder of a child to show him when he should genuflect or kneel. The men were in dark clothes, the inescapable Sunday look of Northern Europe, and those who couldn't cram into the nave stood outside on the porch listening to the magnificent choir, the ancient, moving music, and joining in the chanted responses with the recurrent refrain of *"Gospodi po milo"* (Lord, have mercy on us).

Slowly, during the service, metal trays were passed among the congregation by three priests or acolytes, and the singing was punctuated by the clink of coins dropped on the trays.

As we left the cathedral we saw, in the doorway of the porch, a really extraordinary sight for Soviet Russia. A beggar. An old, blind woman crouched on the steps, held out her hand asking for alms in the name of God and of charity. A number of people dropped a coin or two into her hands even while I watched.

After the Mass our young priest took us on a brisk tour of the compound. He told us that Zagorsk, before it became a town, had been deep in the forest. There the man who later became St. Sergius retired to pursue his devotions. He built a small cell and a small church, and it was there that the Holy Mother of God appeared to him. On this sacred site was eventually built what is now the Cathedral of the Trinity, to which pilgrims from all over Russia come to kiss the fifteenth-century silver casket that contains the saint's relics.

From there we were conducted around the other famous monuments, St. Sergius' well, enclosed in its ornate pavilion, the very handsome tomb of Boris Godunov, the seminary, and so on. But among the whitewashed or painted walls, the plaster extravagances, the gold decorations, the ikons, our guide was continually interrupted by the greetings of fellow priests or religious students, who kissed him on the cheek before addressing him. Ordinary people who wanted to talk to him stopped him without ceremony, kissed his hand, and quite impervious to our presence asked him a question or launched into a discussion of a family matter. One of them tried to follow us into the summer cathedral, which had been locked up for the winter and was only opened for the ambassador after an extended search for the key. But here the priest was firm with the woman who was demanding his attention. "Go away, go away," he said briskly, "don't bother me." And without a break in his gracious manner toward us he continued to show us the magnificence contained in the biggest and grandest of the Zagorsk cathedrals, explaining the huge murals that extend up to the roof of the high narrow domes typical of Russian churches. The purpose of this construction, he said, was to draw up the sound of the singing so that by a trick of acoustics the music would seem to be coming down from the heavens. He pointed out the tombs of Ivan the Terrible's relatives and the seventeenth-century painting, and then with real pride showed us the new mosaic from Kazan and the portraits of Russian bishops painted only ten years ago, long after the Revolution when atheism was pronounced as the proper path for a Soviet citizen to follow. At last the old woman, tired of being ignored, went away.

When we left the Zagorsk religious compound the plaza outside was quite crowded. The little market seemed to be thriving, and there was a cluster of interested villagers staring at our car. As we drove away I turned for a last look at the white walls and the blue-and-gold domes. The beggar at the cathedral porch had changed her position. She was now crouched outside the big arch, still with hands outstretched, still murmuring her plea for alms in the name of God.

There were two places in Moscow I liked very much, that provided for me a pleasant contrast with the pinched and bustling life of modern Moscow, a glimpse of the more spacious, more eccentric, warmer life of another period in the city. One was the town house of Leo Tolstoy, the other the apartment of the musician Alexander Scriabin.

Tolstoy's house, from the outside, is a big, entirely undistinguished structure of mud-colored wood that dates from the early nineteenth century. Inside it is alive with the atmosphere, the work, the possessions, the tastes of an astonishingly vital and expressive family. The entrance hall opens straight into the comfortable, shabby, family dining room. The colors are the good serviceable browns that a practical housewife would choose to obscure the damage that thirteen children could inflict on paint and woodwork. The table is still set for dinner with thick blue-and-white china, the oil lamp in the middle, the big soup bowl at one end, the glass decanters and jugs— for buttermilk and water. The enthusiastic guide informs visitors that Tolstoy was a vegetarian, and that the family was not allowed to drink wine, though champagne was served to guests. On one wall is a portrait of his favorite daughter, Maria, of whom he once said, "She is the only light in my life."

You wander on through room after room, one very cold and formal, which he reserved for important people he disliked and whom he described as "very official and very boring." His own rooms are a jumble of some good pieces of furniture, a number of sentimental relics, a few practical conveniences—a solid screen around his bed to keep out drafts, a heavy, hand-made blanket and quilt given him by his wife Sophie Andrey-evna. His bedroom opens on to a small veranda where he and the children would do calisthenics as part of their Keep Fit program, and beyond is a small yard where he chopped wood in the mornings when he didn't go out to what are now the Lenin Hills to work with the laborers there.

All around are the rooms of the children, each with its special character. The nursery with its rocking horse, its dolls, toys, skates, high chairs. The boys' room with its globes and copybooks. Tatiana's more sophisticated room, cluttered with many paintings, with carefully chosen furniture and carpets. Tolstoy loved this room. He thought it gay and welcoming, and liked to sing and recite with Tatiana's young guests and her beaux.

Everywhere there are big tile stoves to heat the house, and as one walks through the rooms one hears, from time to time, the cozy sounds of a cuckoo clock.

Upstairs is the big hall for the music parties and the amateur theatricals that the whole family enjoyed. Although the decorations are grander than in the rest of the house—white marbled wallpaper, parquet flooring, chairs and sofas covered in dark-gold damask—still the room has an exuberant, expectant air. Looking at the long table set with a dinner service for twenty-four, or the grand piano in the corner, one can easily imagine the parties at which Rachmaninov or Rimsky-Korsakov or Gold-enweiser performed or Chaliapin sang or the evenings when Chekhov or Gorki would talk and argue late into the night while Sophie Andreyevna poured tea and the children became very quiet lest they be sent to bed.

I often used to watch the Russian tourists shuffling through the rooms, on the felt slippers one is asked to wear to save the Tolstoy carpets, and wonder whether this expansive, active family atmosphere seemed odd to them in contrast with their own tight, cautious lives. They always spent a long time in Tolstoy's study, a quiet room at the back of the second floor, gazing at the dark-leather furniture and the wide flat desk near the windows, listening as the guide listed the names of the great books that Tolstoy wrote here from the winter of 1881 onward. None of them ever asked a question or made a comment in my presence. Afterward we would all walk out together into the gray impersonality of the Moscow streets and hurry off in our various directions without even a smile.

Scriabin's flat had quite another feeling about it, far from the elegance of Pushkin's apartment in Leningrad or the bouncing vitality of Tolstoy's house. It is dark and rather shabby, his favorite room dominated by the Bechstein and the strange contraption of bulbs and bells that he needed for his wilder excursions into musical expression. His bedroom is almost monastically simple, hung with white curtains crocheted by his grandmother and neatly mended by some diligent housekeeper. Nothing very much, except that in this flat, as in Tolstoy's house, is contained a kind of life that is no longer possible in the Soviet Union, a life of breadth and intellectual and artistic curiosity, of experimentation, even of faddism. There was room then for personal idiosyncrasies (Tolstoy's vegetarianism or Scriabin's rather ill-informed concern with mysticism) and there was scope to defy convention—after all, Scriabin lived for years in that apartment with his mistress.

One day I received an unexpected invitation from the editorial staff of a magazine called *Soviet Woman* to visit their offices and talk to some of the editors. It was a magazine that I had followed assiduously since I had been in Russia, largely because it is among the few that have an English edition, and I found that I had a number of questions to ask.

I was met in the lobby of a big building that seemed to house a number of publications and led to a large room in which several people were typing at desks along the walls, while the center of the room was reserved for a conference table. The editor and several staff members of the English edition greeted me there—all spoke excellent English—and we settled down to talk and answer each other's questions.

Soviet Woman has a circulation of about 200,000, of which 15,000 are subscriptions to the English edition. It tries to give a fairly broad picture of life in Russia with an emphasis on what will especially interest women—some fiction, some articles, a few picture stories, recipes, household hints, and so on. In the issues I had seen, what seemed to me disproportionate space was given to war reminiscences, to stories concerned with war tragedies, to commemorative accounts of heroes and their sufferings. In one issue, for instance, a mother wrote of a "town named after my son"—about her schoolboy son who at the age of sixteen was tortured and hanged by the Nazis, but died singing the *Internationale*. The name of the village was changed to commemorate the bravery of the young hero. Meanwhile, her younger son became a letter carrier for the underground and later learned to drive a tank, "the desire to avenge his brother's death drove him on. The same emotion burned in my heart. I did not carry a gun. I was a nurse . . ." The same issue carried a picture story called "This Must Not Happen Again." The text began, "The razed streets of Rotterdam. Polish cities in ruins. Bomb traces in London. Refugees on the roads of France. Scorched earth in Smolensk Region . . ." The next issue contained an interview with the woman head of a food factory whose burnt hands were "my souvenir of Stalingrad." But "not until she was shell-shocked could Anna Mukhina be induced to cross over to the other bank of the Volga." And many more stories of the same general sort.

When I asked about this heavy concentration on war and atrocities, one of the editors looked at me in considerable surprise. "But these things are of interest to a very broad audience. It is the central question with which everyone is faced." More gently, he explained, "Our women in the Soviet Union have risen above the kitchen level, and these big matters are of concern to them, and we, naturally, try to give a picture of the life of our women. Often we feel we fall behind the requirements because life here moves on so fast."

This led me to ask about the household sections of the magazine and especially the articles on child upbringing, which I thought might be of only cursory interest to women who have been "liberated" from the chores of child care by state institutions. This was answered by a young, pretty woman staff member. "We need such articles. Our readers often write with problems about their children."

"But I thought most Russian children were put in state nurseries soon after they are born, and remain in state schools of one sort or another until they finish college. I'm glad to hear it isn't so."

"It *is* so, and it is good. With my daughter I thought at first that I would like to keep her at home and take care of her myself, but my friends soon explained to me that it was much better for her to be in the hands of professionals."

I did not tell her that in my opinion this removed half the point of having a child in the first place. Instead, I repeated my question about why, if that was the general opinion, her magazine published so many articles about child care.

She replied, "For some women it is necessary to explain the good things that the teachers do. Also, even with such good nurseries, home problems still arise. With my daughter, for instance, I was very worried because she would not speak to me at all when she came home from the kindergarten in the evenings. This lasted for some long time. At last I asked her teacher what was the explanation. Then the teacher told me that in the kindergarten all the children think of themselves as *tovarischi*. It is their pride. And they must not tell on a comrade."

"So she felt it safer not to talk at all?"

"When I understood the reason I did not try to force her. Such things must be explained to other mothers too."

Questions about the readership of *Soviet Woman* led us into a discussion of the kinds of letters the editors received. "On the whole they are disappointing," one of them said. "They give us too much praise. We welcome suggestions."

"Are there no criticisms?"

"Not really *criticisms*. Some readers say that they want more fiction, but short stories written from a woman's point of view are hard to find. Many write to ask for more fashions and cooking hints, they seem to like both those very much."

None of this seemed to fit comfortably into my picture of a Soviet woman, but gradually I did learn the explanation. *Soviet Woman* evidently caters largely to the privileged Russian woman—the one who has time to read stories in the afternoon, who has the space and the leisure to take an interest in cooking new dishes, and, most of all, to the woman with money to buy the clothes, the models from Moscow collections, that the magazine shows. Significantly enough, the other two major magazines for women are flatly differentiated in their titles for the other classes of Soviet women. *Rabotniza* (Working Woman) has the biggest circulation. *Kristianka* (Peasant Woman) has the next biggest. Neither appears in a foreign language.

When I left the offices of *Soviet Woman* I thanked the editors for their courtesy and attention. They, in turn, asked me formally to write an article, or a series of articles, for them. I tried to look noncommittal even though I was thinking of a number of my foreign friends who had been published in Russia (sometimes without their consent or knowledge) and had never received any accounting or royalties from their Russian publishers. Evidently I was not very successful, because one of the editors said, "Of course we will pay you, as we do all our writers."

"Unfortunately I will not be in Russia very long," I said.

"That does not matter. We will send the money wherever you wish—India, America. Of course, in the currency that you wish."

"Thank you very much for your kindness."

"Please do not mention it. This was what we hoped to ask you today."

"But why me?" I couldn't help asking.

"We would be glad to have *more* Indians writing for us."

As the Moscow winter season picked up speed, there were a good many diplomatic parties at which we came to know and like a number of the people from the various foreign embassies. From them we learned many things not a part of our own experience in Russia. From the Americans we realized that we were in a peculiarly privileged position as tourists. We were not, for instance, followed and watched in our day-to-day activities in Moscow—not that we tried to spot spies or that we would have been very efficient if we had. But judging from the relatively easy behavior of the Russians we met, from their willingness to make an appointment with us or come to our hotel, we assumed that they felt safe, and consequently that we needn't worry.

For the embassy personnel it was quite another matter. They were not only followed, but sometimes got to know the men assigned to watch them well enough to wave an occasional greeting on the street. Though Russians were willing to meet a tourist, to dine with him or go to the theater, they were not prepared to do the same with an embassy person, even when his Russian was much better than Faubion's and the chance of an enduring friendship much greater. Russians were likely to appear at the American Embassy only for official parties, and if a Russian made friends with a junior American official he would be likely to meet him only in public, anonymous places, never at home.

This was not true of the Asian embassies. There one always met Russians who were cordial, cheerful, talkative. But even the Asians had to be wary in a different way. As one of them explained it, "We have to be very careful. If we invite the Eastern Europeans, we can't invite the Westerners. They would come, but we have learned from experience that it makes a very strained party. Groups form in corners, there is very little conversation, everyone leaves early. Only on National Days or some safe occasion like that do they really mix happily. Still it is interesting to be in the middle—that's our compensation." Separately, apparently, they were all friendly and delightful company. But even for the separate cliques it wasn't easy to plan a party because one never knew even a few days ahead whether one might have to attend an official reception given by a top Russian politician at the Kremlin on the same evening. Often the invitations arrived only hours before the party, and a friend told me that on one occasion she was dressed and ready to leave her house for a drink with friends when a Kremlin invitation arrived and she had to change her plans on the doorstep.

At such official parties there were relatively few women. Only the foreign diplomats brought their wives. Apparently the Russian women were invited only if they happened to be important in their own right. For journalists and even for ambassadors, those parties did have their peculiar use—they provided an opportunity to meet and talk (often seriously) to Russian leaders with whom they might otherwise spend weeks trying to arrange an appointment. For us the parties were exciting if only because we could see and exchange greetings with Russians who had, until then, been only newspaper personalities to us.

Among the foreigners there, many entertained and instructed us—sometimes unexpectedly. For instance, an official from an Eastern European country, from whom I had expected only the familiar party line talk, once remarked to me, "Oh, yes, without doubt things are changing for the better—we feel it in our country too. Only the other day one of our schoolteachers asked a pupil, 'What is the longest river in the world?' The boy replied, 'The Volga, of course.' The teacher said, 'No, no! Haven't you heard that things are different now? Now you can give me the proper answer.'"

Once I found myself engaged in conversation with the wife of a diplomat from the Middle East. As usual, we exchanged impressions of Moscow. "I came here not knowing what to expect," she said. "Shortages, coupons, rationing, misery—I found none. At home people think I am lying when I talk like this, but really compared with many of our people the Russians seem to have everything. If the city seems to us dreary, it is only a question of climate and *la mode*—I would never buy my clothes here. But that is a small matter. For the rest I must believe the evidence of my own eyes. Often at home I am asked if there are any Christians in Russia, if people are allowed to worship freely. All I can say is that every functioning church that I have visited is packed. The trouble is usually *not* that you can't attend a service because it is forbidden but that you can't attend a service because you can't get in. Altogether I think they have made a phenomenal recovery after a very bad time."

A fellow guest, overhearing the last part of this speech, joined in. "But other countries that had a worse time have made a better—even a more heroic—recovery. Look at Poland. Russia at least had vast resources, the Poles had nothing. Why be sorry for the Russians? There is such a fuss made here about the miracles of reconstruction. It is nothing compared with other Eastern European countries—I don't even include the West—"

"But there has been a lot of building, a lot of rehabilitation of workers. I have seen—"

"So have I. Apartment houses thrown up very quickly, everything needing repairs in a few weeks. What is the good of that?"

"They had to house their people *somewhere*. Surely quick, cheap housing that gives people shelter even for the time being is useful until they can build the better houses—"

"If they ever build the better houses." Turning to me, the second woman said, "You have no idea of the exasperation of trying to run a house in Moscow. Your life is spent in replacing, mending, repairing, writing letters to ministries, getting no answers—six weeks to get a plumber, a month before the electrician comes to fix the wiring that was faulty in the first place—"

This conversation in one form or another was repeated a dozen times, with different people at different parties. The discussion about the pros and cons of the Russian way of life seemed to be an endlessly fascinating or irritating subject. It never appeared to bore even the most hardened foreigners.

Sometimes in those conversations we would come upon odd fragments of trivial but fascinating information. For example, members of the diplomatic corps are among the few people in Moscow who can drive their own cars but, so one of them told me, there are a number of unexpected hazards. Apart from the normal traffic violations, one can be arrested for driving a dirty car, for driving in shorts, or for driving while eating. Another told us that he, like many other foreign officials, attended classes at Moscow University but he was not permitted to join the basketball team in spite of the urgent pleas of his fellow students. Many people assured us that it was virtually impossible to furnish a house or a flat in Moscow and that, even if you managed by good luck or pull to find an item or two of furniture, it would be prohibitively expensive. Consequently, the carpets, curtains, linen, furniture, and practically everything else, even down to the paint, is usually imported, often from one of the Scandinavian countries. But the fact that seemed to me most bizarre was that at the British Embassy some ingenious person, faced with the hopeless problem of finding silver polish in Moscow, concocted an original substitute—vodka mixed with toothpaste. It works perfectly.

Edward Ivanian called up in great excitement. "I have arranged it!" he said. "I have arranged an appointment with Ulanova!"

"Wonderful! How did you ever—"

"Please be at stage entrance number seventeen of the Bolshoi. Tomorrow, at eleven."

"Of course we will. However did you manage it?"

"Fortunately she is in Moscow. She is rehearsing for the next performance of *Romeo and Juliet*. She can see you after the morning rehearsal."

"Edward, will you be there?"

"No, no. The fewer people the better. She doesn't like to see people."

When we got to the Bolshoi the next day we found that there were, in fact, other people—Russians seldom allow themselves to be interviewed alone. Faubion was so nervous at the thought of meeting his idol that he was certain his Russian would collapse under the strain, so we, too, had brought with us one of the Intourist interpreters—but she, in turn, was so nervous at the thought of meeting the great Ulanova that her understanding of English collapsed.

We were met at entrance 17 by one of the Bolshoi ushers, who led us up a couple of flights of stairs, through a small office into an equally small reception room which, in the geography of the Bolshoi, must have been somewhere behind the first tier of boxes. It was a curiously unreal room. There were no windows. The walls were entirely covered with scarlet damask and seemed to absorb all sound so that one was plagued by the feeling that everyone was talking in whispers. The sofa and the four gilt chairs were all upholstered in scarlet brocade. The floor was hidden by a scarlet carpet. A scarlet plush tablecloth was stretched over the round table in front of the sofa.

Waiting for us in this very red room were Tomsky, a thoughtful and charming man, the art director of the Bolshoi, and Svetlanov, the most brilliant of their young conductors. Ulanova, we were told, would join us soon. She was changing after the rehearsal. Meanwhile Faubion talked to the two men about the organization of the Bolshoi and the interior workings of the most heavily staffed and subsidized theater in the world.

The repertoire for each season, we learned, is chosen by an "art council" consisting of senior actors of the company, all leading artists, elected by the other actors. Usually they pick three new ballets for presentation each season along with the tested favorites. In the 1957-58 season they were doing the Khachaturian *Spartak,* considered very experimental because it is the first of the Soviet ballets to be performed without toe shoes, and *The Flaming Heart,* based on Gorki's folk tales, a new production of the famous *Red Poppy,* which is Chinese in theme, and as a special effort for the fortieth anniversary a combined pageant and ballet about the Komsomol and its activities. The YCL has received five state awards, so the ballet, symbolically, is in five acts, but to my considerable surprise it had not yet been given a title, even though the first performance was scarcely a week away.

Even though Svetlanov talked incisively and interestingly about the role of a Bolshoi conductor, and Tomsky about his complicated role of co-ordinator, we were all half listening for the arrival of Ulanova. When she appeared we were taken unawares—she slipped in through the door almost silently, with no attempt at an Entrance. She shook hands all around, apologized for being late, sat down in the vacant chair, folded her hands in her lap, and waited.

Nobody knew what to say.

After what seemed like an endless pause, Faubion asked if he might plunge straight into technical questions because he knew her time was limited. She nodded without smiling and said nothing at all.

Once Faubion got started on his questions, I had a chance

to look at her more carefully. She is a small, severe, bony woman—she looks much thicker of figure on stage than she actually is—and like most Russian women makes no attempt to hide her age (about fifty), or glamorize herself. She has what Faubion calls "hair-colored hair and eye-colored eyes." She wears her hair drawn tightly back into a braid and then pinned up into a bun. She has neat, undistinguished features, a thinnish mouth and fine, clear, pale skin. She has a briskly businesslike manner, but she never fidgets. When she is listening or when she is thinking she has an air of complete repose.

Faubion was plugging away at his questions.

"How many ballets do you have in your repertoire?"

"Fourteen or fifteen."

"Have you any favorites among them?"

"At the moment, *Giselle,* because it is sentimental. I like that. It used to be *Swan Lake.* My favorite changes according to my state of mind."

Her answers were all direct, short, and curiously cold. However, I listened to them only as a background to my scrutiny of her. She was wearing that Good Basic Black dress that fashion magazines always advise women to invest in. It was absolutely simple, almost austere, relieved only by a tiny white edging at the throat. It was exceedingly well cut. She had on very thin nylons and plain black suède high-heeled pumps.

It is an odd sensation to spend any length of time among people who never gossip—possibly Russians do gossip among themselves, but there is not the kind of public gossip one knows in the West. Information about the family life of leaders or movie stars never appears in the newspapers, the press never reports, say, what a famous woman was wearing on some public occasion. We had heard (from foreigners) that Ulanova had been married four or five times. I didn't know if this was true, but I looked at her hands and saw that she was wearing two magnificent diamond rings, one studded with emeralds, on the thin, rather worn-looking fingers of her right hand. On her left hand she wore a fat gold wedding ring. How strange, I thought, to have no idea at all of the identity of the husband of one of the most famous Russians of our time.

Faubion was saying, "How many hours a day do you practice?"

"I practice one or two hours a day. That much is like coffee in the morning. The rest of your breakfast depends on your appetite. So it is with practicing."

The interview continued along completely formal lines. In answering questions about how much latitude is allowed to a Russian dancer, how far she may mold the choreography to her own interpretation, she said, "Your own expression is important, but you must protect the design. If you don't follow the choreographer, why have one?"

"In the West," Faubion explained, "there is a good deal of flexibility. Markova, for instance, dances Giselle quite differently from Fonteyn, who is again different from Nora Kaye—"

"I have seen no Western ballet," Ulanova said flatly. "When I have been abroad I have been working. I haven't had time just to travel in the West."

Once we got a gleam of rather sly humor from her. Remarking on the interaction between a dancer and the conductor, she stated in her categorical manner that the role of the conductor was the highest. "The foundation of opera and ballet is music. The music is in the conductor."

"What happens if there is a difference of opinion between the ballerina and the conductor as to an interpretation?"

Smiling at Svetlanov she said, "Whoever is strong enough to *convince* the other wins."

Once we got what in Russian ballet circles was certainly a dirty crack. Faubion had asked about the effect on the dancer of the elaborate stage effects, and Ulanova had answered calmly that the stage effects enhanced the atmosphere of the ballet. Then she added, "Of course in some theaters the effects are too much. The swans are flooded out by the lake." This was a dig at the relatively new, wildly popular young dancer of the Musical Theater, Bovt. When we had seen her scintillating performance of *Swan Lake* in a new staging, there had, indeed, in the last act been a most realistic flood on stage which, unlike the Western version of the ballet, brings about a happy ending with the swan released from the magician's spell and reunited with her prince.

At the end of our interview there was a most uncomfortable moment. Before we came to Russia, knowing that we would be interviewing dancers, Faubion had bought several pairs of something called nylon Danskins which he planned to give as presents to dancers in an attempt to soften the imposition that our interviews might represent. We had been told by dancer friends who had visited Russia that the Russian tights are made of a thick cotton knit which wrinkles easily. The nylon tights are much thinner, do not wrinkle as you dance, and stretch to fit almost anyone. Accordingly, Faubion produced his little package and said that this was a present for Ulanova, offered with apologies for taking up so much of her time. Here he turned to the interpreter, because his Russian had worn pretty thin by then, and said, "Please tell Madame Ulanova that these are the best I could find in America, and I know that a hard-working dancer can never have too many tights."

The interpreter, thoroughly rattled, said something equivalent to: "These are the best tights. Russian dancers have not enough."

Understandably Ulanova stiffened. "I have plenty," she said icily. "Since these are so precious, I must put them in a museum."

I don't know if this muddle was ever properly sorted out. Faubion and I left as quickly as we could.

Some days later we were pleased—and puzzled—to receive an autographed photograph of Ulanova as Giselle. But by then, in any case, my feeling about Ulanova had changed because we had been to see her as Juliet at the Bolshoi, a radiant evocation of a young girl in love, in loss, in death, and I had realized that she is as great an actress as she is a dancer. With no apparent effort she communicates every subtlety of feeling and a marvelous warmth. When she came out in front of the curtain to take her bows, she was again her reserved, severe self. Her acknowledgment of the tumultuous applause was almost perfunctory.

Early in November we had what to me was an extraordinary encounter. Having nothing particular to do one evening, Faubion and I decided to walk about a bit and look at the fortieth anniversary decorations. As usual, just outside the Metropole there was a cluster of boys, teen-agers and perhaps a bit older. They surrounded any tourist leaving the hotel, some out of curiosity, some offering to sell the little gilt-and-enamel badges that the Russians seem to love, and some asking for foreign stamps or coins. We pushed our way through them and started walking quite rapidly because it was cold and looked as though it might rain at any moment. We had reached the end of Sverdlov Square when we heard a voice calling, *"Gospodin! Gospodin!"* (Mister! Mister!) and we turned to find a young man running toward us. He was the boy who had come up to our table one night at the Metropole wanting to buy Faubion's suit.

We smiled and asked each other where we were going and what we were doing. "Just walking," Faubion said.

"Then please walk with me," the young man said. "I am going to the Rivoli to meet my friend."

"The Rivoli?"

The young man laughed. "That is what we call it. Short for the Square of the Revolution."

We walked along with our young "beeznessman" and learned that we should call him Vanya. He said nothing further about buying or selling but made polite small talk until we reached the Rivoli. There we were joined by a tall, dark young man with a thin, nervous face and a restless manner. He greeted Vanya affectionately, half embracing him, and then turned inquiringly to us.

"My friend, Igor," Vanya said. He introduced us as American tourists he had met at the Metropole. Faubion told them our names, and he immediately became "Fedya," though I remained *"Gospaja"* (Mrs.).

"Come," Vanya said, "we will all have a drink together."

Igor said, "Good, very good. Ah, American tourists. You are very lucky. But first I have a little beezness. Fedya and Gospaja will not mind. I will finish my beezness in one minute."

"Forget your beezness," Vanya said. "Come for a drink."

"In a minute, in a minute. I must meet this man. He will be here, at the station."

Igor turned briskly and started walking to the Lenin subway station, only a few yards away. We followed him more slowly. Considering the kind of shady enterprises they seemed to be involved in they also seemed remarkably open. The Lenin subway station is almost as popular a place for beezness as Gorki Street. Young men—surprisingly young—were hanging about in twos and threes among the imposing marble pillars and on the sidewalk. Several of them hurried over to Igor for brief, rapid conversations, sometimes only a word or two. He seemed to be the head, or center of some kind of gang—after all, it must take considerable organization to run a network of small black-market deals—and his tense figure seemed to hold a certain authority.

When we caught up with him, Vanya again said, "Come along—forget your appointment."

"No, no," Igor said, looking restlessly around.

Vanya said, "Always business before pleasure." Then, to us, he added in a very affectionate tone, "You can tell he is a Jew. You know what we say? One Jew is a trading post. Two Jews, a game of chess. Three Jews, a symphony orchestra. Well, Igor is a trading post." We all laughed, and Vanya continued cheerfully, "That is why he likes Americans—one American, business. Two Americans, business. Three Americans, business!"

We waited a bit longer, and then Vanya said, "It is beginning to rain. Come along."

"No, no. A few more minutes."

"Well, we will go on. Join us at the Grand Hotel."

"Yes, in a little while."

Vanya slapped him on the back and said in a very friendly way, *"Ty Yevrei"* (You are a Jew).

Just as we turned to leave, a man came up to Igor and demanded in a quiet but commanding voice to see his "passport." All Russians carry cards of identity which they call "passports" and produce on a number of occasions—if they are registering in a hotel, if a policeman asks for it, if they are buying a train ticket for an out-of-town journey. Igor started to fumble in his pocket for his passport. Meanwhile he muttered to Vanya, "Go along, go along, I'll join you later."

Vanya gripped my elbow, and we walked away. By the time

we reached the Lenin Museum, which is on Revolution Square, it was raining quite hard. Faubion, Vanya and I stood with the other pedestrians taking shelter in the museum porch and waited for the rain to subside. Vanya was talking away lightheartedly, but I couldn't listen because I was very upset by that brief, quiet incident at the subway station. The man who had spoken to Igor looked so exactly like my picture of the Russian secret police—thick-set, wearing a black trench coat and a black felt hat pulled low on his forehead—that I was certain Igor was in serious trouble of some kind.

At last I could stand it no longer and insisted that Faubion ask Vanya who the man was and what was happening to Igor.

"Nothing, nothing," Vanya replied airily. "Do not worry."

"But was that man from the secret police?"

"Oh, no, never. We have no secret police now."

"Well, was he from *any* kind of police? Is Igor in trouble?"

"Please do not worry about Igor. He can talk his way out of anything. When he cannot talk enough, he can pay a little. Then everything is all right. Once a friend of his got drunk and threw a beer bottle at a policeman. Twenty rubles fixed it."

"But was this anything to do with being seen with us? With foreigners?"

"Never, never. We welcome foreigners. Now it is all right. A year ago it was risky to talk to foreigners."

"Then what is it all about?"

"Perhaps Igor met a friend. Nothing more."

I didn't believe a word he said.

The rain kept pouring down and we continued to stand in the museum porch, fidgeting and wondering. At last Vanya, seeing that Faubion and I really were distressed, volunteered to go back to the subway station and see what was happening to Igor. He left us standing miserably with our backs to the rain that was driving in between the columns of the porch, and vanished in a second into the damp hurrying crowds. I thought we would never see him again.

Within a few minutes he was back, with Igor beside him. Both were smiling. "Nothing, nothing!" Vanya called out reassuringly. "We will tell you while we drink."

The four of us ran across the street to the Grand Hotel, where, wet and relieved, we began talking animatedly. Over vodka and sandwiches, Igor explained that it was "just an incident. It was nothing."

"But who was that man?"

"That man was a Jew. Like me, he was a Jew. He heard Vanya say, '*Ty Yevrei*' to me and he was very angry."

"But why did he want to see your passport?"

"He wanted to see if I really was a Jew."

I was still bewildered. "I can't see what business it was of his."

"He wanted to know whether I minded or not, whether Vanya had insulted me. If he had, there would have been a fight. The man wanted to fight Vanya for being insulting about Jews. I told him that Vanya was my friend, that he was only joking." He smiled his nervous smile across the table at Vanya, then continued seriously, "You know, one cannot speak against the Jews now. It is against the law."

"Why now?" Faubion asked. "Was it all right before?"

Igor gave us a tired, rather cynical look. "Before, yes. In the days when the papers were full of the treachery of the Jewish doctors toward Stalin. They said that the Jewish doctors were trying to kill Stalin instead of curing him. It was difficult for my family at that time."

Faubion said indignantly, "Surely nobody believed such rubbish."

Igor shrugged. "I was a child. I only know that my father lost his job at the factory. My mother wanted to cry, but she would not. Many people did not speak to us. I remember that. It was difficult to buy food. We did not like to go out of the house because people in our district knew that we were Jews. My father sat all day in the same chair."

"And now it is better?"

Igor smiled sadly. "Now, yes, it is better. My father has retired. He gets his pension. That is something. I am older. That too is something. I stopped my work after middle school to go to work—my parents had done everything for me, the least I could do was to try to give them a decent life now they are old. I started with a construction gang. Now I am the foreman. We live . . . we live."

Faubion remarked, "But that's very good, to be a foreman so young."

"It's a dreadful job," Igor said, frowning. "I have to keep all the workmen on the project, but if anything goes wrong I am responsible. Still it is better than continuing as a student."

"I thought students were rather fortunate," Faubion said. "I mean, the government pays for everything and—"

"Oh, yes, the government pays," Igor interrupted. "Pays for all the necessities, that is. But what about your spare time? One should have a few good things from life. As a student, I would have to say" (his voice suddenly shifted to a childish falsetto), " 'Mama, give me some money,' as if I were a baby saying, 'Mama, give me some milk.' " He raised his glass. "Now, at least I can afford a glass of vodka when I want." We all drank. "But I know when to stop. Look at that man—" He nodded his head, in a slightly contemptuous gesture, at a "simple worker" at a neighboring table. "With every drink he takes he is cutting off his head. He will never be anything but a worker—but can you blame him? Whenever an Ivan has five, ten, twenty extra rubles, he spends it on drink."

"Ivan?" Faubion asked, looking at Vanya, who drank very moderately.

Igor rocked back in his chair, laughing loudly. "Oh, not *this* Ivan. Ivan, any real Russian is an Ivan. And what else is he to do? He'll never collect enough to make saving really worth while. Look at the Russians from the other republics— the Georgians, the Kazaks, the Armenians—they save. They give half their money to their wives and families. But an Ivan? Never! He drinks, he becomes generous, he invites the people from the next table, for a moment he is a big man."

Then Igor told us a favorite story to illustrate his point. An artist was painting a picture of that character beloved of Russian novelists—the saintly fool. He had a lot of trouble finding someone to pose for him, a man with the right look, battered and dissolute but innocent. At last he found the perfect model, a drunken beggar, in the street. Afterward, he paid the beggar 25 rubles and then watched from the window to see what the man would do. He stood on the street corner until he saw the best droshky in town. He hired it, rode two blocks, surveying the world, capturing a dream; then he got out, paid the driver the 25 rubles to cover the brief ride and the proper tip, bowed, and went on his way. "This, you see, is the character of the Ivan—the moment's enjoyment, the grand gesture, and what does the rest matter? But I am a Jew. I will not behave like that. Somehow I will *make* a better life for myself and my family."

"People are always telling us," Faubion said warily, "that it is a good life now—much better than before."

"Better? Oh, yes, better. Before, to talk to you—foreigners —would have been a danger. I would have written your telephone number on a piece of paper like this, secretly." He tore off a corner of the paper napkin, rolled it into a tiny pellet between his fingers and slipped it into his pocket. "Like this, I would save your number so that if I were searched the paper would look like a piece of forgotten rubbish in my pocket. Now," he said with a touch of bravado, "I am not afraid. I can come and see you at the Metropole. What if the militiaman at the door stops me? He can only say, 'What are you buying?' and I will reply, 'None of your business.' In the old days, no. Then it would have meant—" and he placed two fingers of each hand across each other in a tick-tack-toe pattern.

"It would have meant *what?*" Faubion asked.

"This is the sign for prison," Igor told us.

"I see."

"But now, no more. Now life is better. But when you have the necessities, then you want more. Not my parents, perhaps, but *I* want more. A sign of health, I think—don't you? Sometimes we listen to the Voice of America. The music, yes, very good, but they tell lies about our country. We do not want a revolution—a change of government—more fighting—no. Just some better things in our life. Is it not so among workers in America?" Seeing Faubion's solemn expression, he quickly changed his mood. "But why do we talk of such things? Let us order more vodka. You know why I like this place? It has an all-girl orchestra. Wait until it begins to play. Wonderful! Even the singer is good."

We all became more jovial, waiting for the all-girl orchestra to emerge. We talked inconsequentially, drank, and ate chocolates, bickered mildly about who should pay the check, settled on dividing it. When we were about to leave, Igor said, "Fedya, that is a very nice suit you are wearing. How much would you ask for such a suit?"

November 7 came at last, and like everybody else in Moscow, I suppose, we made ready to enjoy a day of celebration and see as much as we could of the colossal fortieth anniversary parade, the culmination of weeks of preparation. For at least a fortnight, on our way home after the theater, we had seen school children, or foot soldiers, or armored divisions rehearsing in Red Square, always late at night when there was virtually no traffic.

The day before, Boris had come to ask if he might bring Maya to spend the afternoon at the Metropole with us. Of course we agreed, partly out of curiosity and partly because Boris had said rather wistfully that he wanted to spend at least part of the great day with the girl he loved. This was impossible at her house because she, her mother, her younger sister, and her small brother all lived together in a two-room flat. Boris and Yelena shared a two-room flat with Yelena's parents, so naturally Boris could not meet Maya there either.

"But, as a married couple, aren't you entitled to a flat of your own?" I asked.

"When we can find one, yes. Our names are on the lists. We wait."

I was inquisitive about their living arrangements, and Boris explained, without indignation, that before he married he had lived with his parents, again in a two-room flat, of which he had shared one room with Valery. Yelena, an only child, had a room to herself in her parents' flat. "Also, they are lucky," Boris said. "There is a big kitchen, big enough to sit." So the simplest course, after they were married, was for Boris to move into Yelena's room.

"Won't Yelena think it peculiar that you don't spend the holiday with her?"

"No, no," Boris said eagerly. "She will think that I am with my parents. That is natural, to see them on this day."

"But without her?"

"She is not friends with my parents. I must always see them without her."

The morning of the 7th was gray and chilly. From time to time there were brief gusts of rain. Jai woke us up in great excitement, announcing that the parade had started. Actually, the people he had seen on the street were participants assembling to take their places. However, from eight o'clock onward we spent most of the morning on our balcony. Fortunately part of the parade marched down the street outside our rooms, otherwise we would have seen nothing of it. Except for the distinguished guests from Communist countries and members of the Communist press and the top-ranking diplomats, no foreigners were allowed in Red Square, where the grandest displays took place. Other journalists had got up very early in the morning to pack into the restaurant of the National Hotel, from which a part of Red Square is visible.

The procession itself consisted of three or four different streams of people and floats which started in various parts of the outlying areas of Moscow, marched through the main roads to converge in Sverdlov Square and Revolution Square and from there, in full strength, to parade through Red Square. The streets of the city were elaborately cordoned off so that once the processions had begun to assemble the city was practically paralyzed.

From our balcony we watched thousands of people lining up neatly, according to instructions, in the street below. There were children carrying placards and balloons, there were "Young Pioneers" with their distinctive scarlet scarves, there were school groups, YCL groups, sports groups. Interspersed among them were women from factories and farms. Often they carried symbols of their work or surrounded a float that represented their particular occupation. One float, for instance, was a model of an electric plant with a red light flashing from its central pylon. Some of the women carried chrysanthemums or paper flowers and leaves. The men were in their usual glum-looking clothes, but that day they too carried pennants and placards and pictures of Lenin.

I was suddenly aware of how much I missed color in the streets of Moscow. In other cities there is nearly always something light, or bright, or pretty, or colorful to catch the eye and give a moment's pleasure as one walks down a street—a well-dressed woman, an attractive shop window, a tricky neon advertisement—but in Moscow on ordinary days buildings, streets, and people were drab. Only the Kremlin, which belongs to another era, seemed to me to have color and fantasy.

Evidently some of the men in the procession had brought along bottles of vodka, for occasionally, instead of the usual stamping and movement against the raw November morning, one would start an active, leaping kind of dance. The bottle would be passed around and soon a ring of people would form around the dancer, clapping in rhythm. Now and then a few of the girls and young men would join the impromptu dance, to the shrieks and laughter of their companions. One of the more enthusiastic groups grabbed their dancer, lifted him off the ground, and flung him in the air. They caught him and flung him up again several times. He seemed to me in imminent danger of at least a broken arm, but everybody was laughing and shouting encouragement. He wasn't injured at all.

It was only later, after the procession started moving and we watched boys and girls and men and women and banners and floats and soldiers going past, that an oddly disturbing fact struck me. There were no spectators along the line of march. The sidewalks, guarded by militiamen, were empty. No crowds jostled each other waving flags, carrying children on their shoulders, cheering, watching, yelling. The parade moved by at a brisk pace under our balcony and the only sound, except for the regular beat of footsteps, was the music that poured all day from the outdoor loudspeakers.

In the middle of the afternoon Boris arrived at the Metropole. Maya reached our rooms about half an hour later. I rushed to open the door to her, with Boris immediately behind me, and caught that first look directed at him over my shoulder. In that instant I knew that I liked her, and that she was in love. She was the kind of light, lively girl who is pretty only because of the animation in her face, the clear changes of expression, the quick coming and going of laughter. She was easy and informal and quite plainly delighted to see Boris.

She didn't seem to me like the conventional picture of an actress. She wore no make-up. Her light-brown hair was brushed back from her forehead and hung straight to her shoulders. She dressed in the usual unobtrusive Russian way. But when she started to play with Jai, we were all captivated by her lively imagination and her remarkable mimic skill.

Between them they invented a game for which no language was necessary. Jai was a hunter in a jungle, and Maya was all the animals in turn. She plunged (with the excited co-operation of Jai) into this game almost immediately, and Boris, Faubion, and I watched spellbound while she became an elephant, a lion, a monkey, a gazelle, a bear, and so on, and Jai stalked her around the chairs and tables.

At last, flushed and laughing, she flopped into a chair and we began to talk. We didn't really talk *about* anything much, except for a few comments and questions about her work. What sort of play did she like acting in the best? "The classics, always the classics. Even foreign classics—Shakespeare, Shaw,

Wilde." Like the rest of us, she deplored the dearth of Soviet playwrights. "We haven't produced a good dramatist since Mayakovsky. But you must remember, this is a new society. It will take time to produce the people who can express it in good art. This cannot be done in a minute. As our society grows, the artists will grow out of it."

But in our holiday mood we preferred to talk trivialities, laugh, make silly jokes, and drink each other's health in vodka. Early in the evening we decided to go out to see what the November 7 crowds in the streets were like. It was already dark, but the center of Moscow was still filled with people. There was virtually no traffic, and the holiday crowds had spilled over into the street. As we walked toward Red Square we were constantly weaving between lines of men and women, arms linked, six or eight abreast, walking along a bit unsteadily, singing and shouting greetings to other passers-by. Some of the men had accordions or guitars. Others—the southerners particularly— would swing into the whirling, heel-clicking dances of their provinces, and soon other southerners would be attracted into forming an enthusiastic audience around the dancer.

The vast enclosure of Red Square was even more crowded with people looking at the lights and staring in a kind of amazement at the illuminated head of Lenin floating eerily high above the Kremlin. I suppose it was really only a translucent balloon on a very long cable that was invisible against the darkness, but it was a thoroughly creepy experience to look up and see the decapitated head of Lenin gazing down on Moscow from the sky.

Some of the people in Red Square were playing an odd, elementary game that Boris explained to us. It consisted of one person walking ahead of his party with his hands at his shoulders and his elbows held away from his sides. Some member of his party would tap his elbow. Immediately he would whirl round and face the others and see that everyone was holding his right thumb in the air and trying to look innocent. He would try to guess who had hit him. This was accompanied by much joking and shoving and laughter.

It seemed a very short time before Maya said that she had to go home, that her mother would be expecting her. She seemed genuinely sorry to leave—I was too; it was easy to understand why Boris was so in love with her. Maya's particular blend of warmth and a kind of openness of expression are almost as rare in Soviet women as her sense of ease and her gaiety. Boris, of course, would take her home because, clearly, even the few impersonal minutes in the subway, sitting a little way apart like all Russians, not holding hands, scarcely speaking, were worth it. I wanted very much to know how their story would end, but I realized that was unlikely as we would be leaving Moscow in a week.

Faubion and I walked slowly back to the Metropole. Moscow revelry ends early, and when we got back to the hotel, after some more wandering around, people were already leaving or being asked to leave.

Our final week in Moscow was a sad one, filled with farewells and last meetings. I found that I had become fond of the city in an inarticulate way. I told myself that we would probably never see our friends there again. Certainly we would never get letters from them and equally certainly we would never write to them (even the ones whose addresses we knew) because one is always haunted by the thought that such a correspondence could get them into trouble.

Shura came to call on us, having heard from Boris that we would soon be leaving. He seemed to be full of his usual insouciance, smiling at the chambermaid who had shown him in, slapping Faubion on the back. He had brought presents for all of us: some painted wooden blocks of different shapes that fitted together to make a model of a Kremlin tower and a mechanical turtle for Jai; flowers for me; for Faubion a tie that I had seen Shura wearing one evening. It was narrow and gray, made of some ersatz material supposed to look like silk, and it was stenciled with a design of Picasso's dove of peace.

He chattered in his bantering manner, then suddenly suggested that he should give us a farewell party. He could arrange it, he said, in the apartment of a friend—the friend with the tape recorder, so that we should have music as well. But since it had been Shura who had explained to us the complications and the expense of such a party, we accepted only on condition that he would allow us to bring the food and drink. He looked deeply hurt and simply shook his head. The party wasn't mentioned again.

Good-bys are always difficult and I noticed that even Shura looked a little constrained before he got up to leave. We promised we would never forget each other. Faubion declared that we would find him if we returned to Moscow. He assured us that he would look us up if he came to New York. He picked Jai up and held him high in the air. "Little boy," he said, "be strong, be happy," and set him down again. He shook my hand vigorously, saying "Good-by, good-by," and gripped Faubion by the shoulders and kissed him on both cheeks. "I will always be your friend," he said, "even though you are a foreigner. You can always trust me as I trust you." To our astonishment, he then added, "If our troops are in Washington, I will do my best— my small best—to protect you and your family."

Jai followed him into the corridor, yelling, "Shura! Look,

Shura, look!" Shura turned to see the clockwork turtle crawling jerkily toward him.

In the mornings we ourselves called on people who had been kind to us; in the evenings Faubion crammed in as much theater-going as he could manage, but we kept one evening free for Maya, who had invited us to dinner at her house. Boris came to pick us up, and together we traveled by métro to quite a remote part of Moscow.

Even through the darkness and the ill-lit streets we could see that this section of the city was practically a separate village. The apartment house itself was simply enormous, running the length of a big city block. The street level was occupied by small shops of all kinds, including a post office. This façade was cut by five or six archways that led into a narrow courtyard from which the entrance stairways to the apartments opened. Above the shops and the arches rose the vast gray expanse of the building, almost featureless because heavy curtains were drawn across all the windows and only thin cracks of light showed here and there. The blocks on each side were occupied by almost identical apartment buildings, making, all together, a self-contained residential community with all the day-to-day needs for living accessible within a couple of minutes' walk.

Boris led us through one of the archways, and in the shabby strip of courtyard we could see clotheslines strung between wooden poles which leaned crookedly this way and that. There were a couple of storage sheds, a padlocked bicycle, and a general air of neglect. Inside one of the entranceways was a small cold hall, and stone stairs leading to the apartments. We climbed up a couple of flights to Maya's door.

Boris had been nervous and quiet. He rang the bell and gave a flourish of knocking on the door for good measure. But when Maya opened the door his manner changed. He was excited and jovial and announced at once that we had brought presents for everyone. He bustled us into the narrow passage, carpeted and dark, and we found ourselves pushing and laughing in an attempt to hang our coats on the wall pegs, banging into the wooden chest against one wall, tripping over the galoshes lined up beyond it. Three doors led out of the passage. One on our right opened into a minute kitchen or pantry, opposite it was the door to the living room, and beyond that the bedroom door.

Maya called to her mother that we had arrived, and a tiny, shy woman came out of the kitchen to add to the congestion in the hall. In the living room Maya's younger sister was waiting, and at last there was room to shake hands formally and to offer our presents. Assuming that they would prefer to have foreign rather than Russian things, we had sifted through our clothes to find suitable presents. For Maya there was a nylon nightdress of mine that I had worn only once, two pairs of Faubion's socks (new) for Boris, a rayon scarf printed with scenes of New York that had belonged to Ruth we gave to Maya's mother, and a pair of Ruth's nylon stockings for Maya's sister. She told us timidly that these were the first nylons she had ever owned.

I was glad that we had brought presents because, judging from the table under the windows, already spread with food, Maya and her family had gone to considerable trouble and expense to entertain us. Boris, who had been carrying a large package of his own, darted into the kitchen and returned without it. I didn't find out until later what his contribution to the party was.

The room was small and seemed breathless with furniture— the round table at the far side, some heavily upholstered chairs, a long puffy couch, a number of little tables and bookcases covered with bits of embroidered cloth and crowded with photographs, a couple of plants in pots, a small bronze reproduction of Peter the Great's statue in Leningrad, a lacquered box, a Ukrainian doll, and so on. The ceiling light in its big red shade gave everything a rather hectic air of warmth. Obviously this was both living room and dining room, and since there was only one bedroom I supposed that one of the daughters must sleep on the couch.

We talked for only a few minutes before dinner, and then Maya's mother gently chivvied us to the table. The younger daughter, her long braid swinging, went to the kitchen and returned in a moment with glasses of tea on a tray. We all drank tea and ate the wide assortment of cold meat and cold fish and red caviar that had been put out for us. Maya's mother unobtrusively insisted that with all this we should eat quantities of black bread and white bread and hot boiled potatoes. It seemed to me a splendid meal. However, I soon learned that it was a great mistake to follow her advice, for this was only the beginning.

Soon the younger girl and the mother picked up the half-emptied dishes and the tea glasses and took them to the kitchen, returning with deep, steaming plates filled with a delicious mixed vegetable and meat soup. We were urged to eat more bread with this, and Boris poured a light red wine for us. And after the soup there was still another course of meat balls in a rich spicy gravy accompanied with mountains of noodles.

While her mother and sister quietly served us, changed plates, ate virtually in silence, and shuttled between the kitchen and the table, Maya carried most of the conversation. She told us about her childhood in Kiev and how she had always wanted to be an actress, about the small provincial acting school where she had studied, and described her terror before she took her final examinations. She told us how her mother had comforted her by saying, "We are the only people who need never be afraid. We have always been simple workers. If you do not pass your examinations, we will continue to be simple workers. There will always be a place for us, the country cannot live without us."

The mother now made one of her rare remarks. Smiling and shy, she said, "Kiev seemed like a great city to me—I had never been to Moscow. My childhood had been in the country—"

"Oh, yes," Maya interrupted, "but my dream was to come to Moscow. I can remember that my father used to tell us, 'If you have two hands and are willing to work, that is all the wealth you need.' But I had other dreams, of another kind of wealth."

Faubion asked, "And you have found it in Moscow?"

Maya turned to him eagerly. "Oh, yes!" she said. "Everything I want is in Moscow!" Her look shifted quickly to Boris, and then down to her plate. "I mean," she added, "I was able to bring my family here. I am doing the work I like. I want to become a better and a still better actress—"

Boris got up suddenly from the table. "Now I will bring my present," he said. He vanished into the kitchen and then reappeared carrying a big cake with icing on it. He set it down in the middle of the table, and then we saw that on its surface, picked out in tiny candles, were the English letters JAI. In English Boris said, "This is the cake for the birthday of your son. Valery told me. He told me that the boy did not receive the the cake that is customary."

I could only smile blindly at Boris, I couldn't quite trust myself to speak. Faubion thanked him properly, in Russian and in English, and Boris waved away the thanks, saying, "It is nothing, nothing. . . . Come, we will cut it here and eat some, wishing for the good future of Jai. Later you will take the rest back to him. We must be careful that we do not spoil the name written on it. He must see his name."

While Boris ceremoniously cut the cake, fresh glasses of tea were brought in, and we all made our wishes and ate a little cake. We sat around the table sipping tea and talking for a while, and I began to wonder when I should make a move to leave. I thought Boris would probably feel he had to come with us, out of politeness, but would certainly want to stay as long as possible with Maya. When, at last, we did get up, Maya rushed out of the room to pack the rest of the cake in its box, and then both of them suggested that they would escort us home.

In a flurry of good-bys and thanks and good wishes and more thanks, the four of us set out for the Metropole. At the door Faubion invited them in for a nightcap, but when Boris suggested that it was rather late, we didn't insist. We stood on the steps of the hotel, and watched the two figures in their dark winter coats walking away across Sverdlov Square toward the métro station. The light from the street lamps caught Boris' blond hair once or twice. Maya's soft brown hair brushed her coat collar as she walked. In less than a minute we couldn't see them at all.

Our last day in Moscow was enlivened only by an unexpected visit from our two "beeznessmen," Igor and Vanya. Somehow, through the hotel grapevine, I suppose, they had learned that we were leaving. They came up to our rooms, sat politely on the sofa and expressed regrets that they would not see us again. The room was scattered with half-packed suitcases and a muddle of clothes and shoes and papers. Igor and Vanya accepted a drink and a slice of Jai's birthday cake, and then Vanya, looking around the messy room, remarked pleasantly, "Often when a visitor is leaving Moscow, there are things for which he has no further use. Is it so with you?"

As it happened, it *was* so with us. There were a couple of

torn shirts of Faubion's, several of Ruth's nylons that had runs in them, a very old pair of snow boots that I had, in any case, planned to throw away, Jai's corduroy pants worn hopelessly thin at the knees, and a few other such items. Faubion pointed out the pile of discarded clothes in a corner of the room, and Igor and Vanya solemnly went over to inspect them. They were surprisingly thorough in their examination, shaking out each garment, holding the stockings up to the light, and at last Igor turned to us and inquired courteously but warily, "How much do you ask for these?"

Faubion said, "We are not intending to sell them."

Igor said, "I am sure we can agree on a price."

"We were going to throw them away."

"Throw them away?"

"But you are welcome to take them if they are of any use to you."

"But, naturally, we will pay for them."

"Please understand," Faubion said rather desperately, "that we do not need them, that otherwise we would simply leave them in the wastebasket of the hotel. Please take them."

Vanya picked up the snow boots. "My mother has no shoes for the winter," he said. "I must thank you from my heart."

They carefully wrapped in newspapers the boots, the clothes, and a number of old American magazines that were lying about the room. They did not wish to be seen carrying the things out of the hotel openly.

Our plane to Tashkent, the capital of Uzbekistan, was due to leave at about three o'clock the following morning. Since we had to be at the airport half an hour before take-off time and since the drive to the airport took at least an hour, there seemed to be no point in going to bed that night. After dinner Faubion and I took the now-familiar walk to Red Square. We stood in the darkness and looked, once again, at the strange beauty of St. Basil's, thick with shadows, silhouetted against the sky. And then, once again, we looked up at the red stars glowing over the Kremlin. It seemed to me at that moment that I knew nothing whatever about Moscow, it was as foreign a city as it had been the day we arrived, but still I wished that we weren't taking the plane that night.

Uzbekistan

FOR MORE THAN an hour before we reached Tashkent the sky had been filling with pre-daybreak light. Soon from the plane windows we could see, in semidarkness, mile after mile after mile of the barren land below us. It was only then that the daunting expanse of Soviet territory took on a positive reality for me. I realized that when we reached Tashkent, after we had traveled 1,500 miles south and east from Moscow, we would still be only about a third of the way across Russia. Faubion told me a story about our friend Dr. Malalasekhara, who had said, when he met Khrushchev for the first time, "I come from such a small island, one of the smallest nations in the world, to your country which covers a fifth of the world's surface." Khrushchev had replied, "But what good is that? Half of it is useless desert." Flying across central Russia it was easy to see the magnitude of the problem of the development of the Russian hinterland.

As the light grew stronger we could make out an occasional isolated pocket of houses forming a large village or small town. At long intervals, around the twists of a narrow river, we could see the neatly contoured furrows that suggest a large collective farm. But in between there were the interminable, frightening stretches of wasteland. When we were within a few minutes of Tashkent signs of life below us became much more

263

apparent. The villages were closer together, we could see the green blur of fields and orchards on the large farms, and soon we got a curiously intimate aerial view of the complicated honeycomb of houses, courtyards, and compounds of the old city of Tashkent. If you walked along the street, there, you would only see the blank, mud, outer wall of the compound, cut here and there with a narrow wooden doorway; from above you get a quick glimpse of the busy, crowded life of grownups, children, and animals that goes on within.

To our astonishment the journey in the much-publicized TU-104 jet airliner service took only about four hours. By ordinary plane it takes thirteen hours, and the train journey has now been reduced from the old fortnight (including overnight stops) to five days. Perhaps it was the speed of the trip that contributed to our shock and delight when we landed in Tashkent. Suddenly we were in Asia. With almost a sense of liberation we stood in the early-morning sunshine at the airport, aware of the spicy, dusty smell of the East, conscious of a slower pace, an older, less driving life, already very remote from the cold northern cities with their bustling people and their feeling of tight determination.

All around us were people with the unmistakable look of Central Asia, short, golden-brown of skin, with straight black hair and strongly Mongol features. A number of the men at the airport were dressed in the traditional Uzbek clothes, brightly colored, striped, knee-length coats, tied at the waist with an equally bright silk sash, high, polished black boots and a small, embroidered skullcap worn on the back of the head. The women were in baggy trousers and tunics, with an open coat flung over their shoulders, boots, and skullcaps that were gaudier in color but similar in design to the men's. The first gesture we noticed was a polite, Oriental one, a greeting or farewell performed by carefully placing the right hand over the heart and making a slight bow. It seemed to give a peculiar charm to even the most casual encounter and impressed me particularly for the strong contrast it offered to the brisk "comradely" greetings of Moscow.

We were met by a pleasant, lackadaisical young man, a typical Uzbek in every way except for his clothes. He was dressed in a British duffel coat worn over brown American-looking slacks. He introduced himself as the guide-interpreter from Intourist and told us that his name was Hafiz. We climbed into the car provided for us, but all the way to the hotel we could scarcely speak to him because we were so busy staring at the streets and people of Tashkent.

Although Tashkent has a population of about a million, it still has the air of a small provincial town that could be as easily in northern India, northwestern China, or Afghanistan. On the streets, as in the airport, there were many people in the characteristic Uzbek clothes, and many of the older women still covered their faces with veils of stiff white material or woven black horsehair, reminding us that now we were in a Muslim country where the power of religion was stronger than the power of the state.

Here in the dusty streets, lined with golden autumn trees, the traffic moved at the unhurried pace of a town used to donkey carts and people who think nothing of walking miles to the market. Hafiz told us proudly, "In the spring Tashkent is a garden, you cannot see it from the air." The trees and vines grow higher than the houses and hide the town under a cloud of green. Otherwise the new town of Tashkent is entirely undistinguished as to architecture. The square cream-washed villas, set back a little from the road and fronted with small untidy gardens or shaded by a grape arbor, have an implacably suburban look. Everywhere the heavy hand of Russian town planners is evident. There are Karl Marx and Lenin streets and squares and avenues. There is a huge new opera house dominating the town's central plaza (the Tashkent Bolshoi). On buildings there are memorial plaques reminding Uzbeks that the revolutionary hero Kuibyshev, lived and worked here for a number of years, but there is also a careful deference paid to two approved Uzbek heroes—Navoi, a fourteenth-century poet and scholar (whom the Russians have labeled a "scientist"), and another poet, Hamsa, who was killed in 1928 "by a rich man." Both have streets and squares named after them. Only the look of the people on the sidewalks or walking casually in the middle of the road and the quick, warm smile they gave us if they caught our eye, suggested that in spite of all this "modern" development perhaps some essentials of Muslim Uzbek life had not been "improved" out of existence.

The only hotel in Tashkent considered suitable for foreigners is on a street corner near the center of town. On each side of it are unpretentious shops and a great number of shoe-repair booths. Inside it is startlingly dingy, with fly-ridden, run-down rooms. However, Hafiz showed us upstairs with a flourish, evidently convinced that we would lack no luxury there. When we told him how pleasing it was to be in an atmosphere so different from Moscow, he nodded understandingly. "Yes, yes," he said, "once I went to Moscow for a holiday. Four days, but what to do? No friends. I could sleep until twelve o'clock. I go to films. I go to shops. I buy souvenirs of Moscow for my family. I return to Tashkent because all the time I was lonely."

We had told Hafiz that we would probably rest until lunchtime and asked him to join us then in the restaurant downstairs. Actually we were all, even Jai, much too excited to do much resting, and I spent a large part of the morning watching the unfamiliar traffic on the street outside our windows: the veiled women walking respectfully several paces behind their dashingly booted, sunburned husbands; the villagers who had driven their donkey carts loaded with fruit and vegetables into town and wore sinister-looking whips stuck in the back of their shirt collars; the gang of small boys climbing someone's walnut tree across the street, jumping down to the road, and then like a flight of birds wheeling off around the corner to some other occupation. The street was flooded with that cool, dry, sunny weather typical of a Central Asian winter, the light had the sharp clarity of the high desert, and the sky was a special, distant blue.

Luncheon was a wonderful meal, filled with new flavors, which confirmed our feeling of being on a continent entirely different from the one to which Moscow belongs. Hafiz found us standing disconsolately outside the door of the restaurant. The door was locked and we assumed that the restaurant was closed although we could hear sounds of activity inside. But Hafiz laughed indulgently and said that the door was *always* locked, it was the simplest way of keeping out the "undesirables." The hotel was known to have the best food in town, and sometimes "undesirable" Uzbeks got drunk and expansive and tried to make their way into the restaurant. On those occasions the headwaiter had only to take a fleeting look at the men, announce that the restaurant was closed, and slam and lock the door to prove it.

Hafiz knocked briskly, the headwaiter duly opened the door, and Hafiz explained that we were Intourist visitors and swept us past the bowing, smiling man. We sat down at a table next to windows that were heavily screened from the street. There were flies all over the tablecloth and the silver and the flowers in the middle of the table. Dead flies mottled the window sill and covered the old-fashioned curls of fly paper that hung from the top of the screens. Hafiz paid no attention to them, didn't even try to brush them away. Instead he picked up the menu and said in his courteous, strangely accented English, "What will it please you to eat?"

In Moscow I had laboriously learned the words on the menu by heart. It wasn't too difficult because during the two months that we were there the menu was never changed. There was never a table d'hôte, everything at the Metropole was à la carte and was identical with the Intourist menu in Leningrad and in any other Intourist hotel. As the winter drew on, the waiters would tell you that some of the vegetables and certain varieties of fruit were out of season and some items, like venison, pheasant, or fresh salmon, were "off" all the time we were there. In Tashkent I was baffled. Except for one or two familiar dishes, such as *ikra* (caviar) and *borsch,* I could make out nothing on the menu.

We decided that each of us would order a different dish and compare our luck, except that for Jai we played it safe and ordered his favorite *plov* (rice mixed with meat and vegetables) and kebabs on skewers. Even that turned out to be far more spicy and interesting than the Moscow variety and was sprinkled with shreds of a carrot-colored vegetable that tasted of turnips. One of us ordered *manti,* which turned out to be a kind of dumpling stuffed with meat and generously sprinkled with fresh dill. *Chakhambili* was a mild curry of chicken or veal, and this was garnished with *petrushka,* a delicious cross between parsley and coriander. There was a miniature lettuce, locally known as Bokhara grass, and *pachison* was an entirely new relish somewhere between a small cucumber and a green tomato. It was pickled in brine and sliced to look like a flower. On the table there was a pepper shaker filled with freshly ground, red chili powder, an essential ingredient of the meal which you add to meat or rice or soup according to the hardiness of your palate, but when I reached for this reminder of Indian food Hafiz told me that women are not supposed to use this hot pepper. Sweet things are considered more appropriate for them. With the meal there were disks of *nan,* unleavened bread that never seems to get stale and is soaked in all soups, gravies, stews. It is also the typical souvenir you buy when you leave Uzbekistan to return home.

I thought it a telling reminder that Uzbekistan belongs as much to the poor continent of Asia as to the Soviet Union that beside the price of each dish on the menu was noted its weight. For example, *borsch* costs 2 rubles, 70 kopeks (27 cents), and after this are the figures 35/550. This means that the basic weight of the meat, or "body," of the soup is 35 grams per portion and when the cabbage, water, flavoring, and sour cream are added, the weight swells to 550 grams. In this way the cautious man can know, as he would at the market, exactly how much he is getting for his money.

Hafiz proposed a long drive through Tashkent for that evening. We were now in siesta country, so naturally neither we nor Hafiz could be expected to do anything in the early hours of the afternoon. He reappeared at the hotel soon after tea, refreshed and cheerful, his black hair slicked back, and at the moment when the sun was losing its heat and the light slanted in great gold shafts between the trees we set off to do the sightseeing he considered necessary. Dutifully he pointed out the schools, nurseries, hospitals, parks of culture and rest in the new part of the town, all, he insisted, "the result of Soviet development." If all this gave me the rather gloomy impression that Tashkent was losing its special character, to Hafiz the rapid growth of Tashkent and the attention it merited from the central government seemed to signalize a welcome injection of new life into the Uzbek capital. "It was quite different when my parents were young," he assured us. He waved a hand at the dowdy provincial roads. "None of this was here then. Now the old people say they fear to leave Tashkent for a holiday because when they return they will not recognize."

We all laughed at his little joke, and encouraged, he went on to tell us that in those days most people couldn't read or write. "And now, please you will look." He stopped the car to show us that on many of the town's street corners where pedestrians clustered were glass cases for the display of the day's newspapers in Russian and in Uzbek.

We drove round a corner, onto an avenue, and suddenly at the far end rose a great range of snow-capped mountains, sharply etched against the evening sky. Tien Shan, the "Heavenly Mountains," that stretch across the southern border of Uzbekistan, dividing it from Afghanistan, Kashmir, and Tibet, begin abruptly and theatrically, almost without foothills —the edge of the vast Central Asian plateau, the Roof of the World.

Faubion and I insisted that we wanted to drive on into the old town of Tashkent to see what it was all like before "Soviet development." Hafiz seemed a bit reluctant to take us, but he did at last agree that we should see the contrast so that we might better understand the achievements of the new town. The Anhar River, the color of pea soup, divides the two sections of the city, and once we had crossed it we were in quite another world. From there we caught glimpses of the snows as the car crawled through the warren of twisting streets, for the houses were flat-roofed and low and no poplars lined the wider roads. Here the level mud-colored line of walls was broken only by the domes of mosques or an occasional fruit tree

growing inside a compound. Sometimes the roads were so
narrow that pedestrians had to flatten themselves against the
wall to let our car past. Most of these lanes and alleys were
unpaved, a bog of mud when it rained but beaten into a smooth
surface by thousands of bare feet in the dry weather.

Here and there we caught a moment, a pose, that could have
come out of an illustrated book of children's Bible stories. A
woman in a bright blue robe, a tall earthenware jar on her
shoulder, standing for a quiet second in the wooden doorway to
a compound. A barefoot child, his black-and-white cap perched
on his shaved head, driving a couple of sheep up the lane. An
old man with a beard, sitting on a doorsill in the evening sun.
But for the most part the life in those compounds behind the
anonymous mud walls was only sensed, a mysterious mixture of
sounds and smells: a mother calling a child, a burst of laughter
floating out, the smoke curling up from where the women were
cooking the evening meal.

Hafiz said that it would all be replaced, one day soon, with
proper housing. There would be no more open drains, no more
animals housed in the same compound with their owners.
There would be new apartment buildings and hygienic living.
Already many of the children were going to the "Russian"
schools in the new town instead of the orthodox Muslim schools
of the old days. Of course they still preferred to speak and read
Uzbek at home, but Russian was now a compulsory language
everywhere, and a "Russian" education would be of far more
use to them in the future. When I asked Hafiz if I might visit
such a school one day he turned to me with real eagerness. "Of
course, of course. I will arrange as soon as convenient."

When we got back to the hotel we invited Hafiz to dine
with us, but he excused himself saying that his brother and
sister-in-law, with whom he lived in "a big house—five rooms,"

were expecting him back. Faubion asked if they were having a party, and if we had delayed him.

"No, not a party. We will be only the family. But my brother's wife cooks very good."

"Better than the Tashkent hotel?"

Hafiz looked embarrassed. "In the restaurant we must use spoon and fork." Suddenly he laughed. "We Uzbeks say that Russians do not like to wash their hands. Therefore they eat from spoons. In the restaurant we also must eat from spoons. At home we eat from hands. Especially for *plov*, that does not taste so good from spoons."

The Uzbeks, he told us, always wash their hands before a meal and when they have finished eating they say *"Armin"* (enough), the signal for the hostess to provide a basin, a jug of water, and a lemon. They wash their hands again, and after that tea is served, either green tea, or strong black tea flavored with cloves and cinnamon and honey.

It was an odd sensation to wake up the next morning to the clatter of horses and donkeys and the screeching of wooden carts instead of the blurred noise of city traffic. I ran to the window in time to see the long procession of carts from the villages around Tashkent coming in to market and decided that the first thing we would do that morning was to join the crowds at the market place.

A market in Asia never fails to be amusing and exciting. It is the place where gossip and news are exchanged, where stories are told and jokes repeated. It is an occasion for the meeting of young people and, eventually, the making of marriage contracts. It is a time for children to enjoy themselves and old people to discuss village affairs. It contains all this and more, besides the prosaic ritual of buying and selling and business deals.

The Tashkent market was no exception. It was held in a large messy bazaar grounds. There was stabling on one side for the animals, and in long rows down the middle and around the edges were selling stalls, roofed with corrugated iron. Between them there was a good deal of open ground, but by the time we got there the stalls and the open spaces were filled with the active, voluble, canny procedures of Asian bazaar life. The smells and the noise were instantly familiar to me from India. There were the flirtation, the talk, the incessant bargaining. The blind and the lame wandered about. The village idiot was harmlessly singing to himself. And there were beggars.

I felt thoroughly at home, and all of us spent a most satisfactory morning. A number of admonitory signs warned people not to litter the market place, nor to trade or sit on the ground. Nobody paid the slightest attention to them. Theoretically, bargaining (like beggars) has been outlawed in Russia, all prices are supposed to be fixed. But this was clearly too much for the Asian nature of the Uzbeks.

Jai had been declaring, with monotonous regularity, that he wanted an Uzbek cap. We found a woman selling them and began the timeless bickering that accompanies such a purchase. At last we settled on a price, but when Faubion handed her the money, she refused to admit that she owed him any change. In a righteous fury Faubion flung the cap on the heap of other caps on the ground and demanded his money back. The Uzbeks who had gathered to watch this transaction murmured approval, and at last the woman found the correct change. After that she grinned with pleasure at the sight of Jai in his Uzbek cap, patted him on the head, and gave him a grape.

So deep is the tradition of the market place in Uzbek that sometimes the old men who are past the age of active trading still come to the market because they cannot bear to stay away from this enthralling nerve center of village and town life. To save face, and to make their own transparent excuse for their presence, the tradition is that they bring some possession of theirs, say a coat, to the bazaar. For this they ask an enormously high price, far beyond the worth of the garment or the pockets of the traders. Then they are free to spend the day sitting on the ground in the sun, the coat spread out before them, talking to friends, catching up on the news, approving or discouraging friendships or possible matches made around them.

The Uzbeks are known to be crafty and enthusiastic traders, and among these old men there is a very popular but fictitious local hero called Affandi. He is a peculiar character, simple to the point of idiocy but unexpectedly wily, innocent but foxy, and the countless stories about him all follow the same pattern. A sharp dealer thinks that he will get the better of the dumb Affandi by persuading him that some valuable item he owns is worthless or by cheating him of a profit in some way. Affandi appears to be entirely gullible, falls in with any suggestion, but always at the last moment the twist in the story brings Affandi out the winner by some elementary trick that the sharp trader has overlooked.

Throughout that morning we stepped between such old men, tripped over watermelon rinds, slipped on rotten tomatoes, examined all the wares in the market, and bought a lot of Tashkent's excellent fruit, especially melons and grapes and pomegranates. We came upon some rather exotic items, some of which we sampled. *Kumiss,* for instance, is fermented mare's milk that has a thin, sweet-sour taste, and seemed to me like a very pleasant summer drink. However, the young Uzbek who was pouring it out into thick glasses from big cans stacked on his cart said that it was alcoholic (which didn't seem possible) and that it was a specific cure for insomnia. A number of people seemed to agree with him because he was never short of customers.

Usma, a green leaf that looks like dandelion, we only asked about. I had thought it some kind of local salad, but in fact it is intended only to be squeezed for juice to be rubbed on your eyebrows to make them black and shiny. Two bunches cost one ruble. Then we saw a kind of Chinese cooking tomato and two sorts of carrots, the "red" and the "gold"—the gold were the ones piled high in ready-shredded fragments, like shoestrings, to use in making *plov.* There were a dozen different kinds of onions, ranging in color from purple to brown and in size from a marble to a grapefruit, as well as the best tiny scallions I have ever tasted.

The stalls where spices were sold were wonderful both for color and for smell. Coriander, turmeric, onion seed, red chilies, green chilies, saffron, a black sweetish spice called *korakand,* and many others were displayed in bowls and baskets, in jars and open trays. From them the buyer chose what he wanted and either had them ground and blended right there or took them home in separate little newspaper cones.

Somewhere in the course of the morning we felt rather hungry. At one end of the market place was a long shed, a kind of open café, where several men in Uzbek robes were standing over a long trough in which rows and rows of kebabs and shashlik were slowly grilling over a bed of glowing charcoal. Following the procedure of other customers at the market, we went over to the railing of the shed, picked up one of the thin disks of *nan* to use as a plate, selected the particular spears of meat that we liked, and then stood in the sun pulling the lamb off the spear with our teeth, taking bites of the bread and using the rest of it to catch the juice. Jai was delighted with this meal and insisted on buying some of the hard-baked bread, cooked in the shape of large doughnuts, which the Uzbek vendors string on a piece of cord, like an immense necklace, or slip on their arms as a series of fat bracelets to carry about more easily. Jai's other choice was a kilo of walnuts, and when we bought them the stallkeeper looked rather worried. "Do not let your child eat many of these," he advised us, "they will give him a headache."

Just outside the market place there was a special, blue-painted stall that always seemed to have a cluster of people around it. We soon saw why. It was an open-air champagne bar selling "fresh" champagne by the glass (as opposed to stale, or day-old, champagne). The townspeople in their work clothes or the farmers in their market clothes would stop here to knock off a quick glass between chores.

It was on our way back to the hotel that Hafiz told us about Tashkent's Donkey Crisis. Jai had noticed that in the market there were both donkeys and monkeys for sale and pleaded piteously for one of each. Hafiz listened thoughtfully for some time and then informed us that donkeys were, in fact, very cheap these days. You could buy one for 10 rubles ($1). The reason was that Tashkent citizens were now forbidden to own donkeys.

As in Biblical Asia—as in modern Afghanistan or Kashmir —donkeys had always been an accepted part of Tashkent life and transport. They took children to school, carried people to visit relatives in the country or on the other side of town. They brought the month's supply of grain, sugar, oil, from the merchant to the housewife. They lived in the back yard or, in bad weather, found shelter under the porch or veranda. They pulled little carts. Some traders made a specialty of buying and selling them.

Then the government cracked down. Donkeys hindered

traffic. Donkeys were not "progressive." Some people fed bread to donkeys while the government felt strongly that all waste bread should go to pigs or sheep who could, in turn, be eaten by people and thus increase the nation's food production. At first donkeys were "discouraged." But eventually stronger measures had to be taken—a prohibitive tax was put on donkey owners. Then a lot of people who couldn't afford to pay the tax and couldn't sell their donkeys because the market was glutted, and consequently had to let them run wild and be carted off in due course by the appropriate authority, were both angry and puzzled. "They do not feel the same," Hafiz assured us, "to visit their family by bus. The government now provides us buses. But it is not like going on your donkey."

Now only people who live in the country, who haven't access to public or collective conveyance for getting their produce to market, may own donkeys. Although the Donkey Crisis caused a lot of comment at the time in Tashkent, nobody really did anything about it. People sold their donkeys for the best price they could get or, in an extremity, comforted their children when the household friend had to be turned forlornly out into the street.

This was only one small example of the detailed attention that the Russian government has turned on Uzbekistan. There seems to be no doubt that this province was chosen by the central government in Moscow to be a model of how a rather disparate area becomes a Soviet Socialist Republic. Uzbekistan used to be part of old Russian Turkestan, Tsarist Russia having seized the region in the middle of the nineteenth century. Nowadays it is correctly known as the Uzbek Soviet Socialist Republic (or Uz.S.S.R. for short), but the old Muslim name Uzbekistan clings and only in official documents is the state given its formal title.

It was the first of the remoter areas to be opened to outsiders, presumably because the Russians were proud of what they had managed to accomplish in a province where a little over a generation ago there had been civil war because Uzbek leaders resented the encroachment of a "foreign" power. The emirs and petty Muslim rulers of local tribes and villages didn't like the threat to their autocracy, and Communist interference with religion stirred up a hornets' nest of hostility. Even in Hafiz' ingenuous, informative tones one could sense the bitterness of those days. "In my father's years of youth," he said about the Russians, "we used to call them *kapur*—infidels. Now we call them *tovarischi.*"

During the interval, the Russians became more prudent and more tactful and the Uzbeks recognized an overwhelmingly superior power. Since 1950 Uzbekistan has been something of a Soviet showpiece. The leaders of China and India have been shown around the area, and now it is open for ordinary tourists to see the achievements of the central government in unification and development. They also hear a good deal of propaganda about how the U.S.S.R. has handled the dual problem of a racial minority (the Uzbeks are a mixture of Turk and Mongol) and a religious minority (Islam is a particularly ardent faith). We did, however, hear at least one rather cynical explanation of Moscow's coddle-and-persuade policy. An elderly Uzbek with whom we talked for a short while over a glass of tea in the hotel restaurant remarked, "Naturally they are careful with us. We produce three quarters of the whole country's cotton, most of its rice, and much of its tea." I supposed that this sort of attitude among the older people served to save their pride and take the sting out of the "Little Brother" approach of the Russians, while acknowledging the fact that Uzbekistan is now a part—a contributing part—of the new Soviet Union.

One day soon after we arrived in Tashkent, Hafiz came up to our rooms and announced that he had made arrangements for me to visit schools in the city. He had been far more thorough than I had expected from the casual nature of my request. We started that morning with a state day nursery and worked our way up to a secondary school.

The nursery was a square white building, sparsely furnished, which impressed me with its air of ordered calm and its virtual silence. The superintendent was a big-boned, commanding woman who seldom smiled, and who made me feel that we had kept her waiting although I knew we were exactly on time for our appointment. She got up from her desk, shook my hand, and through Hafiz informed me that the children in her nursery ranged in age from three months to three years. I was not permitted to see any of them until I had put out my cigarette, scrubbed my hands, and put on a sterilized white overall. Then I was shown into the anteroom where a good deal of flowered cretonne gave a fleetingly cozy air.

This, the superintendent told me, was where mothers came to feed their infants, where they changed into nursery overalls, and where they waited for the babies to be brought to them. A mother was not allowed to enter the play room or the sleeping room, and in the evening she received her child in the anteroom to take him home for the night. Usually a mother feeds her child for about a year unless this period happens to end in the summer. In that case she continues for a couple of months longer because the Russians have a theory that it is bad to wean a child during the hot weather. In any case Russians feel strongly that a child should be breast-fed. Offices and factories give a woman time off at regular intervals so that she can visit her child. In Moscow (and I assumed in Tashkent too), a mother who has not enough milk for her child's needs can buy bottled mother's milk provided by women who have too much.

From the anteroom I was led into a long, uncarpeted room with a cluster of low tables and chairs at one end and a group of toys at the other. The older children were pursuing a variety of activities—painting, playing, wandering about—with considerable composure. I was introduced to one of the two special "walking instructors" and shown the equipment she used, a narrow boardwalk with banisters on both sides, like a miniature ship's gangplank, and a small railed bridge with four steps up and four steps down.

Beyond the play room was the sleeping room, where each crib was occupied by a neat and motionless little bundle wrapped in a green blanket. I thought at first that all the babies were asleep, but when I looked more closely I saw that a number of them had their eyes open. On the veranda that opened off the sleeping room the infants were even more closely covered against the chill air. Even the heads were wrapped, leaving only the face from the eyebrows down partly exposed, covered loosely by a flap of shawl.

After my tour of inspection was over, the superintendent took me back to her office and seated herself at her desk. Her first question was "Have you such nurseries in your country?"

I explained through Hafiz that in India we had some day nurseries but felt, on the whole, that it was an extreme measure for women who had absolutely no way of taking care of their children at home. She looked rather shocked. "But it is much better for the children to be in a nursery," she said.

"Well, we think there is no satisfactory substitute for a mother's love, care, and interest in her own child."

She seemed distressed at this unprogressive view of family life. "I am a mother and a doctor," she told me, "and although I could afford to keep my child at home I would always send him to a nursery. I want to do what is best for him."

At the age of three a child moves from a state nursery to a state kindergarten, where he spends up to ten hours a day. The kindergarten that I visited in Tashkent had an enrollment of 120 and there were six teachers who worked in six-hour shifts. Most of the teachers had been trained in the faculty of what the Russians call the "Pedagogical Institute," but a couple of them were doing kindergarten work as part of their training for being pediatricians. Once a month there were parent-teacher meetings at which the head of the school lectured on the behavior of the children, problems of health, how to teach in vacations, and so on. All this, as well as the painting, reading, music, and handiwork that the children are taught in school, is organized, even in remote provinces like Uzbekistan, according to a master plan set out by the Ministry of Education.

At the age of seven a child moves on to the state primary school for the last few years of his childhood. There, too, the education is standardized, but with minor modifications for provincial requirements. In Tashkent, for instance, I saw classes of children studying Hindi. Uzbekistan shares a short stretch of frontier with India and consequently Hindi has special importance in the area. Incidentally, in those classes I got a brief glimpse of Russian teaching methods, which seemed curiously old-fashioned to me. The children, the girls in their school aprons, the boys in regulation pants and shirts, stand up when the teacher enters and recite in unison the equivalent of "Good morning, Teacher."

The period opens with an inspection of copybooks, all neatly inscribed with yesterday's lesson. Then the teacher calls one of the children to stand in front of the class. In Hindi she says, "Now we will begin our talking practice. What is your name?"

In Hindi the child replies, "My name is Such-and-such."

"Where do you live?"

"I live in Tashkent."

"How old are you?"

"I am ten years old."

The next child is called and put through a similar set of questions. Even though it didn't seem to me the most interesting way of presenting a subject, the children all sat still and attentive—no nudging or whispering in the back rows, no one carving his initials on a desk or gazing dreamily out the window or even looking at us with furtive curiosity. But perhaps that was just because there was a foreign visitor in class and the children were on their best behavior.

Soon after our arrival Faubion had made his usual inquiries about theater or dance performances that we could see. Hafiz looked rather worried. Cotton, he told us, is Uzbekistan's most important crop. It is planted in May and harvested in November and December. To ensure a fast harvest before the cold sets in and also, we gathered, to imbue a sense of the peasant in the young Uzbeks, the older students from the schools and colleges are required to do a certain amount of work in the fields and farms.

Faubion smiled a bit impatiently at this information and said, "Yes, but . . . What I was really asking about was the entertainment life of Tashkent."

"But that is what I am *telling* you," Hafiz insisted. "In these two months there is very little. Because of the cotton harvest."

The eight theaters the Russians have built in Tashkent alone (27 in all of Uzbekistan), as a kind of compensation for other less popular interferences in Uzbek life, are nearly deserted during harvest time because the bulk of their audiences are made up of students and workers in the fields who come into town for an evening's entertainment. Some of the theaters even close down entirely for this period, "because many dancers and orchestras are needed on the farms for the farmers to have entertainment in the evening after harvest work."

Faubion asked after Ismailova, a tiny, dark, slender dancer of extraordinary precision and grace, whom we had seen in London. She is the local equivalent of Ulanova in Uzbek dance, and might possibly be excused from some of the more strenuous duties for the state. Hafiz said, "But it is *November*. Of course her dancing is for collective farms, not in Tashkent."

However, there were a few performances of various sorts that we could see. The Tashkent Opera House, with its big inscription outside, "Art belongs to the People," was putting on an Uzbek opera, giving a chance to younger, more un-polished singers. The inside of the theater is decorated with Uzbek designs, and the various lobbies, anterooms, and cafés are all planned to look like halls in an Uzbek khan's palace, but the great pillared façade and the imposing banks of steps out-side echo the Moscow idea of proper theater architecture.

The opera itself, *Farkhad and Shirin,* also was curiously hybrid. The form was Western, the themes Uzbek. The story was based on a poem by Navoi, who, through his writing, first formulated the Uzbek language and became Uzbekistan's first "patriot." The plot follows the old, Central Asian folk tale, and the music was written in collaboration by a Russian and an Uzbek composer. The conductor, in white tie and tails, was directing a huge orchestra of thoroughly Asian instruments, ranging from parchment hand drums to nasal-sounding flutes, mixed with more usual Western symphonic ones. In the audi-ence were groups of Uzbeks who had come to enjoy themselves in the customary way, *en famille.* In a typical group there might be a couple of the more orthodox women peering at the stage through veils, the older men with their feet tucked comfortably under them on the seat, a marriageable girl carefully placed with a chaperon between her and the approved suitor. They would shout their support of the hero on stage, or their disgust at the villain, or would cluck their tongues appreciatively for a specially good song, all in the manner of the old entertainments.

I was plagued all the time by a sense of incongruity—the Uzbek motifs meticulously followed in the décor of the auditorium, the air of the place, the look of the audience, all for a production that was unmistakably Moscow in style and conception. I fancied that some of those old Muslim ladies must surely be saying to themselves, "What is the world coming to?" when they saw a good Muslim girl whom they had, perhaps, known as the daughter of the local *hakim,* dancing on her points and *exposing her legs.* Surely, in the way of Muslim mothers anywhere, they must have been thinking, "*My* son will never marry a girl like that."

Out of the scattering of concerts, ballets, and plays that we went to, by far the most interesting to me was the first night of *Kholiskhon.* This was a "new" play, meaning that, although it was based on the narrative poem by Khamsa, familiar to most Uzbeks, and had been performed before the appropriate commission for official approval and suggestions, it had not been presented to the public before. Unlike the performances in the Opera House or in the concert halls, *Kholiskhon* was crowded to capacity, and the audience, absorbed in the unfolding of the famous story, would call out *"Dot!"* (an exclamation like Oh!) at the moving passages and *"Dus, dus!"* (Bravo, bravo!) for a particularly good bit of acting or singing. They laughed without restraint at the funny lines, wept openly when the heroine was sad, nudged each other and listened closely to the well-known scenes of climax or treachery.

Kholiskhon is a beautiful Uzbek girl of a fairly rich family, in love with the young and handsome Rustam. They have met in their village and agreed to get married even though Rustam is poor and they are certain to run into strenuous objections from her family. A rich man sees Kholiskhon, falls in love with her, and decides to follow her to find out who she is and how he can capture her to be his fifth wife. He disguises himself as an old-fashioned woman with a veil over her face, a shawl on her head, and an ankle-length multicolored robe. He hides in a special courtyard of the mosque where only women are allowed.

This is a scene for both comedy and pathos. The rich man hears the women talking about their marriages. One has married a rich man even though he had three wives and she had to abandon the man she really loved. "Now he is old," she remarks cynically. "Women too have feelings. Shall I marry again?" Here the audience, knowing Muslim convention, roars with laughter. Another woman, who has gone slightly crazy because she was forcibly married to a man with four wives, sings a song about her sadness, "I was a flower, before my time I became a leaf." The thin music of a long-necked guitar accompanies her, and once again the audience responds enthusiastically, this time with a sympathetic *"Dot! Dot!"*

As the story grows more complicated with plots and counterplots, in numbers of short scenes, the audience is given a wonderfully intimate view of old Uzbek customs, of new Uzbek attitudes, of the ways and privileges of the rich and the worries and hopes of the poor. I particularly liked the scene in the rich man's house and its view of the lavish life of an Uzbek merchant prince. The room contains a couple of low tables, a few inches high, on which the characters place the samovar, the small metal cups of tea, the dishes of nuts and sweets. Then there is a platform, covered with a thick Bokhara carpet, on which the rich man sits cross-legged, lesser people sit on a lower level, and only visitors of equal status join the host on the platform. A hookah, spittoons, and pierced metal braziers holding glowing charcoals have been placed near the master of the house and servants bow deeply when they answer his call or bring him anything. The room opens, through a series of pointed Muslim arches, on to a veranda, partly screened by intricate, lacy plasterwork that filters the light from the garden outside. The bargaining with the marriage broker is an interminable, detailed, professionally shrewd affair which the audience follows with obvious relish as though involved in a marriage contract within their own family.

Kholiskhon's house and garden are more modest, but the most affecting scene of the play takes place there when she wanders late at night among the flowers, her four braids hanging informally down her back, and when she decides to elope with Rustam. Later she relates her feelings to her old aunt, still certain that her love for Rustam is destined for tragedy. "Our dreams will never come true," she says. "We are only women and only good for being wives."

The father's word on the matter is final. He assures Kholiskhon that her future husband is old and will soon die, and then everyone will be far better off. His only complaint is that the rich man has sent a preliminary present of six lengths of cloth. He should have sent ten lengths.

At last the miserable Kholiskhon reaches a decision that astonishes her with its simple boldness. To the wild applause of the audience, she announces, "Instead of crying, I can reject the whole wedding. I can run to Rustam. That is better." (There is quite a long pause here for the full appreciation of Kholiskhon's brave decision.) She confirms it by assuring the audience: "I think only of Rustam. If he dies, I'll die. I'll go my own way."

Of course everything works out all right in the end, with Rustam rich and happily married to Kholiskhon, the wicked punished, and the family reconciled.

The audience seemed thoroughly satisfied, and we, in turn, had learned a little about matters that evidently still agitate Uzbek families. As in so much of the rest of Asia, marriages arranged by parents are still a cause of unhappiness and rebellion in Uzbekistan. As in much of the rest of the Muslim world, polygamy still imposes hard decisions and personal tragedy on women. As is done in most of the Middle and Far East, young Uzbeks break with cultural tradition and form their own particular form of emancipation. The play seemed to hold a very modern meaning for them.

Although Tashkent seemed to us fresh and exuberant and comfortingly Asian after the severities of Moscow, we did eventually remember that our chief reason for coming to Uzbekistan at all was to see the legendary Samarkand. The trip takes twenty hours by train. The daily plane service covers the distance in one hour. We went by plane.

Once again, the arrival at the airport and the drive into the town were an extraordinary experience. Samarkand is set on a low plateau surrounded by jade-green hills and beyond them, on one side, by the desert, on the others, by the snow mountains. Driving in from the airport, you come to the top of one of these hills, and suddenly a flash of piercing blue from the town beyond catches the morning sun, your first sight of the famous azure domes and minarets of the capital of kings, the city that was once among the most powerful in all Asia. As you come nearer, you see that this jagged, dominating structure, surrealis-

tic from a distance, ruined and beautiful close to, is what remains of a once-important group of buildings called Bibi
Khanum. Minarets and prayer towers are eroded into stumps
of turquoise, half the brilliant blue glaze of the tiles lost,
and broken arches, showing their interior mud-colored brick-
work, open on to rubble and crumbling courtyards. But over
one of the arches the plaque of Arabic writing is still clear and
brightly colored. It reads: "Only the sky compares in beauty
with this mosque." In that moment Samarkand's past is as real
as the new color-washed houses that have been built around
the scattered ruins to form the new town of Samarkand.

All the time you are in Samarkand the ruins are never out
of your consciousness. The briefest walk from Samarkand's only
hotel ("For cultured service come to the Communal Hotel,"
says the sign) or the shortest excursion into town takes you past
one or another of the monuments to Samarkand's past glory,
and those sudden bursts of blue seen from a street corner,
through a shop window, while walking in the park, color all
the unimportant, uneventful life of present-day Samarkand.
Though this life contrasts strangely with Samarkand's history
which is so famous a distillation of romance, magnificence, and
turbulent excitement, the constant juxtaposition of the two is a
part of Samarkand's special magic.

Samarkand—the name means "Place of Sugars"—was an
important center of trade and government long before the
Christian era. Alexander the Great destroyed the city in 329 B.C.,
when it was called Maracanda. Gradually it was rebuilt and
resumed its dominant position, so that those indefatigable
Chinese travelers of the seventh century who wandered about
Asia and wrote voluminous letters of description and comment
to their people at home were able to list Samarkand as one of
the greatest trading cities of the world, the central depot of the

old silk route that connected China with the West. One ancient writer pointed out that in Samarkand the pressure of trade was so great that every boy of fifteen was immediately urged to enter business, and to be a successful merchant was considered the highest achievement.

In 1220 Genghis Khan, during his great sweep across Central Asia, razed the city once again while more than a hundred thousand soldiers fought vainly to defend it. But by the end of the thirteenth century Samarkand was, once again, according to Marco Polo, a "very great and eminent city."

It was not until the middle of the fourteenth century that Samarkand produced its hero of heroes, the man who started his career as a robber of passing caravans, tricked and bargained and fought his way to power, then killed the ruler, married his wife, and made himself king. By Western writers, fascinated with his story, he has been called Tamerlane or Tamburlaine. But his name was Timur, and because he was slightly lame (*leng*) he was locally known as Timur-i-leng. His mighty kingdom, one writer explains, stretched from Irtish and the Volga to the Persian Gulf and from the Hellespont to the Ganges. Now, after all those distant wars and conquests against Turks, Egyptians, Persians, Mongols of the Caspian, Russians of the Urals and the Volga, all that Samarkand holds of Timur and his empire are his tomb, the legends about him, and the buildings he erected in his capital city.

When we set off diligently to look at these buildings we soon found that each one had its true story and a legend. The guidebook and the shy but conscientious Intourist guide told us, I suppose, the historical truth. But the Uzbeks we met at the ruins or talked to in the hotel restaurant told us the legends. Bibi Khanum, for instance, the jagged, splendid monuments that we had first seen on our way in from the airport, was built by Timur during the years 1399 to 1404 to commemorate his victory at Delhi. Ninety captured elephants carried the stones that went into its erection. It was hastily built—Timur was imperious and eager—and after less than a hundred years began falling apart. The architect's plans were apparently faulty and the inevitable disintegration was speeded by mild but frequent earthquakes. The towers and pillars collapsed at strange angles, the walls crumbled, and walking through the present crazily beautiful ruins, seeing that incredible blue of the tiles against the softer blue of the noonday sky, I thought the truth quite dramatic enough. But the legend is even more appealing.

An old man, a citizen of Samarkand, sitting on some worn steps in the shade, told us that he liked to come to Bibi Khanum often, to sit on these steps, to look at the high cracked archway, and to "think about philosophy." "It is a good way to spend your time when you are old," he said in Russian that was almost as clumsy as Faubion's, "even for a simple worker whose children and grandchildren are grown." He told us the other story. Bibi Khanum was to be the greatest college in the kingdom and was erected by Timur's Chinese wife while he was away at battle. It was to be a surprise and a homage to him when he returned in triumph. The only architect of the time who was competent to build so grandiose a monument and could guarantee its completion in time for Timur's return was in love with the Chinese queen.

For his services she offered him money, jewels, position at court. He asked only to kiss her cheek. Timur's wife started to kill the architect for his effrontery, but then, as he pointed out, the building could not be created.

The queen then said (so the story goes), "Choose any beautiful girl of the kingdom instead of me." And according to proper Oriental convention, she illustrated the logic of her request metaphorically. She took two eggs, one brown, one white. "See, the colors are different"—she cracked the eggs—"but the inside is the same."

The architect parried by taking two glasses. He filled one with water and one with vodka. "See, the color is the same," he said, "but the taste is different."

Apparently outmaneuvered, Timur's queen agreed to the architect's bargain. The building was completed within the specified time. When the architect demanded his reward, the queen allowed him to kiss her, but first put her hand on her cheek so that he would kiss only her fingers. The architect kissed her with such passionate intensity that a mark burned through her fingers onto her cheek.

Timur returned, saw the mark on his queen's face, heard the story, and swore to kill the architect. But the architect, chased by Timur, ran up one of the minarets and was never seen again. However, all this scuffling and chasing rattled the foundations of the buildings, and that is why they have fallen apart.

Our Intourist guide was a pink-complexioned boy, stocky of build and very bashful of manner. He was plainly worried about us. After a couple of days of ruins and monuments, he said, rather apologetically, "There is nothing more to see in Samarkand. You will wish to return now?"

We told him that we would like to stay on for a few days.

"May I ask why you feel so?" He seemed really astonished.

Faubion said something about the charm of Samarkand, the magic of the name alone, quite apart from the beauty of the ruins.

Our guide still looked puzzled. "It is a quiet life here. That is very well for me, I am a country boy. But I have been in the capital. A very busy life there. Too quick for me."

"Didn't you like Moscow?" Faubion asked. "Even for a change?"

"Moscow? I have never been there. I was speaking of Tashkent. Do you not wish to return now to Tashkent? There is much to do in Tashkent."

We finally managed to persuade him that we liked the slow pace of Samarkand, enjoyed walking down the sleepy main street, between the candy-pink houses with their blue doors and window frames, that we found a lot of interest and amusement in the noisy little market where we sat and sipped green tea and watched the country people and their donkeys come clattering in to sell their cloth and embroidery, their food and furs. But evidently he wasn't entirely convinced, because one morning he came to our rooms at the hotel, full of energy, to say that he had found something interesting for us to do after all. He found us standing on the balcony. He had pointed out to us when we first arrived that we had the best view in the hotel—not, we discovered, of the mosques but of the townspeople. We enjoyed watching them walk past singly or in family groups, the veiled women and the girls with their long black braids walking respectfully a few paces behind their men. We could see the farmers and shepherds, in their dashing fur hats and brightly sashed robes, assemble on the restaurant steps after the market was over and emerge some time later rather drunk, singing Uzbek songs or putting Uzbek words to tunes we had heard in Moscow.

That morning we had been watching a funeral procession in the street. The coffin, draped in red, was in the back of an open truck apparently borrowed from some collective farm. Banks of flowers surrounded the coffin, and in a flower-decorated jeep behind were members of the family. After the jeep came the mourners led by a small brass band which played sad music.

The whole procession, moving at a walking pace, circled twice through the town. Our young guide watched with us for a while and then put his hand on his heart and made a slight bow in the direction of the coffin. Rather embarrassed by this gesture, he explained, "I am not Muslim, but that is the custom in this country. Very quickly I learn and follow their customs."

"You are not Uzbek?" I asked. His hair was brown rather than black, but his deep sunburn and his broad, rather flat features gave him a vaguely Uzbek look.

"I will always live in Samarkand, but in the old days my family came from Ukraine." Some years before the Revolution there had been bad times, trouble, not enough land or food. His family had moved to Kazakhstan, which was still almost pioneer country, an untested wilderness, where they and other harassed farmers tried to make a living from the soil. Only after the collective farms were organized did they feel some security. "They would never leave the collective now. It is their life. They wish to die there happily because they have been able to live there. Just to live, that was everything that they ask."

Their boy, however, asked more. "I was ambitious," he told us, "for education." There was no college near the collective, so he came to the closest one, in Tashkent. There he joined the Young Communist League, and because he studied hard at his English he was able to become an Intourist guide and interpreter. You have to be a Komsomol member for such a job. Then the only drawback, as he had told us, was that the giddy pace of Tashkent was too much for him, too exhausting after the measured life on the collective. He was delighted to be sent to Samarkand. He read Uzbek history, learned the language, he wanted to be good at his job. He was engaged to an Uzbek girl whom he had met at college. He had even found a place for them to live after they were married, he said, staring shyly at his boots. He seemed to feel that all his wildest ambitions had been achieved.

The thrilling excursion that he had planned for us that morning was a visit to the Persian Lamb Research Institute of Samarkand. It was a square, two-story building a couple of blocks from the hotel, and there we were greeted by a group of jolly young scientists who seemed scarcely able to contain their delight that we had come all the way to Samarkand to see their institute, the only one of its kind in the world. Enthusiastically they led us through their "library" of lambskins, all filed and indexed according to color, texture, and design, the largest such collection anywhere—white, gray, black, red, and every variation between.

In the course of that morning I learned a great deal more than I ever expected to know about Persian lambs, about their diet and grading, about the differences between broadtail (the fur of an unborn lamb) and karakul (the fur of a day-old lamb), about the auctioning of skins in Leningrad, their shipment to the West, and their impressive dollar earning power. The poorer furs are sold in Russia for coat collars and caps. The best go to America—$30 apiece for karakul, $33 for broadtail. I remembered that in Moscow a Persian lamb coat sells for $2,000 in a department store. I never saw anyone wearing one.

One of the eager young scientists told us that Uzbekistan was the heart of the Persian lamb trade and that Bokhara was the best Persian lamb area in Uzbekistan. Inevitably the crisp scientific approach, the graphs and tables on the laboratory walls, were wildly at variance with the romance of the names —Bokhara (best in quality and quantity, the oldest producer of this fur), Samarkand (ranking third in production, but improving). It was not a moment for sentimental recollections. To the efficient young men Bokhara is the gypsum desert, excellent feeding grounds for Persian lambs. Samarkand needs more vitamins in the salt licks to produce better furs.

At only one point in our tour did the briskly practical attitude of the workers appear to show a crack. One of the young men, spreading out the smoothest and most delicately grained of the skins (from a 135-day-old unborn lamb), said, in a soft voice, "See, how like the finest Arabic writing." He ran his hand gently over the design in the fur. "Like inscriptions on a mosque."

We walked back to the hotel feeling rather cheerful, thinking that perhaps these surroundings, the incredible blue of Samarkand's domes and minarets to recall the past, the casual, messy, Asian life of the roads or bazaars to give a different view of the present—surely these things must have their own effect on the Western Russians. The young scientist at the institute was a Moscow boy. Surely he must have sensed with relief —as we did—the different air of Samarkand after the determined pressure of Moscow life or the drab chill of the north.

Apart from our visit to the Persian Lamb Research Institute we did nothing very much in Samarkand except return again and again to the ruins. The most imposing was, I suppose, Gur-Emir, the shrine where Timur was buried. A big archway of tan brick, set with light- and dark-blue tiles gleaming like enamel, leads into an absolutely simple courtyard. In one corner is the massive coronation stone of the emirs of Bokhara, captured in the sixteenth century, a block of white marble with carved panels around the sides. In the dead silence of the courtyard nothing can be heard of the town's mild activity, only the occasional sound of the bells on the animals being driven along the road outside or the thin wail of the muezzin's call. Nothing moves except possibly the solitary figure of a devout Muslim wearing the white turban of the Believer.

Immediately ahead is the great bleached façade of the shrine with its recessed arches and haphazard fragments of old mosaic. Above it, like an immense blue melon, the dome of Gur-Emir curves against the sky. Inside, it is cold and dark, although the walls are whitewashed and parts of the panels of carved onyx that used to surround the tombs can still be seen. There Timur was buried, at the feet of his religious mentor, and beside his sons and grandson. His sarcophagus is made of a rare black stone from China (he died suddenly when he was preparing to conquer China), which is considered so valuable that in the eighteenth century it was stolen by the Shah of Persia. He was, at last, persuaded to return it. Now that smooth black slab contributes to the overwhelming atmosphere of death that pervades Gur-Emir.

Timur, a sort of constructor-king, was responsible for most of the mosques, tombs (including his own), and religious universities still standing in Samarkand. One or two of the mosques on the outskirts of town, dedicated to the protection of travelers or of shepherds, are older. Timur's enemies at the time, watching the passion and energy and money that went into the construction of his great monuments, and considering the poverty of his subjects, used to compare him to a streetwalker who earned money to support her children. The idea was noble; the practice, ignoble.

But after Timur's death his grandson, Ulugbek, succeeded to the throne and continued the pattern of Samarkand's building, and one of the most beautiful of the architectural wonders that remain is his Registan, a set of three matching buildings, once again characterized by sky-blue domes and minarets. Only one of the buildings has an unusual feature, over the entrance a large mosaic of a tiger, flaming out in all his yellow and black stripes—exceptionally representational for a Muslim religious monument which normally contains no depiction of human or animal figures.

Ulugbek, according to fact as well as legend, was a progressive ruler, experimental, original, and a great astronomer. His passion was his observatory, the largest of the time. Apparently this concern was too mysterious for his contemporaries, and a group of orthodox Muslims killed him and destroyed the observatory. All that remains now, on a hill outside the town, are two huge metal tracks of a giant sextant with which he plotted the movements of the stars.

Ulugbek's last building was a minor tomb for one of his wives, and of all the lovely things we saw in Samarkand this remained my favorite. It belongs to a cluster of tombs in a remote part of the town, a miniature casbah of steps and winding paths, where wives and sisters of successive rulers are buried. The predominating colors, as always, are blue and white, but at the entrance the tall wooden columns and the ceiling above them are painted red and green—the reason is explained in an inscription outside the tomb: "May this mosque lighten the weight of grief." The wooden doors of each small tomb are inlaid with ivory and mosaics. The inside walls are filigreed and perforated, and the ceilings molded into elegant honeycombs. The sunlight slants sharply down on the walled steps between the tombs. Deep shadow picks out the stone tracery and the pointed arches. Flights of birds wheel between the shiny blue domes.

Around this nest of tombs is the largest graveyard in Samarkand. Good Muslims like Ulugbek's wife particularly wanted to be buried near the tomb of one of Islam's most sacred saints, Kasim ibn Abbas. He was given the name of Shaki-Zinda (the

Living King), and the group of tombs—in fact, the whole hill —is named Shaki-Zinda to commemorate his holiness. In the early fourteenth century Kasim came to the great capital of Samarkand, the crossroads of East and West, in order to convert the Unbelievers. He was so successful that some of the local fire worshipers, resentful and defeated, killed him.

Predictably, the legend is different. According to the story handed down among the people of Samarkand, Kasim was a failure. The Unbelievers refused to be proselytized. So Kasim took off his own head, carried it under his arm, and walked into his tomb. This miracle so astonished the people that everyone, including the fire worshipers, accepted the faith at once. Kasim was also a writer and somewhere he wrote, "Those who are killed on Allah's path are not dead, they are living still," and this dictum came to be the summing up of his life and earned him the name of the Living King. Apparently numbers of people in Samarkand today believe he is still alive, and even those who don't believe feel it very important to be buried near his tomb. In this way, symbolically at least, they will not have died, just disappeared.

From these faraway legends, from the fine Arabic inscriptions and the glitter of the mosaics, we would return to the hotel, our heads full of the ruins and the spectacular, dead history of Samarkand. Sometimes in the evenings we would drive out into the country—ten minutes would take us out of town—or go down to the river Zeravshan, surrounded by cotton fields dotted here and there with storage sheds and farmhouses, and always beyond the fields would be the great wall of the snow mountains. On the way back, we would look ahead to the squat houses of the town, a few pylons, even a factory chimney, all made insignificant by the towering wreck of Bibi Khanum or the blue domes and minarets of Timur's capital.

There were only a few days left before our Russian visas expired and so, reluctantly, we had to leave Samarkand. In the morning our Intourist guide came with us to the airport. His fiancée was arriving on the Tashkent plane which would take us on the return trip. He was smiling and self-conscious when he introduced us to a tiny, dark girl who was too shy to say more than a word of greeting. We saw them standing on the landing strip, waving good-by as we entered the plane.

In the usual Russian way, we all crowded up the steps together, the people at the head of the line taking the seats in the front, and the others filling in the other seats in an orderly way. I found myself sitting next to a young Uzbek woman. Her braids were wrapped around her head in the traditional fashion. She wore high boots and a loose robe with a man's jacket over it. We smiled at each other, but said nothing until the plane started.

At the moment when the plane left the ground she gripped my arm. Her eyes were tightly closed and she was breathing hard. She was clearly in some sort of distress, but I didn't know if she was feeling sick, having a heart attack, or what. I looked around desperately for Faubion, who was a couple of seats behind me, and at the same time caught the eye of a young Uzbek across the aisle. He hurried over, and so did Faubion. They both leaned over the girl. The young Uzbek took my seat. "This is my wife," he explained in Russian, and then said something comforting to the girl in Uzbek while Faubion and I stood in the aisle watching nervously.

After a few moments he turned to us again. "She is frightened," he said. "She has never been in a plane before. We are going to the city."

"We, too, are going to the city," Faubion said.

"I have been before, but my wife never." He tapped her on

the shoulder and indicated something out the window, but she continued to keep her eyes closed and her fists clenched. He smiled at Faubion and me standing helpless beside him. "We are passing over the farm," he said. "She will feel better if she looks." He said something more to her, urgently but soothingly. She opened her eyes long enough to take a quick look out the window, and suddenly she became interested. She turned her back on us to stare down properly. She shook her head, evidently in disbelief. "Yes, yes," her husband insisted, laughing. At last she looked at us, smiled, and returned at once to her inspection of the green farmland under the plane. Her husband said to Faubion, "You will stay in Tashkent?"

"Only for a day, and then to Moscow."

"Moscow," the young man said wonderingly. "One day perhaps we will even go to Moscow."

Within an hour we were in Tashkent. Within a few days we had left Russia altogether.

Set in 12 Point Intertype Garamond
Format by Anita Walker
Manufactured by The Haddon Craftsmen, Inc.
Published by Harper & Brothers, New York